C000270130

John Heymer was bo[rn] [in] 1934 and went to Sou[th Wales to] become a coal miner. [He joined two] years later for National Service and signed on for three years in the Royal Fusiliers. He then returned to the pit but, after being buried in a roof fall, joined the Monmouthshire Constabulary. Heymer spent a couple of years in Headquarters as a training instructor and another couple of years in the photography department before being appointed scenes of crime and crime prevention officer. In between those appointments he worked the beat.

John Heymer is now retired and lives in South Wales with his wife. They have three children and two grandchildren.

THE
Entrancing Flame

The Facts of Spontaneous
Human Combustion

JOHN E. HEYMER

WARNER BOOKS

A *Warner* Book

First published in Great Britain
by Little, Brown and Company in 1996
This edition published by Warner Books in 1997

Copyright © John E. Heymer 1996

The moral right of the author has been asserted.

A CIP catalogue record for this book
is available from the British Library.

ISBN 0 7515 1562 0

Typeset in Bembo by M Rules
Printed and bound in Great Britain by
Clays Ltd, St Ives plc

Warner Books
A Division of
Little, Brown and Company (UK)
Brettenham House
Lancaster Place
London WC2E 7EN

This book is dedicated in general to all the victims of Spontaneous Human Combustion and to the loved ones whose lives have often been irremediably shattered by the trauma of a sudden confrontation with the seemingly unnatural and unimaginable horror of SHC. It is dedicated in particular to the memory of Jean Lucille Saffin whose family, since her death in 1982, have insisted that her death resulted from SHC and not from some mysterious unknown accidental cause cited at the inquest.

Contents

	Acknowledgements	ix
	Preface	xiii
1	Revelation	1
2	Odyssey	5
3	Henry Thomas	14
4	Annie Gertrude Webb	31
5	An Acausal Connection	37
6	The Experts	47
7	The Lavoisier Syndrome	54
8	A Little Learning	65
9	The Fireman and the Tramp	75
10	Anomalous Phenomena	82
11	Preternatural Combustion – The Facts	93
12	The Procrustean Stretch	107
13	Miscellany	115
14	Of Dinosaurs and Fossils	126
15	Quod Erat Demonstrandum	131
16	Ashton and Soudaine	147
17	Trances	156
18	Atomic Flames	169
19	The Entrancing of Jeannie Saffin	179
20	The Investigation – Past and Present	189
21	Static Flash Fires	202
22	Preternatural Combustion in Oregon, USA	211
23	Cigarettes Can Kill?	223
24	The Burning Question	229
25	A Paranormal Event?	234
	Conclusion	238
	Appendices	245
	Index	255

Acknowledgements

I would like to acknowledge the assistance of certain persons, namely: Bill Treharne Jones, BBC *Newsnight* producer; Larry E. Arnold of ParaScience International, USA; Professor Ron Westrum of Ypsilanti University, Michigan, USA; Bob Rickard, editor of *Fortean Times*; Philip Schofield and Heidi Hannell, of *Schofield's Quest*.

I wish to express my gratitude to both Kath and Don Carroll for their unfailing courtesy and patience.

I would also like to thank all those who contributed their stories in response to *Schofield's Quest*, namely Sandra and Mike Stubbins, Debbie and Dianne Clark, Susan and Joanne Motteshead. My special thanks to Peter Sadler, who came to my aid on a couple of occasions with his theories and experiments.

Preface

If you are intending to read this book in the hope of learning more about a 'supernatural' phenomenon, then you have the wrong book. For centuries Spontaneous Human Combustion has been considered to be one of many aspects of the 'super-natural'. I have endeavoured to bring the phenomenon into the realms of the real world.

Spontaneous Human Combustion happens – there is no doubt about that. For reasons examined in this book, the Establishment chooses not to acknowledge the existence of SHC. In their denials of the phenomenon they often create even more incredible mysteries.

I served for more than twenty-five years in the Gwent police, before retiring in 1981 as a scenes of crime officer with forensic training. I dealt with a case of Spontaneous Human Combustion in 1980. I have spent the past nine years, since 1986, research-ing the subject and am now even more convinced that the phenomenon is a relatively rare yet natural event.

By keeping an open mind and examining the arguments for and against, I believe that, by the end of the book, the reader will know that Spontaneous Human Combustion is no myth. Many instances of Spontaneous Human Combustion are never recognised as such and even the relatives have no idea that anything untoward has occurred when a person has burned to death supposedly as the direct result of carelessly dropping a cigarette onto their clothes or bedding. Any person who has lost a relative to Spontaneous Human Combustion and has been given an unsatisfactory explanation by the authorities will know that there is more to it by the time they have reached the end of this book.

I would like to know of more cases and I ask anyone who has had personal experience of, or has lost a relative to, the 'entrancing flame' to write to me c/o Little, Brown, at the address below. I will then interview contactees by telephone, providing they are in the UK. I will write to anyone abroad. The address to write to is: Little, Brown and Company, Brettenham House, Lancaster Place, London WC2E 7EN. For those of you on Internet, my E-Mail address is jeh@astar.demon.co.uk.

The reader may get the impression that I dislike and distrust scientists. This is not the case. I have the utmost admiration for scientists and am greatly interested and impressed with their discoveries. In espousing the cause of Spontaneous Human Combustion I have inadvertently found myself at odds with a few Establishment scientists who deny the possibility of Spontaneous Human Combustion in spite of the considerable amount of evidence in support of the hypothesis. However, as you will find in the following pages, such persons constitute a fairly large minority, especially in the Establishment. You will also learn that such an attitude, on the part of certain, even eminent, scientists is not a new development. Paradoxically there have always been those who, while constantly engaged in the search for new discoveries, seem convinced they already know it all.

I know of no scientific investigation of the SHC hypothesis. All the tests and experiments of which I am aware have been conducted on the hypothesis that the 'wick effect' is the true explanation.

THE
Entrancing Flame

CHAPTER ONE

Revelation

I stepped through the door into another dimension – momentarily thrust down into Dante's Inferno. The room was as hot and steamy as a sauna. It was bathed in a hellish orange/red glow. There was a not unpleasant sweetish, yeasty smell to the atmosphere, reminiscent of an old-fashioned bakehouse. The walls, ceiling and every surface were coated with a strangely greasy black soot. The density of the soot increased with its height up the walls. Immediately inside the door stood a television set. It appeared to have been designed by Salvador Dali. The plastic control knobs on the front of the set had been melted and reformed into surrealistic shapes – arrested in mid-flow as they cooled while slowly oozing lava-like down the control panel of the set. The valves of the set were still glowing with power but no picture showed on the tube.

A single light bulb emitted an orange glow as it hung down, naked, from its holder in the centre of the soot-blackened ceiling. On the floor, immediately below the bulb, lay a pair of men's shoes upon which lay the misshapen remains of a plastic lampshade. The heat in the room had softened the shade until it drifted from its fixings, sliding down over the bulb to fall onto the shoes below where it lay, a shapeless, colourless blob that somehow brought about in me a heightened sense of unease.

Both the light bulb and the window panes were coated in an orange sticky substance which filtered the light thus causing the unholy glow. One pane of window glass was cracked, presumably by the strange heat source that had melted the lampshade and the knobs of the television set. It was a nightmarish experience. To step from a pleasant, bright, clean and neatly furnished room into this steaming, garish orange glow was so totally unexpected that the effect was disorientating in the extreme. However, there was much worse to come.

The room was furnished with a table, chairs, a settee and an armchair. Both settee and armchair were fitted with loose covers. A rug lay on the fitted carpet in front of an open coal-fire hearth. On the carpet, in front of the hearth and partly on the rug, lay a mass of ashes. At one edge of the ashes, furthest from the fireplace, was a partially burnt wooden-framed armchair.

During the course of my twenty-four years' service in the police up to that time I had witnessed more than a few truly horrific sights. But this was the first time that I actually felt my hackles rise. Lying on the carpet between the ashes and the shoes was *a pair of male human feet clothed in socks*. The undamaged feet protruded from short lengths of trouser-leg bottoms. From the upper, burned, edges of the trouser legs emerged blackened leg bones which progressed to white, calcined bones, disintegrating at mid-thigh. The collapsed powdery bones merged into an amorphous mass of ash where the torso should have been. The remains of the trouser legs had a thin, charred edge, as if cut by a laser beam. The transition from undamaged cloth to ash was immediate, with only the thinnest line of scorching to show that the trousers had burned. Beyond the burn line on the trousers the remaining material was in perfect condition. At the opposite end of the ashes lay a blackened, featureless skull, which appeared to have been shrunken.

Although the sight of the extremely sparse remaining portions of a human being was in itself horrific there was something about the socks and remaining portions of trousers that particularly troubled my mind. I could not say why, in the context of such a totally bizarre scene, those items should prey on my mind to the extent that they did. For years to come, whenever that scene came to mind, it was the sock-clothed feet and the portions of trousers that always figured largely in my mind's eye. I was constantly aware there was something incongruous about the pieces of clothing. Fifteen years passed before I realised why the trouser legs bothered me so. The reason will be revealed at the appropriate stage of this book.

I was looking down on the scarce remains of Henry Thomas, a seventy-three-year-old man who had, for the most part, been incinerated far more effectively than can be achieved in a crematorium. The complete torso and arms, including the bones, had been reduced to ash. This horrendous incineration had taken place on the carpet of the victim's living-room floor.

Nothing else, other than the armchair in which he had apparently been sitting, had suffered any fire damage. The flounced loose covers of the settee, situated less than two feet from the ashes, were not even slightly scorched. While trying to equate the impossibility of the scene with the undeniable fact of its reality, the reason for the weird lighting effects dawned upon me. The light, transmitted by both the window and the light bulb, was being filtered through a deposited layer of condensed, vaporised flesh. It was the same glutinous substance that gradually builds up on the inner surfaces of the domestic oven in which meat is regularly roasted.

As I struggled to maintain my grasp on reality I felt much like Alice having stepped through the looking-glass. Familiar frames of reference were suddenly missing. I now understood why my colleagues in the adjoining room, who had summoned me to the scene, were so subdued and non-committal on my arrival. It was a truly awe-inspiring situation. I was instantly and absolutely convinced that the scene I beheld was the aftermath of Spontaneous Human Combustion.

Until that day my only knowledge of the phenomenon had been largely obtained from reading *Bleak House* by Charles Dickens, which I read with more than a little scepticism. The scene I was viewing coincided so exactly with Dickens' description of the death of Mr Krook by Spontaneous Human Combustion that it was obvious he knew what he was writing about. This mind-blowing experience was to be responsible for permanently altering my mind-set. I would no longer so easily dismiss reports of unusual phenomena solely on the grounds of their seeming impossibility. I was immediately converted into an 'asceptic', with regard to Spontaneous Human Combustion. I have coined the term 'asceptic' in the sense of 'not sceptic' as it befits my state of mind better than 'believer'. The term 'asceptic' is less dogmatic than 'believer'.

I did not instantly become so amenable to reason with regard to other disputed phenomena. My conversion to a fully open mind came about gradually and was largely occasioned by the constant refusal of some sceptical (especially forensic) scientists to recognise any facts which tended to support the Spontaneous Human Combustion hypothesis. Over the next fifteen years I was to discover that some scientists are capable of the utmost folly when it comes to providing 'explanations' for facts that refuse to conform to the presently accepted interpretation of the physical 'laws'. Unfortunately it is the scientists with negative views of SHC that mostly express opinions on the subject. The more open-minded scientists tend to keep their opinions to themselves for reasons which will be examined in this book.

CHAPTER TWO

Odyssey

In January 1980, while serving in the Gwent police CID as a forensically trained scenes of crime officer, I dealt with an incident that has been the subject of controversy ever since. It was the instance of the alleged phenomenon Spontaneous Human Combustion which I related in the previous chapter. In manifestations of the phenomenon the *living victims* are supposedly reduced to ashes by fire from within their own bodies. I shall be constantly using the phrase Spontaneous Human Combustion throughout this book. In order to reduce the tedium of repetition I shall use the accepted contraction of SHC from here on.

Everyone who attended at that incident either believes it to have been SHC, or in the very least does *not* believe it to have resulted from the ordinary processes of combustion. The forensic scientists, however, took a different view. Their solution was, and is, the 'candle' or 'wick effect'. They maintain that human beings can burn away like twopenny candles, even in conditions so devoid of oxygen that burning furniture ceases to burn. I shall be dealing with the 'wick effect' in a later chapter.

The newspaper reports referred only to the bald facts of an elderly man dying in a fire at his home. The verdict was accidental death. I was not called to give evidence at the inquest so I do not know how the matter of the two feet and the pile of ashes on the carpet was glossed over.

At this time, however, I had no interest in the SHC phenomenon and felt no great urge to preach the gospel of SHC. In the years that followed I made no attempt to learn any more about the phenomenon. From what I had read on the subject it seemed to be firmly situated in the realms of the supernatural. Never having felt any sympathy with things supposedly supernatural I was quite content to remain mildly mystified regarding the incident. I was more interested in the view of the experts which seemed to me incapable of fitting the facts.

Six years after the event there began a chain of circumstances that was destined to lead me deeper into the controversy. I have since appeared on numerous television and radio programmes in the UK, Australia, America, Canada and, most recently (in 1995), on European Discovery satellite TV. I have also written a number of articles for international publications such as *New Scientist, Fate Magazine* and *Fortean Times*, all on the subject of SHC. In July 1994, I had the pleasure of addressing the first Fortean Unconvention 94 held at London University, which was organised by the management of the *Fortean Times*. As a result mainly of my articles in *New Scientist* I was contacted by numerous people who provided me with relevant data and food for thought. I also heard from some rather strange people too.

The one person who made the greatest difference to my outlook on life was Dr Ron Westrum, Professor of Sociology at Eastern Michigan University, USA. He sent me a quantity of material that he had both acquired and written during the course of his continuing investigations into 'Social Intelligence About Hidden Events'. His studies relate to many different aspects of human behaviour that are not generally known. Some types of aberrant behaviour can be widespread throughout a country or even the world yet, while suspected, is denied by those who should be in the know. This denial by those who should know also relates to phenomena such as meteorites in the past and ball lightning in the recent past up to and including SHC at present. He also studies the reaction of people in general when faced with anomalous phenomena. It all boils down to the fact that some people will go to great lengths to avoid having to recognise inconvenient facts which do not fit in with their theories, beliefs or teaching. There are, it seems, a great many anomalous events that are either ignored or explained away. SHC is just one of them.

Over the years I have inadvertently become an 'authority' on the subject of SHC. The process has been slow and, to start with, unintentional. Each time I have appeared on radio or TV or written an article I have received more data from interested people. All the data would have had very little meaning were it not for two amazing coincidences that gave me a clue to the nature of the phenomenon. The coincidences could well be classed as 'Jungian acausal connections' by anyone familiar with Jung's essay on 'Synchronicity'. More importantly, the same coincidences gave me reason to suspect that there are a great many more cases which are normally hidden by the usual circumstances of a house fire.

I am becoming more of the opinion that, while there is no official conspiracy as such, there is a tacit agreement on the part of the Establishment to play down reports of SHC so as not to disturb the public unduly. In an article published in *Fire* magazine in August 1986, Senior Divisional Officer Douglas Leitch of Strathclyde Fire Brigade, makes a superficially plausible attempt to explain away SHC. He fails to convince on several important points which I will deal with later in this book. However, I quote a relevant part of his text:

I would suggest that there is more need for fire scene investigation specifically relating to body destruction than spending

valuable research money on what would, if proven, only cause
alarm and distress to members of the public.

Daddy knows best. Ignore the scratching at the door; pre-
tend not to hear it. With luck, whatever it is will go away.

I cannot prove absolutely, by direct methods, that SHC is a
fact for reasons that will be made all too apparent. I can only
hope to prove, to the readers' satisfaction, that the answer is not
the much vaunted 'wick effect' which opponents of SHC
quote incessantly as though it were an effective incantation to
ward off the evil spirit of SHC. On occasion, I shall be asking
the reader to seriously consider the facts and to use their
judgement when weighing up the various pros and cons of
the SHC versus 'wick effect' controversy. Consider the facts
and weigh up what I and the sceptics have to say regarding the
interpretation of those facts. Though common sense can
sometimes lead us into error it does, for the most part, stand us
in good stead.

Sceptical scientists are adamant that common sense is no
substitute for the rigorous 'scientific method' of investigation.
I agree with them on that point with the reservation that the
scientific method is not always suited to the investigation of all
phenomena. Scientists engaged in quantum physics are certainly aware of the inadequacies of the scientific method. As I
shall demonstrate at a later stage, some scientists are as guilty as
any lay person when it comes to propagating invalid assumptions which have long been based on common sense rather
than observation. These assumptions are readily tested by
means of simple experiments.

Though the subject matter of this book is hardly a matter
for humour there will be times when a modicum of humour
inevitably creeps in. This story has unavoidable elements of
farce. The unexpurgated statements of some of the experts and
their ill-conceived 'experiments' constructed in futile attempts
to prove the 'candle effect' constantly result in pure farce. This

farce is not of my invention; I neither claim the credit nor take the blame for it.

Sceptical experts have not committed themselves to print very often in denying SHC. Certain of the sceptical experts incautiously attempted to demonstrate the validity of the 'wick effect' on the various TV programmes in which I took part. The first of the programmes, 'Newsnight' on BBC television, left the question open, while the second, 'QED', also a BBC television production, claimed a resounding victory for the scientists who appeared on the programme. The third and latest (1995) was a Yorkshire Television production shown on the satellite Discovery programme and called 'Arthur C. Clarke's Mysterious Universe' which, in the main, favoured the SHC argument. As the programme was made for showing first in the USA it was toned down somewhat. No mention was made of the fact that the victims were alive at the start of their incineration, neither were the photographs of the remaining extremities shown.

Some of the devices and arguments used by the sceptics require little effort on my part to destroy them. The main thrust of my argument is that the famous 'wick effect' theory, which the scientists strove so hard to validate, resulted from a monumental misunderstanding of a paper published by Professor Gee of Leeds University in 1965.[1] The misunderstanding has been perpetuated for the past thirty years.

I shall make liberal use of quotations and for this I make no apology. Quotations, aphorisms, etc., are the distillation of the wit and knowledge of some of the greatest minds that ever lived. I believe in making full use of their vastly superior wit and wisdom when the quote is apposite and expresses my thoughts better than I. It is right that such gems of wisdom should be kept in constant use rather than stored away in dictionaries of quotations – as corporations hide away works of art in safety vaults.

This is my first book. Though I claim the credit (if any) and accept the inevitable brickbats, it virtually wrote itself. Having written various magazine and newspaper articles on the subject of SHC I found I was experiencing increasing difficulty in cramming the relevant facts into the too small format of the magazine article. On reading my last heavily edited and emasculated newspaper article I realised that a book has been struggling to break out.

Though I have carried out the necessary research to ensure, to the best of my ability, that my facts are correct, I have not been required to exert myself too much. Most of the knowledge I have drawn upon has also been kicking around in my head as the direct result of fifty years' omnivorous study of anything and everything. In common with Erich von Daniken I too am an autodidact (self taught) and as such continue to seek knowledge every day of my life.

Whenever I relate an incident that I have witnessed, be assured that the facts of the matter are as reported. I learned my craft (writing) not as a journalist or author but as a practical police officer for twenty-five years. When one has to obtain evidence to put before a court, knowing that lawyers will pounce on the slightest inconsistency, one soon learns to stick to the facts. Journalists 'gild the lily' as a matter of course – police officers do so at their peril. My hard-won skills of gathering and presenting evidence have not diminished. Have no fear that you are to be subjected to a hotch-potch of dreaded police jargon. I never found the need to resort to jargon while in the force and I have not developed a taste for it in the years since my retirement. Jargon is a poor substitute for original thought.

David X. Halliday, forensic scientist at the Metropolitan Police Fire Investigation Unit, stated on the BBC 'QED' programme in 1989, 'For some people, belief in spontaneous human combustion is an act of faith and no amount of evidence will convince them otherwise.' As I was the only active proponent of SHC on the programme I have a sneaking suspicion that he was referring to me. We have crossed swords on several occasions on the vexed subject of SHC. In reply to his charge I would say that I do not 'believe' in SHC or in anything else. 'Belief' implies or requires an act of faith. I prefer knowledge, based on facts, or an acceptance of possibility rather than blind faith. Thus I accept the possibility of SHC. Far from being convinced otherwise by the so-called 'evidence', to date I have yet to see one scrap of evidence that militates against the SHC hypothesis. I have no need to believe in the existence of SHC. I am certain SHC is not a 'supernatural event' and am equally certain that it can be satisfactorily explained in terms of present-day physics. I do insist, however, that the 'explanations' do not insult my intelligence. I accept the possibility of SHC having personally witnessed the aftermath of such an alleged occurrence. At no time has any sufficiently credible explanation been given by sceptics to show convincingly that the incident was anything other than SHC. While the experts can provide no proof to the contrary, and persist in making statements and demonstrations that are an insult to the intelligence, I have no alternative other than to accept the possibility of SHC.

In the following pages I review the 'evidence' carefully applying the acid test of reason and even resorting to the use of the much maligned common sense. Thus viewed, the 'evidence' transpires to be of 'many things: of bones and fat and candle wax – of stuffed armchairs and springs . . .', but *not* the impossibility of Spontaneous Human Combustion.

My involvement in the events chronicled in this book has inevitably resulted in my personality being stamped upon it. Instead of being a dispassionate essay it is certainly biased, though I hope not unfairly, towards the SHC hypothesis. This bias was brought about by the fact that no supposedly scientific explanation could stand up to critical analysis. It is my experience that a 'scientific' explanation of anomalous phenomena is any explanation – no matter how ridiculous –

proposed by a sceptic of SHC. I declare my interest so as to pre-empt accusations of unfair bias.

As far as I am aware this is the first book on the subject of SHC that has been written by one who has the double advantage of having witnessed the aftermath of such an occurrence while also being a forensically trained investigator. As far as I am able to ascertain previous books on the subject are mostly compendiums which have been written by journalists who have 'researched' the subject purely for the purpose of producing a saleable book. Their research has not gone beyond rewriting the more famous of the historical reports of SHC and interviewing witnesses to some modern occurrences of alleged SHC. Such writers have not the knowledge, experience or training to enable them to differentiate between cases of SHC and actual instances of the 'candle effect' and even flare-ups resulting from excess body static.

In this book I shall deal in the main with cases that I can verify by reference to official reports, witness statements and pathologists' reports or by interviewing the actual witnesses myself. I shall only bring in other cases when I can provide some useful comment as a result of my research or when I find certain inescapable similarities between my cases and some of the others. As sceptical scientists are so ready to dismiss the singular anomaly as unworthy of consideration – a mere aberration or blip on the graph of the normal – I have, on occasion, been obliged to utilise other well-documented cases so as to provide statistical evidence, even though the statistics are, of necessity, small.

It is my contention that Spontaneous Human Combustion is an umbrella term covering four different and separate phenomena of which two are different types of Spontaneous Human Combustion: one which is always fatal and one which the victim can survive. The four separate phenomena are briefly: the 'wick effect'; SHC where the victim is reduced to ashes; the flameless type of SHC which seems to attack only part of the body (see chapter 17) and the static electric flash burns (see chapter 21).

Notes

1 A Case of Spontaneous Combustion, Professor Gee, *Medicine, Science and the Law* Vol 5, 1965.

CHAPTER THREE

Henry Thomas

'When you have eliminated the impossible, whatever remains, however improbable, must be the truth.'

CONAN DOYLE

I was confronted with the bizarre scene of Henry Thomas's death by incineration on 6 January 1980. My duties encompassed three different functions, namely photography, fingerprints and forensic science.

During my tour of duty I attended all scenes of sudden death resulting from murder, suicide or accident that occurred in my division which covered the whole of the western half of Gwent. In the case of non-criminal deaths I photographed the scene and corpse for the benefit of the coroner's officer reporting on the death. I would also examine the scene for any indication as to the cause of death. Often I would attend at the post mortem examination of the corpse by the Home Office pathologist to photograph any relevant findings.

There is nothing more disgustingly stomach-churning than to be present at the post mortem evisceration of a human corpse that has been immersed in water until it starts to disintegrate due to advanced decomposition. A human corpse lying undiscovered for a week in a prefab during a heatwave runs a close second. I have dealt with and handled corpses in various stages of decomposition during my twenty-four years in the force prior to Henry Thomas's demise. At that time I would have been hard pressed to imagine a death scene that could bother me.

Being a life-long avid reader I had, over the years, read various accounts of SHC. This phenomenon allegedly manifests itself as a living person suddenly erupting into flames which reduce the body to ashes – apart from the odd extremity or two. Although there are many supposedly factual accounts of the phenomenon I tended to maintain an open mind on the subject with a possible bias towards disbelief. To my thinking, SHC was slightly further up the scale of credibility than UFOs. My opinion was based partly on the fact that so many accounts, written by authors with no first-hand knowledge of the phenomenon, persistently equated SHC with other, allegedly supernatural, phenomena. The causes of SHC were variously ascribed to the wrath of God, ball-lightning, magnetic storms, Haley's Comet, the illiberal imbibing of spirituous liquors (a hot favourite with the Victorian temperance movement), etc.

Half an hour before my unsuspecting venture into the alleged realms of the supernatural, I was in my office looking forward to a quiet Sunday afternoon updating the records of my week's work. The phone rang, interrupting my labours. The control room officer at Ebbw Vale police station requested my attendance at a death in a house fire at the Rassau Council Estate, Ebbw Vale. As usual I requested particulars of the incident. To my surprise he declined to oblige. He said, mysteriously, 'We think you had better see for yourself.' I had never before been requested to attend a scene 'blind' so to speak. I did not labour the point, assuming that he had good reason for his reticence.

The Rassau Estate is located on the side of a mountain in the northern extreme of the county. In mid-winter it is one of the coldest places in Gwent. As I approached the house I was surprised not to see any fire engines or the usual sightseers in attendance. Normally, at any house fire, one has to beat one's

way through hordes of onlookers whether day or night. The
street was curiously deserted. The front door stood open. I
entered the house and was immediately struck by the absence
of the distinctive smell that results from a house fire, however
small. On entering the lounge I saw two of my uniformed
colleagues, a supervisory sergeant and a uniformed constable,
Terry Russell, who was the coroner's officer for this incident.
Gwent police did not appoint coroner's officers as such.
Whichever uniformed officer was first on the scene automatically became coroner's officer for that case. They were both
strangely reticent.

Rassau council houses were not then centrally heated and
were far from warm. With no visible signs of any form of
heating, the house was surprisingly and unnaturally warm –
especially as the front door was standing wide open. So far I
had seen none of the usual signs of a house fire. By now I
strongly suspected being set up for a practical joke. Such prac-
tices are not entirely unknown among police officers. I said to
my colleagues, 'All right, where's the fire?' The sergeant
pointed to a closed door and said, 'In there John'.

When a fire is confined behind closed doors smoke normally seeps out around the doors and soot is deposited on the
paintwork of the surrounding door frame. The paintwork
around the door was perfectly clean. Close examination of
door and frame revealed no trace of smoke seepage. I opened
the door rather gingerly, half expecting a joker's booby trap. I
entered the room and left the realms of sane normality.

As I gazed at the surprisingly small pile of ashes and the dis-
embodied feet I was reminded of the scene of Krook's death
by SHC in Dickens' classic *Bleak House*. I was certain that I
was looking at such a scene. The two officers, who had arrived
at the scene before me, knew that what they had seen was
something that just should not be. We all sensed that the laws
of physics had been inexplicably suspended or breached in
some strange fashion. My uniformed colleagues had little

experience of fire deaths and so were not overly familiar with the effects of fire on a human body. However, they knew instinctively, as they viewed the bizarre scene, that such damage to a human body just could not occur in such circumstances.

The unbelievable effect of the transition between one room and another, between the real and the surreal, was such that I had to step back and forth through the doorway, between the two 'different dimensions', just to verify that the whole mad scene was real – it was. The room was laden with anomalies. Nothing had burned that had not been in contact with the body. The remains had been discovered some three hours before my arrival. At the time of the discovery there was no fire. Though the weather was particularly cold (well below freezing), the front door had been left open since the discovery of the event. Hours after the body had been reduced to ash the room was still radiating heat. The amount of heat released in that room must have been terrific. The walls were still radiating sufficient heat to make the house comfortably warm even though it had no insulation or double-glazing and was situated near a mountain top.

The ashes lay on a rug and a foam-backed, fitted carpet, both of which were only burned where they were in contact with the ashes. The charred portion of the rug and carpet were saturated in melted human fat. I later discovered that on the floor under the fitted carpet were thermo-plastic tiles. A hot saucepan placed on such tiles will leave a permanent mark on the surface. When the carpet was removed and the floor washed there was no sign to be found to show that any heat had been applied to the tiles. They were all unblemished. Were one to light a fire of sticks and wood on a foam rubber-backed carpet, covering thermo-plastic tiles, then I venture to suggest that, before the fire had been burning for an hour or so, the carpet would have burned through. In addition, obvious damage would be caused to the underlying tiles. But in this case, the charring of the carpet extended for only an inch or so beyond the boundary of the ashes.

The only inanimate and really flammable object in the room to have actually burned, apart from the charring of the carpet, was the wooden-framed easy chair in which the victim had been sitting when he started to burn. This chair was mostly reduced to ash, with the exception of part of the right-hand side of the wooden frame. Part of the fabric cushioning was also unburned.

In the fire grate lay the dead ashes of a coal fire containing a quantity of partially burnt coals. On the hearth lay a bundle of sticks ready for the laying of a fresh fire. On the front of the hearth lay Thomas's plastic-framed spectacles – they were undamaged. The front edge of the tiled hearth, a few inches from the ashes, was blackened with smoke. The surface of the hearth was clean and tidy. There was no sign of any coals having fallen from the fire. It had apparently gone out through lack of attention, though there were plenty of unburned coals in the grate.

Until the room was entered, by the person discovering the remains, it had been sealed tight. The window of the room was steel-framed and a good draught-tight fit. Both doors to the room had been sealed with draught excluder. The room was so well sealed I am certain that, with both doors tightly closed, the coal fire did not normally burn very brightly because of an insufficient supply of air.

Many years previously, when I lived in a town at a similar altitude to the Rassau (Blaenavon, Gwent), I completely sealed the living-room door with draught excluder to reduce the persistent icy draughts. I found that the fire would not burn properly unless the door was open. One had to be constantly poking the fire to keep it alight. I soon realised that the cause was lack of air due to the all too efficient sealing of the door. I removed the top strip of draught excluder from the door and the fire burned quite well from then on. The doors of Henry Thomas's

Scene of the Henry Thomas incineration. Drawing by John E. Heymer

living-room had both been sealed all around the frames.

The reason why I was unable to detect any signs of smoke seepage around the door before entering the room was that the frames were so effectively sealed that smoke was unable to seep out. As the smoke could not get out so the air could not get in. The room was virtually hermetically sealed.

Here was a further anomaly. In a room full of combustible materials the only object to burn, apart from the partially burned chair, was the least combustible object of all – a human body. The human body is approximately 75 per cent water. Thus the body of a person weighing ten stones (140lbs) would contain about 105lbs or ten and a half gallons of water (water weighs 10lbs per gallon).

As a scenes of crime officer, I was required to ascertain how certain situations leading up to death came about. Both training and experience enabled me to read a situation and form reasonable conclusions. Having got over the initial shock of finding myself involved in a case of SHC, I thoroughly examined the scene and arrived at the following conclusions. The chair had burned quite well, while in contact with the burning body. When the one side of the chair burned away sufficiently to give way under the weight of Henry Thomas's body, it collapsed and deposited the burning body on the floor. Free of the burning body the unburned remains of the chair ceased to burn. The body continued burning until only ash remained – apart from the lower extremities and the skull. At the time I did not know whether Henry Thomas was alive or dead when combustion commenced.

I am convinced that the fire originated in the region of the abdomen. The blackened, though complete skull, and completely untouched feet are strong indications that the fire commenced in the middle of the body and burned outwards towards opposite ends. Here we are faced with a seeming paradox. The bulkiest portion of the body, containing the most water, is the part that burns away completely. I will attempt to resolve this paradox in a later chapter. At that time I had no idea at all as to how the corpse might have burned. I only knew instinctively that it was not a normal process of combustion. All my succeeding research in the years to follow would bear this out.

The most puzzling anomaly of all is that a readily combustible object, such as the chair, which initially is burning well, ceases to burn once the oxygen in the room is exhausted – yet the water-laden body continues to burn until the torso, including the major bones, is consumed. The process of combustion is also known in scientific circles as oxidation. Combustion cannot proceed without the presence of oxygen in some quantity. That the doors were sealed and the burning chair self-extinguished proves that the necessary oxygen for combustion/oxidation was not present soon after the initial flare-up. Yet the water-laden body burned to ashes. Few, with a modicum of common sense, would argue that there was not something strange in the incineration of Henry Thomas. Yet as I shall relate, forensic scientists insisted that the incident was entirely unremarkable and not worthy of investigation.

In all the accounts of SHC that I have read, both fictional and factual, mention is mostly made of a foul stench. As I mentioned earlier in this account I was not aware of any unpleasant odour. But, as I also mentioned, the front door of the house had been standing open for some hours as had the doors to the room, so any unpleasant odours could have long since cleared. Even so, at that time the heat in the room was still oppressive. When I spoke of this occurrence with Thomas's next-door neighbour he recalled how, on the evening of Henry Thomas's death, he had gone into his rear garden. He said that his nostrils were assailed by a foul smelling smoke which he saw to be issuing from the chimney of Thomas's house. He assumed that Thomas was burning some rubbish on his fire grate and thought no more of it as the smoke did not invade his house.

Having photographed the scene I went to Ebbw Vale police station to arrange the attendance of forensic scientists from the Home Office Forensic Laboratory at Chepstow, Gwent. On arriving at the station, a young constable told me he had solved the case and knew the cause of death. He said that death was due to SHC. He then produced a book of *Worldwide Mysteries* which he had been given for Christmas. In the section dealing with SHC there was a photograph of the remains of Dr J. Irving Bentley. Dr Bentley had died in 1966 in Pennsylvania, USA, in circumstances usually attributed to SHC. On examining the book I was immediately struck by the similarity between the scene in the photograph and the actual scene I had just left. The photograph showed a portion of a bathroom in the floor of which a hole was burned. Over the hole, propped against the bath, stood an undamaged aluminium walking frame with rubber feet. There were some ashes around the hole and the lower portion of a human leg and foot which was undamaged and clad with a slipper. All who had been to the scene of Henry Thomas's death were struck by the amazing similarity of the two scenes.

I called out scientists from the forensic science laboratory. The more common procedure is for scenes of crime officers to examine scenes and collect specimens and samples for submission to the laboratory for examination by the forensic scientists. The scientists are normally only called out when it is considered that the investigation would be better served by them searching the scene themselves. I considered an occurrence of SHC to be of sufficient scientific interest to warrant the attendance of the scientists. I also thought they would appreciate an opportunity to examine such a rare occurrence. I was about to become acquainted with a rather common (but as yet unsuspected by me) mind-set that I have since named 'the Lavoisier Syndrome'. I will elaborate on this syndrome later.

The forensic scientists duly arrived and, to my dismay,

immediately dismissed the possibility of SHC. They declared it
to be a proven impossibility. They said the phenomenon had
been scientifically investigated some years ago and was completely explicable by a process known as the 'candle effect'. I
asked how the 'candle effect' could reduce a human body,
containing gallons of water, to ashes on the living room carpet. They said that the victim's clothing had somehow caught
fire and, in burning, had melted the surface fat which was
soaked up in the clothes as if by an exterior wick – the molten
fat thus fuelling the flame. Their reading of the scene went
something like this: The body of a man has been reduced to
ash on the floor of his living room. For the man to be so
reduced to ash he must have come into contact with a source
of ignition. There had obviously, at some time in the recent
past, been a coal fire burning in the grate. The spectacles of the
deceased were lying on the long, outer edge of the hearth.
Obviously Mr Thomas had fallen for some reason and landed
headfirst in the fire. He had thus caught his head on fire and
had then burned to death. Nothing remarkable or mysterious
in that. If it is said quickly enough and no thought at all is
given to the odd peculiar circumstance or two, or three, then
their 'explanation' seems almost reasonable. Closer inspection
by the scientists revealed a small scrap of charred fibrous material adhering to the top fire bar of the grate. This was eagerly
pounced upon and declared to be a piece of the skin from the
forehead of the deceased. It was obviously deposited there
when he fell into the fire. His perfectly clean and undamaged
spectacles were also deemed to have fallen from his head in
the fall.

In vain I pointed out the clean state of the grate and the
undisturbed pile of chopped firewood in the grate. Neither fitted in with a person having fallen into the fire and then
having extricated himself. Such an occurrence would surely
have resulted in some disturbance to the fire coals and the
chopped sticks and even the rather unstable companion set of

fire tools standing in the grate. The position of the spectacles suggesting they had been placed there by the deceased while sitting in his chair watching television. They did not look as though they had fallen there when their owner fell into the fire.

My arguments were in vain. The scientists were adamant that SHC was a non-starter and the cause of the fire must, of necessity, comply with the normal rules of combustion. Ergo, the deceased fell into the fire and was so ignited. The analysis of the 'forehead skin' would support their reading of the situation. I then asked how did a man come to fall into a fire headfirst, catch fire, pick himself up and sit down in his armchair apparently to burn away without making any attempt to extinguish the flames? They had to agree that Thomas had been seated in the armchair during the initial stages of his combustion. They did not dwell upon the patent absurdity of a man, whose head was in flames, sitting down in an armchair and making no attempt to quench the flames. Common sense dictates that any person in such a situation, still having control over their movements, would either go through the door into the kitchen a few feet away to douse themselves in water or would, if out of control, stagger about the room blindly. The last thing a person in that situation would do is sit down in an armchair or any other chair.

The victim's slippers were on the carpet just beyond his unburned feet. The position of the slippers strongly suggested that he had settled comfortably in his chair to watch television. The chair was facing the television set, which was switched on. He had apparently eased his slippers off his feet while sitting with his legs outstretched. The electric light was switched off. (The fact that the light was off was included in both the statements of the victim's sons-in-law who broke into the house and discovered the remains.)

I would expect an elderly person to make up a coal fire with the room light on rather than off. If the fire needed stoking it would not be giving out much illumination. There was nothing to suggest that Thomas had in any way been in contact with the grate. Bearing in mind the position of his slippers and spectacles it is highly likely that he had removed the spectacles, placing them on the edge of the hearth within his reach. He had also eased off his slippers and settled down in the armchair probably for a nap. He had probably become drowsy while watching the television.

Though I was an experienced scenes of crime officer I did not feel able to continue to argue the point. I must confess that the sample of 'forehead skin' did tend to give me pause for thought. I left the scene to the scientists and went to my next job. That was the end of my official involvement with the incident once I had sent in the film to HQ for processing. Had I known that I was to become embroiled in controversy over the matter of SHC in the years to come I would have made far more searching inquiries at the time instead of leaving physical evidence for the forensic scientists to ignore.

A few weeks later I learned of a most interesting detail. My superintendent, Bob Haines, who had been at the scene, called me to his office. He said that he had the forensic report on the sample of 'forehead skin' obtained from the grate. Analysis of the charred fibrous tissue showed it to be of bovine origin. He said, 'So, it seems John, that there was this passing cow . . .'

The streets and gardens of Rassau were often invaded by marauding bands of ravenous mountain sheep in the winter months – but cows are non-existent at that altitude. The grazing is too sparse for cows. I would hazard a guess that the 'fibrous tissue' was the remains of some leather article that had been disposed of on the fire.

The remains of Henry Thomas, such as they were, were later examined by the Home Office pathologist, Dr G.S. Andrews. He subsequently reported to the effect that he saw quite a few cases each year where elderly persons fell asleep in bed or in an armchair and died from smoke inhalation. The smoke in these cases resulted from a burning cigarette, dropped when they fell asleep, setting fire to the bedclothes or chair upholstery. I too have dealt with such cases. There was, however, a world of difference between those cases and that of Henry Thomas. In all such cases I attended the bodies were for the most part hardly damaged, if at all, whereas the bedclothes or furnishings were often considerably damaged. The fire brigade was usually called to such cases and extinguished the fires before the houses were destroyed. Mr Thomas had contrived to burn away to ash while disturbing the furnishings to such little effect that no one, not even his next-door neighbour, was aware that there was a fire. Mr Thomas was also a non-smoker.

One further bizarre twist was revealed at the post mortem examination. Henry Thomas was *alive* when he started to burn. Dr Andrews commented in his report to the coroner that the pink colour of some remaining muscle tissue indicated the presence of carbon monoxide in the blood. This was indicative of the deceased having inhaled the products of combustion shortly before death. The pathologist ascribed the cause of death to 'burning'. The inquest verdict was accidental death. Had Henry Thomas been judged to have fallen dead, from heart attack or stroke before burning, the verdict would have been natural causes.

I have described the scene of the death of Henry Thomas in both subjective and objective terms. Police reports are normally purely objective and rightly so. It is not right that juries or magistrates should be influenced by the subjective feelings and emotions of police officers. I have departed from the usually strictly objective approach because I am not compiling a report for the courts. I am allowing myself a little licence in the hope that I shall not bore my readers. Such licence does not mean that any facts are invented or indeed exaggerated to give a false impression.

It may surprise some readers to learn that police officers are prone to subjective emotions. Do not be fooled by appearances. To perform efficiently in harrowing circumstances an officer cannot allow grief to immobilise him. Other participants in the incident can collapse in shock and horror but police officers cannot afford to give way lest chaos ensues. Over a twenty-four year period, prior to the death of Henry Thomas, I had learned to divorce myself from the horrors of injury, suffering and death. One cannot be of much use at a road accident dealing with living people minus limbs and virtually disembowelled if one succumbs to the horror of the situation.

Over the years I became so inured to horror that I was able to enter a fire-damaged room and photograph the scene which included the bodies of three children, aged eighteen months to three years. While firemen, having arrived too late to save the children, were unashamedly weeping I was able to concentrate completely on focusing and composing my camera shots. I saw no babies – only a 'scene'. I could switch off from the most harrowing of incidents as long as they were normal. What really threw me with the Henry Thomas incident was the utter impossibility of the event. Being suddenly confronted with the 'impossible' affects one in a most profound manner. Life is just not the same afterwards.

During the latter stages of writing this book I was both dismayed and saddened by the actions of police officers claiming compensation for 'post traumatic stress' resulting from their attendance at the Hillsborough football stadium disaster in 1989. It is not often that I find myself in agreement with judges – most of them seem to live in cloud cuckoo land. However, I entirely agree with the comments of Mr Justice Waller when he dismissed the claims of the 'stressed' police officers. He said in his judgement:

> *It is part of a police officer's duty to deal with situations which might cause psychiatric injury to ordinary people. The fact that*

people are professional rescuers must be taken into account. They
will not be persons of ordinary phlegm, they will be persons of
extraordinary phlegm being hardened to events which would to
ordinary persons cause distress.[1]

Such claims by police officers does the force no service in the
eyes of the public. If a police officer does not have the moral
fibre to stand such stress then he/she should resign and remove
themselves from the possibility of suffering such trauma.

Ordinary people, touched by the phenomenon of SHC,
have been irrevocably changed. In some instances the early
death of individuals witnessing such events are believed by relatives to have resulted from them stumbling unprepared upon
such horrific scenes. Others have suffered mentally ever since
the death in such fashion of a close relative.

To return to Henry Thomas, though the only piece of 'evidence' in support of the forensic scientists' theory (the fibre of
'bovine origin') turned out to be a red herring, no further
action was taken to ascertain the true circumstances of his
death. The forensic scientists and I were agreed that the death
was not due to any criminal action or suicide. We were not
agreed as to the manner in which Henry Thomas met his
death. I awaited the outcome of the inquest – eager to see
what the press would make of such a strange death. To my
chagrin, although it made the front page of the local paper, the
South Wales Argus, there was no mention of the unusual circumstances of the death. The report merely related how an
elderly man had been found accidentally burned to death in
his home.

I was tempted to check with the newspaper reporter as to
why the bizarre nature of the death had not been reported.
However, it was a disciplinary offence for a serving police
officer to disclose any information to the press without
authorisation. Discretion overcame my curiosity.

Six years after the event, in 1986, I discovered that members

of the press attending the inquest had been kept in ignorance
of the circumstances of Henry Thomas's death. They heard
nothing at the inquest to indicate that anything unusual had
occurred. Such cavalier treatment of the facts by coroners
seems to be the norm when inquiring into deaths which are
allegedly due to SHC. The usual high standards of proof are
relaxed and verdicts are arrived at which do not accord with
the known facts. Many more open verdicts should be recorded.
Even though one may be totally opposed to the concept of
SHC one has to admit that the circumstances of his death
were somewhat unusual and at least worthy of comment.

The forensic scientists, who are supposed to take nothing
on trust, formed a view of the situation which was based on a
series of unsubstantiated assumptions. They assumed Henry
Thomas to have fallen into the coal fire. There was no shred of
evidence to support that assumption – especially after the
analysis of the fibrous tissue. They assumed he had caught fire
following his assumed fall. They then assumed that he had sat
down in his chair while on fire. Finally they assumed that he
had been consumed by a process dubbed the 'wick effect'
when there is very little evidence that such an effect is possible in such conditions. I knew what I had seen was
'impossible'. I also knew that I had not imagined the situation.
I even had my photographs of the scene should I start to
doubt the evidence of my eyes. Having seen the 'impossible' I
felt no need to deny what I had seen or to try and explain it
away by some ridiculous mental acrobatics. Neither did I feel
the need to embrace the 'supernatural' to explain my experience. I do not believe in any form of supernatural
phenomena. We, and the entire universe, are part of nature,
therefore anything which occurs within the universe, no matter how bizarre, is a part of nature and, by definition, natural.
All anomalous phenomena are natural – they may not be normal, after all that is what makes them anomalous. So
anomalous happenings are not supernatural, they are merely

supernormal. Yesterday's anomalies are today's mundane. Today's anomalies are tomorrow's mundane. The difference between the supernormal anomaly and the mundane is just a matter of time and knowledge. Denying anomalous occurrences only delays their inevitable transition to the realm of the mundane.

In Chapter 1 I stated that the skull of Henry Thomas appeared to be shrunken. This is often the perception of people on viewing the remaining skull at the scene of SHC. However, it seems that they and I are mistaken. The skulls only appear to be shrunken because, devoid of their covering of flesh and fat they are considerably smaller than the complete head. The pathologist stated that the skull was intact together with the upper part of the vertebral column. He further stated that, together with the lower part of the legs and feet, they were the only bones to survive – '. . . – all the rest of the bones had been broken during burning or had disintegrated.' He did not mention whether or not the brain survived.

One final comment with which to end this chapter, the calcined bones of Henry Thomas, together with the bone ash, were brilliant white in colour; not grey or black. Had the calcined bones been cast in plaster of Paris they could not have been any whiter. At the time I did not know the significance of this fact. I will reveal the relevance of the fact in the proper chronological order. Had I known of this fact at the time then it might have changed the whole course of the controversy which has continued to surround the subject of SHC.

Notes

1 *Daily Telegraph* 11 April 1995

CHAPTER FOUR

Annie Gertrude Webb

Annie Gertrude Webb was a spinster, aged seventy-five. She was an epileptic and lived alone in Corporation Street, Newport, Gwent. On Saturday 2 February 1980, she had only returned home from a short stay in hospital a couple of days previously, following a short course of treatment.

Shortly after nine o'clock that morning, a life-long friend of Annie, living nearby, was alerted by Annie's next-door neighbour. The neighbour had noticed that the windows of Annie's living room were blackened with smoke on the inside and he was unable to get any response from knocking on her door. He knew that Annie had given her friend a key to her house.

On entering the ground-floor living-room they found the room full of smoke and in total darkness because of the soot-coated window glass. Their nostrils were assailed by a strange, foul stench which was overlaid by a strong smell of gas. The room contained a gas fire. The fire switch was later found to be in the 'on' position yet the fire was unlit and there was no gas escaping from it. The neighbour immediately turned off the gas supply at the main, fearing an explosion. He was unaware that the gas meter, which was coin operated, had run out.

They then opened the kitchen door to let out the gas and to let in some daylight. On examining the scene they were confronted with the horrific sight of Annie Webb reduced to a pile of ashes, two lower legs, half a bare right arm and a blackened skull. That the remains were those of Annie was obvious from the plastic hospital name tag on the wrist of her surviving arm.

Just as Henry Thomas's surviving lower legs were clothed in the lower portions of his trouser legs so Annie Webb's lower legs were clothed in stockings. They were of a substantial nature and somewhat loose on her legs. She was of slim build. Her stockings were only burned as far as her legs were burned. The burning pattern was an exact parallel to that of Henry Thomas.

The room was quite small and cluttered. The gas fire was situated on one wall. Along the wall on the right of the fire (when facing the fire) stood a dining chair and a stuffed armchair. Immediately in front of the fire about five feet away was a table set with a cup and saucer, a teapot with cosy and some bottles of sauce and milk. The items on the table could have been placed there in preparation for an evening meal or breakfast. The table was covered with a plastic table cloth, under which there was a conventional cloth of some woven material such as cotton. A further dining chair lay on the floor between the table and the fire and to the left of the fire. The remains of Annie Webb were encompassed by the gas fire, the chairs and the table. Her feet were just under the table.

The dining chair and armchair to the right of the fire were in contact with the ashes of Annie Webb and were both partially burned. The dining chair was lying at an angle with its top supported by the wall bearing the gas fire. The edge of the plastic cloth, nearest to the burned armchair, was burned slightly and scorched. The remaining dining chair, though in contact with her lower right leg just below the burn line was undamaged.

The incinerated remains of Annie Webb. Copyright Chief Constable, Gwent Police.

Police Constable 201 Wheatstone was the investigating officer for HM coroner. He was an observant officer and noticed that Annie had plugged practically every gap around the window and door through which draughts could enter the room. As in the case of Henry Thomas, she had virtually hermetically sealed the room. P.C. Wheatstone said in his statement, relating to the sealed door and window, 'I have been told that the fire was therefore starved of oxygen and prevented from spreading'.

Once again we are faced with the paradox of a grossly incombustible human corpse being reduced to ashes in conditions so devoid of oxygen that a fiercely burning wood and plastic foam-filled armchair and dining chair cease to burn. When the room was first entered even above the smell of the incinerated body there was a strong smell of gas. As I mentioned earlier the gas supply was by way of a coin-operated meter and it had run out. Had the fire been extinguished in the normal manner when the gas ran out then there would have been no great smell of gas. Certainly not strong enough to be instantly recognisable over the smell of the incinerated corpse. I strongly suspect that the gas fire was extinguished during the incineration of the corpse because of the lack of oxygen. Gas requires oxygen to burn just as any other fuel does. There can be no combustion without oxygen and the same rule applies to SHC.

If the gas had run out before or during the conflagration then surely there would not have been a noticeably strong smell of gas. To leave such an amount of gas in the fetid atmosphere of the sealed room that it was still strongly present, when all had ceased to burn, then a considerable amount of unburned gas must have been released into the atmosphere of that room. This could only have occurred by the gas going out, because of the lack of oxygen, and continuing to flow until the coin ran out.

The victim's epilepsy and the proximity of a lighted gas fire gave rise to the obvious, yet erroneous, conclusion that she had suffered an epileptic fit and fallen headfirst on to the gas fire and so burned to death. This would be the second person to be incinerated in their living-room after being assumed to have fallen headfirst into/on to a fire in the county of Gwent in just over three weeks.

The gas fire was a standard three-burner type with a fixed guard to prevent clothing, etc, from coming into contact with the flames. The middle ceramic burner was blackened and broken. These facts were taken as evidence that the head of the deceased had struck the fire, catching fire and breaking the ceramic burner. As the head burned so the ceramic middle burner was supposed to have become blackened by the proximity of the burning head. No traces of skin or hair were found on the protective grille, which was neither bent nor damaged in any way. A tea cloth (clearly visible in the photograph) remained, neither burned nor even scorched, about a foot above the burners. Had Annie's burning head been lying against the grille then the cloth would have caught fire or at the very least have been plainly scorched and soot coated.

Six years after this incident I went to the home of ex-Police Inspector Colin Durham in Newport, Gwent. He had visited the scene of Annie Webb's incineration and was convinced that the cause of ignition was not the gas fire. He was convinced for the same reasons that I have described above. Colin took me into a room of his house in which there was installed a gas fire similar to the one in Annie Webb's room. I saw that the centre ceramic burner was broken in two and blackened. Colin explained to me that when the fire is set on low heat (which is how the fire is mostly used) it is only the centre ceramic block that is lighted. That block gets nearly all the use. Consequently it is the one that is blackened and also the first one to break with the constant expansion and contraction of normal use.

So, Annie Webb's fire showed only signs of normal use. There was not one shred of evidence to prove that she fell against the fire and was thus ignited. In the normal course of events the results of the examination of the fire would be taken as proof positive that she had not been in contact with it. However, when the spectre of SHC looms then the normal rules of common sense do not apply. Any vague possibility (and some not so possible) is dragged in to 'explain' the death and 'prove' that SHC was not the cause. The object of the exercise at inquests held into these cases of SHC is to explain away rather than to explain.

Like Henry Thomas, Annie Webb was alive when she started to burn. The pathologist's report stated that the cause of death was yet again – 1a. Burning. Analysis of a blood specimen revealed a carbon monoxide content of 15.5 per cent. Miss Webb was teetotal and a non-smoker. She had inhaled a significant amount of smoke before she died.

The pathologist stated in his post mortem report that the body had been almost completely destroyed and reduced to ashes. All that remained that was recognisable was as follows: the left leg below the knee and the right leg to above the knee; the right arm; and the blackened skull containing a very heat-shrunken brain. All internal organs were destroyed except for the left lung which was heat contracted and charred. The right arm only survived because when she fell to the floor her right arm was flung out and away from her torso. This differs from Henry Thomas's case – he burned while sitting in an armchair with both his arms in contact with his burning torso, so both his arms were destroyed. For the record Annie Webb was not obese; she was not even fat. In fact she was quite slim – this is quite obvious from the photo showing her remaining right arm and legs.

Once again, as in the Henry Thomas case, we are faced with the puzzling fact of the unburnt stockings on the remaining portions of Annie Webb's legs. With the exception of the surviving right arm, the remaining skull, ashes and lower limbs are exactly the same as Henry Thomas's remains.

CHAPTER FIVE

An Acausal Connection

In 1985, Bill Treharne-Jones, a producer for the BBC's 'Newsnight' programme placed advertisements in national newspapers asking for anyone with personal experience and knowledge of SHC to contact him. My colleague, ex-Police Inspector Colin Durham, got in touch with Bill Jones and supplied him with the details of the case of Annie Webb. At that time I had no knowledge of Annie Webb and Colin Durham knew nothing of Henry Thomas. Although both cases occurred in the same county and within a month of each other, nothing ever appeared in the local press other than the fact that a couple of pensioners had died tragically in house fires.

Colin Durham assisted Bill Jones in his inquiries and interviews. They obtained the permission of Annie Webb's brother, as next of kin, for the coroner's records and police photographs to be released to Bill Jones for the purpose of his investigation into the subject of SHC.

They went to the photography department at Gwent Police HQ in Cwmbran for the photos relating to Miss Webb's death. While there, they were asked by the photography technicians why they were not using the case of Henry Thomas.

Colin Durham admitted that he knew nothing of the case. As far as he knew the case of Annie Webb was the only case of SHC that had occurred during his entire service in the police. Once Bill Jones was shown my photographs of the Henry Thomas case he decided that he had to interview me as well.

Colin Durham contacted me and I agreed to the interview. I thought it was just a matter of telling Bill Jones my story to assist in his information gathering exercise. They both came to my home and we spent an interesting couple of hours discussing SHC in general and the case of Henry Thomas in particular. Bill Jones was most impressed with my story and then he and Colin Durham went on their way. I thought that was the end of the matter. Until that time I was not particularly interested in the subject of SHC. Now and again, in conversation, the subject would crop up and I would recount my experiences and give vent to my exasperation at the lack of interest shown by the forensic scientists who attended my case. I was not entirely convinced at that time that the phenomenon of SHC did in fact exist. The only thing of which I was absolutely sure was that Henry Thomas had not died in the manner that the forensic scientists insisted he had.

Some time later I was redecorating my living-room. I was not in too good a mood as I was suffering from a dose of flu and I hate decorating at the best of times. I had to get off the step ladder with my hands stuck up with paper paste to answer the phone. It was Bill Treharne-Jones wanting to know if I was ready to start filming. I told him that I had no intention of doing any filming. I had absolutely no desire to appear on TV. Suddenly I had an extremely frustrated TV producer on the phone. He said that he could not make a programme without pictures; it was, after all, a TV programme he was producing. I said that I had not agreed to appear on TV and I had not even been asked to take part in the programme. Bill said he thought I had understood that I was required in the programme when he interviewed me. In the end I capitulated and agreed to do the programme. That decision marked a major turning point in my life.

I had read the standard works on SHC which contained the usual pictures of ashes and unburnt portions of limbs euphemistically referred to as 'extremities'. These pictures were in the main the same as the scene I had witnessed at Ebbw Vale. Come the day of the filming in Ebbw Vale I arrived at the hotel where the BBC film crew were staying. Most of the crew were somewhat tardy at putting in an appearance after the previous night's 'discussions' in the hotel bar. I am not the most patient of people and I detest waiting. To keep me occupied and quiet, Bill Jones gave me the photos and coroner's reports on the death of Annie Webb to peruse.

Once again I was looking at a classic scene of SHC: totally destroyed body, apart from the blackened skull and the ubiquitous 'extremities', coupled with minor damage to furnishings. I read through the pathologist's report and the witness statements. Suddenly I was electrified. A short, handwritten addendum to the typed statement of Annie Webb's friend was to bring about a total change in my life. It made me an active investigator into a phenomenon which I instantly knew was not the much-vaunted 'candle' or 'wick effect'. The hand-written sentence that changed my life read, 'deceased had put paper in window and round door to keep draughts out – this was normal for her.'

Nothing in the report of Henry Thomas's death mentioned sealing against draughts. Whether anyone else had noticed I do not know. If someone had noticed it was not on record. As I related in my examination of the death scene of Thomas, I had examined the doors and windows and found the windows to be tightly fitting and steel-framed, and the doors to be sealed top, bottom and sides, with a proprietary draught excluder. I was not required to make a report of my examination of the scene. As no crime was involved my only function was to take the photographs.

As I read that hand-written sentence I experienced a revelation. Suddenly I knew that the fact that both the rooms were sealed was no mere coincidence. The connection between the two cases did not come to me then – just the feeling of absolute certainty that there was more than chance surrounding the two deaths. Here we have the amazing coincidence which Carl Gustav Jung would have termed an example of 'synchronicity' or an 'acausal connection', that is, two related happenings that are connected other than by the usual cause and effect principle. By pure luck I was handed the document whose relevance could be understood only by myself – I was the only person that knew both rooms were virtually hermetically sealed.

We filmed the programme and in January the following year it was screened. The programme was quite well done and in general left the question of SHC still open. The film showed a reconstruction of me attending at the home of Henry Thomas (which was then occupied by a young woman, Mrs Morris, and her children). I was filmed in the actual room explaining what I had seen there. During the course of the day we discussed the tragedy with Mrs Morris. She of course, knew all about the event. She said that when she moved in the walls were still covered in a greasy soot which she had tried to remove without success. She had painted over it but it kept showing through. Finally she had coated the walls with a heavy hessian-type material which was successful. More surprisingly she told us that when she had cleaned and polished the thermo-plastic tiles on the floor there were no marks to show where the body had been incinerated. Those tiles are the sort that mark very easily when in contact with quite low heat.

The Newsnight programme also showed an interview with retired London Fire Brigade station officer, Jack Stacey. He recounted his experience extinguishing the still-burning body of a tramp named Bailey at Vauxhall in London in

1967. This case is dealt with in detail later in Chapter 9.

Professor Gee, senior pathologist at St James' Hospital, Leeds, was shown briefly demonstrating his experiment in support of the 'wick effect'. Professor Gee had a paper published in 1965 in which he described his experiments in detail. (This is also dealt with fully in Chapter 11.) Professor Gee gave a verbal account of the 'wick effect' scenario. He said that the involved person collapsed due to a heart attack or something and fell into the fireplace or against some form of ignition. He said, 'Being an old lady and since these usually occur in the wintertime they're probably wearing a considerable number of clothes.' He continued to say that they became ignited at one end, say the head, rather like having a candle with the wick around the outside, the wick being the clothing and the body the candle. He said that as part of the clothing burned it melted the fat which then soaked into the clothing and in burning melted the next layer and so on down to the bottom of the clothes. He further stated that as the clothing of old ladies normally ends around the knee that would explain why the burning usually stopped in that region. He then showed how he had wrapped a piece of human fat around a test tube, which was in turn wrapped in cloth, and burned it in the draught of an extractor fan. The interviewer was astute enough to comment on the fact that there was no bone in the test package. The professor replied, 'No – there was no bone in it, that's right. But, of course the bone would be saturated with fat anyway in this sort of process and so it would burn really quite well. In fact, this is far from the case. As reported later in this book, though the fat content of the bone will burn away in such an experiment the bone structure itself is hardly affected.

Later in the programme an interview with the manager of a large London crematorium was shown. He was given pictures of spontaneous combustion to study. He had never heard of the phenomenon. On looking at the photos he was visibly taken aback. He stated, '. . . it seems as though the fire may have come from within.' He then went on to say that he thought the subject needed a lot of explaining and that it was frightening. When it comes to the destruction of bodies by fire then a crematorium manager has to be ranked as an expert in that field. The same applies to the fireman, Jack Stacey, with years of practical experience of the effects of fire on bodies.

A forensic scientist, Stephen Leadbetter, was shown humping about 10kg of books in the British Museum library to 'research' the phenomenon of SHC. He contributed a quote from a French surgeon, Dupuytren, who wrote in 1830 that the phenomenon was easily explicable by 'force of reason'. Force of reason showed that people rendered themselves helpless by imbibing too much alcohol and as a result fell into an open fire and burned away in their own fat. Leadbetter ended his contribution to the investigation with the observation, 'People either like a mystery or perhaps like to make a mystery.'

The programme had dealt with the cases of Thomas and the tramp, Bailey. Thomas was not an alcoholic, neither had he fallen in a fire from which he was too drunk to remove himself. Bailey, admittedly, was an alcoholic – but not only was there no fire for him to fall into there was also no possible form of ignition in the house to initiate his burning. Leadbetter had seemingly adopted the politician's trick of answering a question that had not been posed rather than face the more difficult proper question. I say 'seemingly' because, when viewing pre-recorded TV documentaries, one can never be sure that people have actually said what they appear to be saying with all the 'creative' editing that goes on. The programme ended with a clinical psychiatrist committing the fallacy of arguing from the particular to the general. He stated that, 'People [not some people] have a wish for supernatural beliefs . . .'

In May of the same year, *New Scientist* published my first article on the subject of SHC. I related the Henry Thomas case and first proposed my hypothesis of water in the body breaking down by 'some as yet unknown biochemical action' into the gases hydrogen and oxygen. I wrote, 'If conversion of the gases occurred at a suitable rate, then the resulting flames would be confined to the body. As it consumed the body, the burning hydrogen would use up all the oxygen, leaving none to support the combustion of other materials.' I further stated that ignition could result from body static.

Two editions of the *New Scientist* later brought a reply in the letters section. This was the first occasion that David X. Halliday of the Fire Investigation Unit of the Metropolitan Police Forensic Science Laboratory crossed my path. He stated the case for 'prolonged human combustion' which is the 'wick effect' under a different name. David X Halliday also put forward the theory of long slow burning while not noting the absolute necessity of adequate oxygen for any speed of burning. He also apparently overlooked the fact that Henry Thomas was reduced to ash and failed to comment on my hydrogen/oxygen theory. I thought it strange that no one commented on the fact I had categorically stated that Henry Thomas was alive at the start of his incineration. Eventually I got around to reading my printed article. I was unable to find any mention of that fact. I checked with the Forum editor of *New Scientist* who assured me that he had not cut the reference out. At the time I was writing my articles on a Spectrum 48k computer with a 'Tasword' word processing programme which automatically numbered the pages as they were printed out. I unfortunately omitted to print out one of the pages. As I had taken the trouble to ensure that the end of each page coincided with the end of a paragraph the missing page was not noticed. It was on that page that I mentioned the fact of Thomas being alive.

I later had a long conversation with Halliday by telephone. There was no meeting of minds. We disagreed on everything. At one stage I said that I had assumed that Henry Thomas had placed his spectacles on the edge of the hearth. Halliday told me in no uncertain terms that I must not assume any single thing when carrying out a scientific examination. He insisted that every single assertion must be proven beyond a shadow of a doubt. But the forensic scientists who attended the death scene of Henry Thomas had assumed that Thomas fell into the fire, that he set his head on fire in the process and had then sat down in an armchair to burn to ashes. None of their assumptions could be supported by evidence. Our paths were to cross again in the future 'QED' 'scientific investigation' of the subject of SHC.

In my researches I came upon an article by Alexander Ogston, MD, Assistant-Professor of Medical Jurisprudence at the University of Aberdeen. It was published in the *British & Foreign Medical – Chirurgical Review* (vol. 95, dated January 1870). Dr Ogston's article appeared in the section, 'Original Communications' under the title, 'On Spontaneous Combustion'. It is, quite possibly, the same source that Leadbetter used for it mentions Dupuytren's 'alcoholic' solution.

Dr Ogston stated that he had discovered fifty-four writers on the subject of SHC in the medico-legal literature of the day – Dupuytren was one of the writers. Of the fifty-four writers, Dr Ogston found that thirty-five expressed definite opinions on the validity of the phenomenon of SHC. Five were entirely sceptical, namely Drs Caldwell, Caspar and Taylor and the chemists, Bischoff and Liebig. Three believed in increased combustibility (preternatural combustion), namely Dupuytren, Stille and Guy. Ogston concludes, '. . . while the remaining twenty-seven, including the illustrious names previously mentioned (Fodere, Orfila, Gordon Smith, Paris, Briand, Breschet, Devergie, Henke, Apjohn, and a host of others) believe in the spontaneous ignitability of the human body.' So, in his own time, Dupuytren was in a very small minority regarding the existence of SHC.

One of the respected researchers of the day, one Fontanelle, reported on how alcohol was unable to assist in the burning of flesh. He demonstrated that portions of flesh soaked in alcohol will burn only so long as the alcohol burns in them. Rather like our Christmas pudding flambé, once the brandy is burned the pudding remains unburnt.

Further on in Ogston's article, Dupuytren is quoted as having written in the *Lancette Française* for February 1830 (no. 97) that he had, in frequently burning portions of bodies, found no difficulty in consuming them, especially the fat parts. 'I do not know,' he adds, 'a single example of spontaneous combustion in a lean and dry individual: all were, without exception, extremely fat.' My own research has revealed that the majority of cases of SHC involve individuals who are far from fat, whereas the wick effect is more likely to involve the fatter person, unless there is a suitable independent fuel supply involved.

Dupuytren continues with his explanation (that so impressed Stephen Leadbetter) to the effect that the victims of SHC are in the main fat old ladies much given to imbibing spirituous liquors who fall down drunk into or on to a fire and, because of their inebriated state, are insensible of their burning or incapable of removing themselves from the source of the fire and are thus incinerated. Devergie and others ridiculed this explanation, remarking that while the flame of fat is white, the flame in cases of spontaneous combustion is blue. (Throughout history, people witnessing occurrences of SHC have mostly reported that the colour of the flames is blue.) Beck, in a footnote to his *Medical Jurisprudence*, disposes of Dupuytren's views with the words, 'without derogating from his acknowledged talents, I will only add that Dupuytren was a better surgeon and anatomist than a chemist.'

One final quote from the good Dr Ogston before we leave him to sink back into oblivion: 'One fact, however, is rather remarkable, that none of those who totally disbelieve in the idea of spontaneous combustion, profess to have seen a single case analogous to those observed by its supporters.' This rather convoluted statement means that none of the sceptics have actually seen a case whereas the believers have. The same holds mostly true at the present time. Even when a modern sceptic is actually present at a case of SHC his prejudice and 'knowledge' cause him to see just another case of the 'wick effect'. Without an open mind it is impossible to see, for seeing is largely a function of the mind. The eyes are merely the instruments by which we can observe the world around us. What enters the eyes is converted to signals which are in turn interpreted by our brains. How we see the world depends entirely upon how we interpret those signals. All incoming data are interpreted according to what we know and, perhaps more importantly, to what we think we know.

CHAPTER SIX

The Experts

During my time at the police training college where I received my initial training, I was taught that forensic scientists could perform marvels if only we (the police) could provide them with the necessary forensic evidence. We were assured that every person always left some trace of their presence at the scene of a crime which, if detected by the forensic scientists, could place that person at the crime scene. All we had to do was produce the person, together with the clothes and tools, weapons, etc., he had used during the crime and the forensic scientists would prove the connection.

I spent the first ten years of my service utterly convinced of the infallibility of the forensic scientists before my naïvety came into headlong collision with the harsh world of reality. In the early 1960s, prior to the introduction of the 'panda system', I was stationed in a semi-rural area. I had received a complaint from the local Forestry Commission that a very hard-working thief had cut down thirty or so full-grown elm trees (pre-Dutch Elm beetle). I caught the public bus to the sub-divisional station and borrowed the sub-divisional van. The scene of the crime was way out in the sticks and could only be reached after several changes of buses and a very long walk.

On arriving at the decimated wood I found that all the missing trees had been felled with an axe. Only one axe had been used as was immediately obvious from the striation marks across the wood chips lying around the remaining tree stumps. The striations were caused by various nicks and some quite sizeable chunks missing from the cutting edge of the axe blade. The striation patterns were the same on all the chips, ergo one axe. I visited a few farms and found that one particular, and not very popular, local farmer had recently replaced a great deal of his fence posts with newly split elm posts. It did not require the services of the CID to figure out that the elms were now being pressed into service to contain a certain farmer's dairy herd.

I paid the suspect farmer a visit and had the dubious pleasure of trying to persuade a naturally taciturn individual to admit to an offence to which I had no witnesses, after being obliged to caution him in no uncertain terms that he did not have to say anything to me let alone admit to a crime. The caution, which had recently been revised, still caused me to froth at the mouth every time I had to administer it. There are assumptions in English criminal law to the effect that certain things are as stated even when they are patently not so. It is a legal assumption that every person, including the newly arrived immigrant or any visiting foreigner, even though he can speak not a word of English, is fully conversant with the whole of the criminal law of this country. In other words, 'ignorance of the law is no defence'. That being so, why can it not be assumed that people know that they do not have to admit to a crime? If we are concerned with *justice* why should a guilty person not admit to their guilt if they so wish? For some strange reason that I have never succeeded in fathoming, the revised caution (thought up by a clique of judges not by Parliament) was brought into effect so fast that officers on the beat had not yet received copies of it. The previous caution which had stood for fifty or so years required an arresting officer to caution a person once the officer had made up his mind to charge that person with a crime. That meant one could ask all the questions necessary to obtain evidence of guilt. The new caution required that any person suspected of committing any offence should immediately be cautioned. In effect if a person is driving a car with a defective sidelight then he must be cautioned before being asked any questions. That same person has to be cautioned again if arrested and again before being asked to make a statement. If he agrees to make a statement then the caution must be written down and signed by him before starting the statement. He is again cautioned before being charged. In effect every time a police officer looks at a suspect he has to caution him against admitting to the crime. If any reader is wondering at the increasing rise in the rate of crime then they might wonder, in the light of the caution, whether the judges should not shoulder some of the responsibility.

However, I digress. While bandying words with the taciturn suspect axeman I noticed a large tree-felling axe standing against the barn wall. I picked it up and saw there were so many chips out of the cutting edge it resembled a steel replica of a stone-age flint axe. I took possession of the axe and returned to the woods where I collected several specimens of chips from the ground as samples. I then cut several further chips with the axe as control samples. When holding a control sample next to an original sample it was apparent that mostly the exact same patterns flowed across from one chip to the other. There were some differences which were to be expected as the axe would have sustained some additional damage since those particular trees were cut down.

I returned to my station quite jubilant. I told the detective sergeant what I had done and that I needed the CID Morris Traveller to take the samples to the forensic science laboratory which was then situated at Cardiff. To my astonishment the sergeant proceeded to indulge in what was to my ears near blasphemy. He questioned the competence of the forensic scientists and my motive for wishing to take my samples to the forensic science laboratory. He asked me if the suspect was pleading guilty. I replied, in a rather superior fashion, that the suspect was obviously not pleading guilty; if he were then I would not require the services of forensics. He said that if it was a not guilty plea I was wasting my time. I was adamant that I wanted to submit the axe and wood chips for forensic examination. He told me that I could go by all means but I would have to find my own way without the benefit of CID transport. He would not allow their one vehicle to be used for chasing geese – forensic or otherwise.

I returned to my station to find that one of my friends, Special Constable Idris Lloyd, better still, Special Constable Idris Lloyd, van owner, had come on duty, complete with van. Idris promptly volunteered to transport me and my samples to Cardiff. We left for Cardiff after I had found the requisite forms for the submission of articles to the forensic laboratory and filled them in. As we drove to Cardiff I could not help but wonder why there was a box on the forms in which I was obliged to state whether or not the defendant was pleading guilty. I could not see how the defendant's plea could possibly have any influence on the ability of the scientists to examine my samples and the axe and conclude that the axe had or had not cut all the sample chips. In due course the axe and chips were safely delivered to Cardiff.

Two or three weeks later when I came on duty one morning my sergeant handed me the axe, together with the chips and the report of the forensic laboratory. As far as I can recall, after thirty years, the report boiled down to the fact that the examining scientist, while admitting that there were certain points of similarity, could not say with any degree of certainty that the same axe had cut all the chips. Having relieved myself of a few choice expletives I asked what I should now do. My section sergeant advised that I return the axe and apologise to the proud possessor of the brand new elm-posted fence.

The next hour found me back in the divisional van pulling into the suspect farmer's yard. I could not bring myself to apologise and, as I approached the farmer, about to hand over the axe, I had a sudden flash of inspiration. I said to him, 'I have had this axe and the woodchips examined by the forensic scientists at Cardiff. I now know that this axe cut down the trees.' He replied, 'All right, I admit it.' He then made a full written confession with all the appropriate cautions. I have no doubt that I was assisted by the fact that at that time there was on TV a very popular series called 'The Expert'. Marius Goring played the lead part of a forensic scientist who, as is always the case in these TV shows, carries out every stage of the investigations and without fail nabs the villain each week while the bumbling police officers fall over their own feet chasing innocent people in all directions. He was a sort of forensic Perry Mason. The power of TV is such that the mere mention of forensic scientists was then usually sufficient to produce an admission of guilt from the accused.

That was the day my eyes were opened to the fact that even forensic scientists can have feet of clay. Over the following years other incidents occurred which served to reinforce the fact of their fallibility. Many a conviction has been overturned on appeal when certain irregularities have been discovered in the laboratory procedures of a particular forensic scientist. Cases which did not rely on the forensic evidence to gain a conviction get thrown out on appeal once it is revealed that the same forensic scientist gave evidence as was found guilty of procedural irregularities in another case. By the time I clashed with the forensic scientists over the Henry Thomas incineration I was well used to the fact that they were far from being as clever or infallible as TV programmes and novels portray them. Forensic scientists are no different to any other group of people when it comes to ability in their chosen profession. All groups comprise the good, the bad and the mediocre. The really good are always outnumbered by the mediocre.

In this scientific age we have become used to the debunking of anything that does not fit into the scientific frame; in other words anomalous phenomena. Sceptical scientists refuse to accept as evidence any fact (which in any other situation would be accepted as solid proof) as proof of the existence of any of the so-called paranormal or psychophysical phenomena.

In June 1986, I received a letter from Don Brothwell, Reader in Zooarchaeology at London University. Though I received the letter at that time I did not get to read it until a few years later as my Siamese cat had knocked it off my desk with some other letters and they remained lodged between the desk and the wall until I moved the desk. (I must confess that I assumed my cat was the guilty party – he hasn't denied the offence.)

Don Brothwell stated that he had read my first article in the *New Scientist*. His own work includes forensic aspects of ancient bodies. He was interested in the case of Henry Thomas which he found puzzling (unlike some Home Office forensic scientists who were so convinced that Thomas died by the 'wick effect' that they weren't puzzled). The letter contained eight questions relating to the scene of the incineration of Henry Thomas. Brothwell wanted to know what temperature was needed to melt the lampshade and TV control knobs, how hot were the ashes of the body, how flammable was the material of the trouser legs and so on. Of course I could not provide the answers he requested. The only sample taken was the fibrous material from the top bar of the grate which supported the forensic scientists' theory that Thomas had fallen headfirst into the open fire and so set his head alight. (The reader will recall that, on analysis, the fibrous material proved to be of bovine origin.)

I found one of Brothwell's questions extremely interesting and very pertinent to settling the SHC 'wick effect' controversy. In question six he asked if there had been any estimates of the temperature required to 'calcine' the bones. He wished to know whether the bones had been whitened and fissured or merely blackened. He also asked if anyone had attempted to estimate the temperature by examining the calcined bones. He also stated that if any fragments of the bones had been preserved, the firing temperature could be ascertained by electron spin resonance.

Sadly, no samples were taken and kept. I felt embarrassed at my inability to answer Don Brothwell's questions. However, his letter shows that there are scientists capable of obtaining some definite answers to the mystery of SHC. If, as he proposed, an electron spin resonance test were to be made on the bones of suspected cases of SHC, the resulting discovery of the firing temperature would certainly settle one argument. I described the calcined bones of Henry Thomas as being pure white like blackboard chalk as opposed to John DeHaan's description of the calcined bones and ash in the Oregon 'wick effect' murder case which were grey. It is believed that the firing temperature in 'wick effect' cases is in the region of 500°C. If the firing temperature of the white calcined bone remains of a SHC case were to be ascertained as in the region of say 1300°C then it would be obvious even to the most determined sceptic that there was a very unusual burning process involved. Such a process could well be such as I propose in Chapter 18.

CHAPTER SEVEN

The Lavoisier Syndrome

'Accurate knowledge is the basis of correct opinions.'
ANON.

*'Faith manifests itself not in moving mountains but
in not seeing mountains to move.'*
ERIC HOFFER

The 'Lavoisier Syndrome' was first described in my article on the subject of SHC and the death of Henry Thomas which was published in the *New Scientist* magazine in May 1986. The Lavoisier Syndrome is a condition afflicting a considerable section of the scientific community. The syndrome is not a new manifestation, neither are scientists alone in suffering from its effects. Some experts and specialists have been displaying symptoms of the syndrome throughout recorded history. It is the common state of 'believers' in general to be so afflicted.

A wise, self-taught American dockworker/philosopher, Eric Hoffer, said, 'Faith manifests itself not in moving mountains but in not seeing mountains to move.' A mountain is a pretty obvious object. However, the Lavoisier Syndrome creates a mental block which prevents the afflicted person from seeing mountainous facts which do not conveniently fit into his theoretical landscape. How can a man solve a problem he cannot or refuses to recognise because to do so is considered to be heresy?

This is a suitable juncture at which to explain my reasons for naming this inability to see the obvious the 'Lavoisier Syndrome'. Antoine Lavoisier was a famous and great French chemist in the eighteenth century. In fact he is considered to be the father of modern chemistry. In 1772, a committee of the French Academy of Sciences was called upon to debate persistent reports of falls of meteorites. The committee was given two meteorites to examine.

'Knowing' that stones cannot fall out of the sky, Lavoisier's committee reported that the witnesses to these heavenly bombardments were either mistaken or lying. The subject of meteorites continued to surface and be denied by the experts throughout the remainder of the eighteenth century.

In 1790, the parishes of Creon and Juillac in south-west France were literally showered with meteorites, some of which weighed 20lbs. The meteorites caused considerable damage to crops and property. The local mayor and some 300 villagers signed an affidavit attesting to the truth of the incident. The affidavit was sent to a physicist, Pierre Bertholon. He published it, while publicly deriding the actions of so many people in attesting, in a legal document, to an event which was obviously wrong as it was 'physically impossible'. It is difficult to see how any man, no matter how learned, can dismiss such testimony so lightly and so publicly. Is it likely that 300 people could imagine they saw stones fall from the sky? Imagination can hardly damage crops and property.

Admittedly, in light of the level of knowledge at that time, such an occurrence would appear impossible. It would fly in the face of reason. That, however, was not sufficient reason for the meteorite testimony to be dismissed out of hand as perverse lies or a mistake. Physical 'laws', derived from observations, indicate probability. Only observed facts can result in certainty and, paradoxically, not always then. When reason is at odds with observed phenomena then reason must always be questioned.

In general, the scientific world will only accept facts which are amenable to proof by the 'scientific method'. Physical phenomena occur whether they are capable of being proved by the accepted scientific method or not. Meteorites shower down on earth daily as they have done since the earth was formed and so they will continue to do, regardless of the opinions of scientists or any other doubters.

Let us examine the 'scientific method' of ascertaining facts relative to any aspect of the physical world. The scientific method requires any experiment, when correctly set up and performed, to yield a certain verifiable result. For the 'truth' of that result to be accepted in scientific circles the experiment must be capable of being performed by any other person in the same fashion and must yield the same result every time. This is known as replication. If an experiment cannot be replicated by others then the results of the experiment are rejected.

It is an undeniable fact that the immense body of knowledge now in existence and being constantly added to has resulted mainly from the application of the scientific method of investigation. This does not necessarily mean that such is the only method of obtaining knowledge. I must plead guilty to a more than casual interest in paradoxes. One paradox, seemingly incapable of resolution, goes thus: why do so many scientists, engaged in seeking answers and making new discoveries, so often act as though they already have all the answers? They persist in denying the existence of phenomena which do not fit into their own self-constructed and constantly changing frames of reference. The mass of extant knowledge is enormous and is doubling every few years. It has long been impossible for any one man to know all that is known relating to his particular speciality. In the time of Sir Francis Bacon (the sixteenth/seventeenth centuries) a man could be well versed in all the sciences and still able to turn out excellent poetry in his spare time. Now every discipline is split into smaller and more tightly defined specialities – the effect of which is similar to fitting a horse with blinkers. Mountains on the periphery of the vision are just not seen. The tunnel vision of specialisation prevents researchers from seeing a solution outside their special fields.

Specialists are inherently inefficient whether human scientists or some other species. On the survival of the fittest scene the highly specialised species are always the first to go. The phenomenal success of man on this planet is due to the fact that he is the most unspecialised animal on earth and thus infinitely adaptable.

Many experts are contemptuous of the opinions of people not qualified in their field. They seem not to realise that most of the disciplines in which they exercise their expertise resulted from the discoveries and inventions of individuals with no qualifications in those fields. Thomas Edison did not finish grade school. At twelve years of age he was earning his living selling newspapers. He went on to invent the Edison screw electric lamp, the phonograph, the cinematograph and a host of other appliances, from which have sprung whole industries and branches of science crammed full of highly qualified experts. Many such experts in these fields would not now give credence to the opinions of such an untutored person as Edison.

Possession of 'expert' knowledge can be a distinct disadvantage. Had the Wright Brothers possessed the knowledge of their 'expert' detractors then they would not have wasted time building a heavier-than-air machine that could not possibly fly. They would have spent their efforts advising other ignoramuses that they were attempting the impossible. However, the brothers (erstwhile newspaper publishers and builders of bicycles) happy in their ignorance, built their airplane and the rest is history. They did not know enough to dissuade them from their endeavours. I find it strange that the experts, who knew that heavier-than-air machines could not fly, never wondered how the heavier-than-air birds managed. But then, the birds were doubtless too stupid to know better. Man was already taking to the skies in hot air balloons which were of course lighter than air and could thus float. Did the sceptics not notice that birds flew and did not float? The Wright Brothers, together with birds, effectively demonstrate that ignorance can be bliss.

Scientists in general are dominated by the scientific method. However, it is not an infallible tool of discovery. A tool it is and, like all other tools, it is more suited to some applications than others. Physicists engaged in subatomic particle research (quantum physics) know the futility of attempting to predict the behaviour of particles. In subatomic physics there are no certainties – only probabilities. Just because physical phenomena are more amenable and their behaviour more predictable at the macro level does not mean that such phenomena must always behave in a predictable manner.

Common sense demands that where the scientific method is incapable of testing certain observed phenomena it is the method that should be rejected not the phenomena. If such a method cannot be found then it should at least be accepted that, for the moment, some things are not amenable to our present methods of examination and analysis. The apparent phenomenon which is incapable of being subjected to the scientific method of examination should not be dismissed as hallucination merely because it does not conform to man-made criteria.

A common objection to taking phenomena such as SHC seriously is that it is contrary to 'the laws of nature', 'the laws of physics' and 'the universal laws'. From whence came these 'laws'? Did Moses bring them down from the mountain, engraved in stone, with the Commandments? There are no such 'laws'. They exist only in the minds of men. For the most part they are as immutable as the laws that are made in Parliament but are changed with a lesser frequency. They are merely man-made hypotheses which appear to work and which suit our purpose until they are of necessity rewritten.

As knowledge advances so certain hypotheses or 'laws' are scrapped and replaced with updated versions which comfortably embrace the new discoveries. Thus Copernicus upset Ptolemy's applecart and was himself upset by Newton. Einstein revised Newton's universe and his theories are now in the process of being reworked by Stephen Hawking. So it has always been and no doubt will be *ad infinitum*. The old makes way for the new. This constant changing of the 'laws' is not an easy matter. It is seldom achieved without a certain amount of 'blood letting'. Academics fight it out with drawn pens in the various scientific publications until eventually another herd of dinosaurs shuffle off stage right. An advance in knowledge is often delayed by the unreasonable clinging of the savants to discredited theories – the more so if the outmoded theories are their own.

The Lavoisier Syndrome is largely responsible for the continued denial of observed phenomena. Peer pressure plays a large part in delaying the acknowledgement of phenomena outside the accepted frames of reference. A research scientist is only as good as his reputation. To progress in his chosen field he must continually publish papers, articles in scientific journals and, best of all, books. All must be approved and accepted by his peers. To be respected and provided with the necessary facilities for his research he has to conform. Should he have made his name and be world famous then he can afford to express opinions and adopt views that would be the ruin of less well-established colleagues. There is, however, a limit to just how offbeat his opinions can safely be. Any scientist daring to publicly express a belief in the validity of the SHC phenomenon would immediately become suspect. His road to the Nobel Prize would suddenly become potholed and strewn with numerous obstacles and diversions. He is thus obliged to conform.

Let me tell you a story. In 1939, JLB Smith, a South African ichthyologist (a zoologist who studies fish), was presented with a fish which had been caught by native fishermen. The fish was highly unusual and they knew of the strange man who studied fish. Guessing correctly that he would pay a good price for the fish they trudged for hours through the heat of the day to his residence. By the time they arrived the fish was pretty ripe. However, it was still in a sufficiently good state for Smith to eagerly purchase it. The fish was a coelacanth which had supposedly been extinct for fifty million years.

Did Smith turn cartwheels and shout for joy? Did he even shout 'Eureka'? No. He kept quiet for a long time, suffering recurring nightmares in which he dreamed he found a coelacanth. Morning after morning his waking relief ebbed away with the dawning realisation that his nightmare was all too real. He was so conditioned by his training and so bound by his 'knowledge' that he suffered agonies before he screwed his courage to the sticking point and released the details of his historical find. He suffered all those agonies because he feared the ridicule of his peers. He later vividly described his mental torment in his book entitled, *Old Fourlegs*, the non-technical name for the coelacanth.

The common or garden variety of forensic scientists in Britain are employed by the Home Office and, as such, are civil servants. The work they do is, in the main, far from exciting. It consists of repeatedly running the same tests over and over; day in day out. They are not, for the most part, in the vanguard of those engaged in making momentous discoveries. As with other civil servants their ascent up the promotion ladder results from passing the appropriate examinations and serving the requisite time at the various stages. Their progress, though slow, is certain, as long as they do nothing to blot their copy book. A very large blot would result from any expression of belief in such a suspect subject as SHC. The training of analytical scientists is such as to brainwash them into a blind belief in the scientific method of investigation. Civil servants are not noted for their dash and verve. The number of forensic scientists having to plead guilty to harbouring original ideas would not be overly high.

The whole world knows perfectly well that a human body cannot catch fire and be reduced to ashes, including the major bones, merely through a carelessly dropped cigarette or a spark from an open fire. But such scenes are relatively common. That they result from a misplaced cigarette or spark is a wrongful assumption, the validity of which has never been proven. All tests to date have been unsuccessful and so tend to support the SHC hypothesis – if only by default. Too many untenable assumptions are made by lay persons. What is really amazing is the large number of supposed experts who also make the same unfounded assumptions.

Not many people have witnessed a person being doused in methylated spirits or paraffin and then having a lighted cigarette deliberately thrown onto their clothes. I am certain that any reader being so mistreated would be in no doubt that they were about to become the centre of a fatal conflagration. It is common knowledge that a lighted cigarette and clothes soaked in meths or paraffin constitute a recipe for disaster. It is also common knowledge that a cigarette dropped into a bucket of paraffin or meths will result in an explosion of fire. *Wrong! Wrong! Wrong!* I will relate in a later chapter how I conducted my own experiments and proved that cigarettes are unable to cause a fire in any of the above circumstances.

Show many a forensic scientist a small heap of ashes with an odd foot or two on the periphery and he will claim that it is quite common for humans to be so reduced by the mere touch of a cigarette. Were humans so readily combustible then the atmosphere would long have succumbed to the greenhouse effect hastened by the continuous contamination from the thick, foul smoke of human candles.

Opponents of SHC cloud the issue and attempt to confuse and silence any lay person daring to question the impossibility of such an occurrence, by solemnly intoning such phrases as 'preternatural combustion', 'candle effect', 'long, low-temperature combustion'. Such terms are entirely without meaning in the context of a living person being reduced to ash in a sealed room wherein the atmosphere is devoid of the necessary percentage of oxygen (in excess of 16 per cent) to support the combustion, slow or fast.

The principle which has ruled scientific endeavour since the creation of the Royal Society is 'Take nothing on trust'. This principle should be extended with the addition of the following words: 'Dismiss nothing without proper investigation'. Adherence to such a precept is laudable in the common run of scientific analysis and investigation. This precept does not prevent close examination of such seemingly preposterous claims as that made by the mayor and 300 inhabitants showered in meteorites. To dismiss such a claim and to refuse to examine the considerable physical evidence is, to say the least, unscientific. Though this incident occurred in the eighteenth century the same attitude prevails today.

Sceptical scientists are all too ready, as indeed are other experts, to refuse to accept that persons other than they can see or correctly interpret physical occurrences. In their unreasoning reluctance to recognise the facts of SHC they deliberately or subconsciously fail to see the obvious and stretch, out of all proportion, certain facts to fit their argument.

In Greek mythology there was a bandit named Procrustes who lived by the roadside in the land of Attica. He was ideally situated to offer refreshment and accommodation to people travelling the lonely road. Procrustes had two beds, one short and one long. He insisted that his lodgers fit the bed he chose for them. Perversely, he insisted on the short bed for the tall persons and the long bed for the short persons. Naturally the lodgers never did fit. Procrustes provided a devastatingly simple solution to the problem. He sawed off the legs of the tall persons so they fitted the short bed. The short persons were stretched on the rack till they were tall enough to fit the long bed.

In such Procrustean fashion do the opponents of the phenomenon of SHC treat the facts of the case. They perversely persist in cutting and stretching selected facts of SHC incidents until they fit, albeit uncomfortably, into the currently wrong-sized twin beds of physics and chemistry.

Following publication of my first *New Scientist* article, Professor Ron Westrum congratulated me on having the courage to write the article and so lay myself open to the inevitable criticism of the sceptics. At the time I thought he was exaggerating the situation. I have since found that he was correct.

I had been constantly confounded by the inability of, or refusal by, forensic scientists to see what was so plain to me. At times, in the face of such concerted opposition, I began to doubt my interpretation of the evidence of my own senses. Luckily I have always marched to my own personal drumbeat and was able to retain my faith in myself in spite of being out of step. However, it was still a great relief to hear from Ron Westrum. I was more than pleased to discover that a Sociology PhD actually made a study of the behaviour of scientists when confronted with anomalous data. Ron Westrum sent me copies of some of his articles dealing with the reluctance of experts to see unwelcome phenomena. I was amazed to find that in one of his articles entitled, 'Blinded By The Light', he chose, as I did, the reaction of Lavoisier and colleagues to the reported meteorite strikes to illustrate his theme. Scientists are subject to the same faults, foibles and vanities as anyone else.

Though I am content to stand up and argue matters with sceptics on my own it is still comforting to know that there are others, especially academics, of like mind. Though solitary by nature and nurture I have no wish to be totally isolated. I shall expand upon the nature of Ron Westrum's work in a later chapter.

CHAPTER EIGHT

A Little Learning

'A little learning is a dang'rous thing.'
ALEXANDER POPE, AN ESSAY ON CRITICISM.

'The man who makes no mistakes does not usually make anything.'

E.J. PHELPS.

In 1940, in the preface to his essay, 'What is Life?', Irwin Shrodinger (physicist) wrote to the effect that humanity has long yearned for an all-embracing, unified system of knowledge. As we have progressed and developed ever-increasing specialities we have an even greater need for such an overall unified system of knowledge. There is however, no possibility of any one person comprehending all knowledge. Schrodinger argued that certain persons should be prepared to take an overview of various disciplines and endeavour to synthesise facts and theories so as to develop more comprehensive theories and discover greater facts. He acknowledged that such people should be prepared to make fools of themselves on occasion when they would inevitably get it wrong. There indeed lies the rub – not too many academics are prepared to look foolish.

I have long engaged in the synthesis of facts and theories relating to different disciplines. Consequently I have made many mistakes. I have also triumphed and confounded specialists on several occasions in different fields of expertise.

Fifty years after Shrodinger wrote his insightful essay knowledge has increased at an even greater rate than he could have foreseen. He wrote that it was then next to impossible for one man to know more than a small portion of the whole. It is now impossible for one man to know all there is to know in his own particular branch of science. It is, moreover, extremely difficult to keep up with the daily advances in a single specialist branch of a science. The unhappy result of this necessary breaking down of the sciences to ever smaller and smaller specialities is that the wood can no longer be seen for the trees. Scientists are now toiling away each in their own little section of the wood, investigating a certain species of tree, completely unaware of the many and varied types of tree growing in neighbouring areas of the same wood.

A helicopter pilot, overflying the wood at a certain height, is able to see that the wood is a kaleidoscope of different types of trees at different stages of growth. He may not know much about a particular tree, but, unlike them he is familiar with the wood as whole. The pilot is in a position to observe that trees of the same species in different locations have different rates of growth. He might possibly be able to observe the conditions that cause such different rates of growth. The scientists, studying the same species in isolation, would not be aware that the two groups differed.

The present practice of specialists burrowing away in tightly encapsulated fields of investigation has led to them acquiring extremely specialised, esoteric states of knowledge. Whatever study time they have is entirely taken up in keeping abreast of developments in their own field. The result is that on any other subject they are virtually clueless. It is no coincidence that year after year the BBC 'Mastermind' award goes to a tube-train driver, taxi driver or housewife. There is no shortage of academics in the competition yet they are often beaten by the ordinary person who, for the most part, possesses few, if any, academic qualifications. This singular lack of knowledge on the part of specialists on any subject outside their speciality is recognised by educational psychologists. They have named the state 'professional cretinism'.

We now come to the reason for this digression. Had I gone through the usual channels of formal education it is not beyond the bounds of possibility that I might have achieved a degree and possibly a doctorate. With such letters after my name no one would question my right or ability to write this book on such a controversial subject. I do not possess such palpable signs of education attesting to some degree to my store of knowledge and/or ability. It is therefore necessary for me to list some of my achievements in lieu of formal qualifications.

I have no O' levels or any other educational qualifications, yet I have a far greater breadth of knowledge than the majority of university graduates. For a variety of reasons I spent my formative years, during World War Two and after, being shunted around between numerous relatives and complete strangers while my parents enjoyed the war each in their own fashion. Being constantly on the move and always the new boy I soon developed an intense dislike for school. However, I loved learning and spent a great deal of my childhood in libraries or holed up reading library books when I should have been in school. The subjects that I studied, at my own whim, were of so much greater interest than the dates that various villains ascended to the throne of England or how much wheat was grown in Canada. I studied lycanthropy, witchcraft, astronomy, Einstein's Theory of Relativity, spherical trigonometry, seven figure logarithms and many more in no particular order. At fourteen years of age I found a Bible on a bombsite. I read it from cover to cover and became an atheist, hence my disbelief in things supernatural. I went from subject to subject as the whim took me. I have continued to study in such fashion right up to my present age of sixty-one. I hope to continue to do so until I die somewhat in excess of 100 years of age.

When I joined the police force, after three years in the regular army, I passed all the exams including the mathematics exam which had many questions relating to fractions. I was at that time unable to do fractions. Having discovered decimals some years before I could not see the logic of fooling around with such cumbersome equations. Finding myself on the spot with my future at risk I hastily converted the fractions in the questions to decimals and solved the problems. I then converted the answers back to fractions. My Chief Constable told me at the subsequent interview that though my education was not all that it could be I had demonstrated a more than adequate share of common sense and intelligence. He considered these attributes to be of more consequence than formal education and so accepted me into the then Monmouthshire Constabulary (now the Gwent Constabulary). During my three months' training at Bridgend Police Training School I consistently came top in every single examination without ever staying in at night to study. I consistently beat into second place an ex-National Service Officer and university graduate. My lowest marks were in excess of 90 per cent. I won the book prize for consistently coming top in the exams. The prize was a copy of the *Concise Oxford Dictionary*, which I still have.

As late as 1978, I spent three months on a scenes of crimes course at Durham Police Headquarters. Once again, at the advanced age of forty-four, I consistently finished every exam well before the allotted time and came top in every one of the nine examinations, including three photography examinations, despite there being on the course three ex-professional photographers with City and Guilds and HNC qualifications. I constantly asked questions in class and wrote up my notes and never spent any free time studying the subjects. I was able to take the course so effortlessly in my stride because it was one small arc of my continuous learning curve.

My unquenched love of learning and constant thirst for

knowledge has resulted in my acquiring a vast store of information which spreads across many different subjects. I have on occasion been criticised by experts for not being wholly versed in their particular subject. They doubt that I am entitled to express an opinion on a subject that I have not studied in such detail as they. One can easily become bogged down with detail. Some things are better observed at a distance which allows one more breadth of vision. More than one expert has quoted Pope's well-known first line of the following phrase from his 'Essay on Criticism':

A little learning is a dang'rous thing;
Drink deep, or taste not the Pierian spring:
There shallow draughts intoxicate the brain,
And drinking largely sobers us again.

This is quoted in criticism of my propensity for absorbing the bones of a subject rather than spending a lifetime studying it in detail. I do in fact 'drink largely' of the lake of knowledge rather than at a tributary spring inasmuch as I know something of a great many subjects. Knowing a little of this and a little of that often results in an insight into a problem that the experts not only cannot solve but often swear is incapable of solution. I also make a lot of mistakes as I feel my way sometimes with insufficient knowledge but I learn from my mistakes which, when all is said and done, is how we learn naturally. 'The man who makes no mistakes does not usually make anything.' E.J. Phelps.

At the end of my first week on the fingerprints course I solved the problem of obtaining fingerprints from a water-logged corpse. I did this over the weekend in my own time as the instructors had said that they would be grateful if any of us could come up with a better method than the one they were using. At the time they were coating the sodden fingers of a corpse with layers of strippable paint (the hands had been amputated and were kept in the refrigerator). This paint was plastic and water based and could be stripped off once a thick enough layer had been built up. The thickness of paint would display a negative impression of the prints. These would be inked, photographed, reversed for colour and finally printed. It took a long time for the paint to dry on the cold and clammy, salt-water sodden fingers and would take several days to build up a sufficient thickness. Included in my store of knowledge was the necessary know-how for moulding and casting in several different media. I felt sure that after a few hours' experimenting I would be able to cast flexible prints of the corpse on to a pair of surgical rubber gloves. I was given permission to buy the materials I needed and spent a few hours over the weekend perfecting a satisfactory method.

I soon developed a process whereby I was able to transfer the prints of my left hand on to a surgical glove worn on my right hand. It was then a simple matter to ink the prints and roll them on to the fingerprint forms. The result was a perfect set of prints. The moulding materials I used would not be unduly affected by the cold clammy skin of the corpse except that it would take marginally longer for the medium to set. I estimated that I could have the corpse printed in less than an hour.

I am afflicted by an inability to leave things alone once the original objective has been achieved. When learning a technique or experimenting I constantly go off on a tangent as my mind is stimulated and ideas come thick and fast. One of the first questions that is asked of the fingerprint experts on the course is, 'Can fingerprints be forged?' It seems that someone on every course always asks that question. The answer is always the same, 'No'. Having solved the problem of the sodden corpse my thoughts naturally turned to the ultimate challenge – forging fingerprints. It seemed such a natural progression to follow on from the work I had already done. I soon completed a 'lift' consisting of real prints and forged prints.

Come Monday's fingerprint class I gave the fingerprint 'lift' to my instructor and asked him to take it to the North Eastern Criminal Records Office Fingerprint Department and ask them for their opinion on the prints. NECRO was attached to the training school. The following morning I met the instructor outside the classroom as we were both about to enter.

He handed me the lift and said that the fingerprint experts could find nothing unusual about the prints. I told him what I had done and proudly displayed my glove and explained how I had solved the problem of fingerprinting waterlogged corpses. His reaction was strange to say the least. Instead of falling on my neck with tears of joy, and praising me for the clever one that I was, he merely looked somewhat discomfited and said, 'Yes, well John, we'll be late for class. We'd better get moving.' We went into class and not another word was ever said about either the corpse prints or the forged prints.

It is my sceptical opponents that have all the diplomas. I do not begrudge them their achievements, neither do I regret not having such qualifications myself. Had I taken the formal route to an education I might now be another 'professional cretin', set in my ways and 'knowing', beyond any shadow of a doubt, that such things as SHC just cannot be. I am not constrained to view problems with the educational tunnel vision of most experts. There are those who have sufficient strength of character to emerge from the formal education process with their critical faculties untouched. Two such mavericks that spring readily to mind are Dr Vernon Coleman and Professor Hans Eysenck, both of whom are viewed with jaundiced eyes by their professional peers for their outspoken criticism of medicine and psychiatry and their refusal to conform.

I would find life much easier if I did in fact have a PhD or at least a BSc. I would then be taken more seriously by major publications. It is not enough to be right when criticising the Establishment. If one does not have impressive formal qualifications then the media are in general uninterested. I will give a classic example.

In April 1987, an article of mine was published in *Prediction*. In the article I criticised a supposedly scientific test carried out at the University of California by Shawn Carlson of the Physics Department. Some months previous Carlson's article relating the tests and conclusions were published in the prestigious international science magazine *Nature*. The article caused a sensation in the press, tabloids and broadsheets, all trumpeting how Carlson had finally scientifically proven astrology to be baseless.

I have no belief in astrology, though I was familiar with Michel Gauquelin's studies of the correlation between birth signs and occupation. I was curious as to why Carlson should have spent so much time, effort and money in an endeavour to discredit astrological natal predictions. I felt that he would have been much better employed looking into the fact that people undergoing two years of psychiatric therapy for neurotic disorders showed the same remission rate (roughly two-thirds) as those receiving no treatment.[1]

The test, which was in two parts, was carried out with a large number of students and some participating reputable astrologers. The astrologers had to construct natal charts depicting the personality traits of the students. Each student was given three natal charts. They had to pick out the chart which they considered best fitted their subjective assessment of their own personality. A little reflection is sufficient to make one realise that people tend to pick assessments of their personality or character that are flattering though untrue rather than true but unflattering. If the students scored correctly at a ratio of one in three then the score would equate with chance and would be claimed as a success for the scientific hypothesis. If the score was significantly greater then the astrological hypothesis would prevail. Carlson also introduced a scientifically acceptable personality assessment known as the

California Personality Inventory consisting of 480 true-or-false questions. This was introduced to refute any claims by the astrologers when they failed that people do not readily recognise their own personalities. Once again the students had to choose their correct CPI profile subjectively.

The second part of the test required the astrologers to pick out the correct CPI assessment according to their natal assessment. Once again they had to pick the correct one out of three. The results of the first astrological test were one in three correct and equalled chance. However, the scientific claim to victory was grudgingly omitted because the students scored exactly the same with the CPI. Carlson stated:

> *From the results of Part 1 we notice that the test group scored at a level with chance, consistent with the scientific hypothesis. However, we cannot rule against the astrological hypothesis because the test subjects were also unable to select their own CPI profile at a better-than-chance level.*

At this point Carlson should have called it a day. Instead he endeavours to excuse the obvious fact that the so-called scientific CPI process is of as much use as a natal chart. He lists the following reasons why the students perversely failed to pick out their correct CPI assessment:

> *Some subjects may have recognised correct information about themselves but subconsciously chose a CPI which did not describe them as well, to avoid admitting they had certain character traits. Such denial in a large percentage of the subjects would tend to cancel a positive effect.*

He continues, 'The CPI may not test the kind of attributes by which subjects may easily recognise themselves', and, 'People may be unable to recognise accurate descriptions of themselves.'

This is a supposedly scientific double-blind study, in which a scientist is parading a number of excuses for students failing to validate an allegedly scientific personality assessment method. The same excuses apply equally to the astrologers' natal charts. Having conceded his failure to demolish the astrologers with Part I of the test Carlson then claims absolute victory with Part II, in which astrologers were unable to match the CPI profiles to their personality/character analyses based on the students' natal charts.

I have given only the briefest account of Carlson's article which consisted of six pages of very impressive and intimidating computer printouts, histograms, charts, tables and a great deal of text describing *ad nauseum* the meticulous efforts of Carlson's team to ensure that astrology had a fair shake. If one only read the blocks of print in heavy type it seemed that the scientific hypothesis had been proved. It would seem that the journalists just skipped through the bold print conclusions instead of reading all the data.

The title of my article was 'Double Blind or Double Standard?' Carlson's test certainly used double standards. The astrologers were found to be wrong on the basis of a test that had already been proved of no more value than the natal charts of the astrologers. Due, no doubt, to my lack of qualifications my article was rejected by both national and regional newspapers. The publication of my critique of Carlson's conclusions in *Prediction* passed without comment.

By choice I remained a constable throughout my service. This allowed me the time and freedom to pursue my whims. In so doing I gained a reputation as an eccentric.

Note

1 *Psychology is About People*, H.J. Eysenck, Pelican Books, 1982.

CHAPTER NINE

The Fireman and the Tramp

When I got in through the window I found the body of a man named Bailey lying at the bottom of the stairs leading up to the second floor. He was lying partly on his left side. There was a four-inch slit in his abdomen from which was issuing, at force, a blue flame. The flame was beginning to burn the wooden stairs. We extinguished the flames by playing a hose into the abdominal cavity. Bailey was alive when he started burning. He must have been in terrible pain. His teeth were sunk into the mahogany newel post of the staircase. I had to prise his jaws apart to release the body. The fire was coming from within the abdomen of the body.

Thus reads the major portion of the statement dictated to me by Jack Stacey, retired London Fire Brigade station officer.

At 5.21a.m. on 13 September 1967, one of a group of office cleaners phoned in a report of some strange blue flickering flames showing inside the upper windows of a derelict house at 49 Auckland Street, Lambeth, London. The ladies were waiting at a bus stop on their way to work when their attention was drawn to the first-floor window of the derelict house. They could see the flickering blue light but could not see the source of the light. They presumed that it was burning gas so they phoned the fire brigade from a nearby telephone kiosk.

Station Officer Jack Stacey and his crew were on the scene within three minutes. They had the fire under control by 5.26a.m. Jack Stacey was first up the ladder and through the window. The house was owned by Lambeth Council and was derelict. There was no gas or electricity on site. Bailey's clothing was searched and failed to reveal any matches, lighter or other form of ignition. In short, there was nothing in the house that could have caused Bailey to catch fire.

When interviewed on the 1986 BBC 'Newsnight' programme, Jack Stacey stated:

The flame itself was coming from the abdomen. There was a slit of about four inches in the abdomen and the flame was coming through there at force, like a blowlamp – a bluish flame which would indicate that there was some kind of spirit involved in it. There's no doubt whatsoever, that fire began inside that body. It couldn't begin anywhere else. That's the only place it could have begun – inside that body.

Inquiries in the area by the local police revealed that Bailey was a well-known tramp. He was known to be an alcoholic and most probably imbibed methylated spirits –which was a common practice at that time with such down-and-out alcoholics. It was also known that he was a non-smoker.

The coroner, Dr Gavin Thurston, concluded that death was a result of the ignition of the contents of the stomach. I suppose that, like Jack Stacey, Dr Thurston considered the alcohol imbibed by Bailey as the source of the flames. I am unable to agree with that supposition. How could the stomach contents burst through the wall of the stomach and the abdominal muscles to reach the necessary air/oxygen for combustion? And where was the source of ignition ready to ignite the spirit if it could burst through?

Alcohol could not burn 'at force like a blowlamp' unless it was under pressure like a blowlamp. I am prepared to concede the possibility, however unlikely, of a pressure build-up in Bailey's stomach sufficient to burst his abdomen (though a massive burp would be far more likely to ease the pressure). What I cannot possibly accept is that pressure from a human stomach could be maintained when the hole in the abdomen is four inches wide.

How could that level of pressure be maintained for at least seven minutes? The cleaners first observed the blue flames at 5.19a.m. The fire continued to burn until extinguished – with some difficulty – by Stacey at 5.26a.m. So the blue flames were roaring from Bailey's abdomen for at least seven minutes. It was a most remarkable occurrence which was witnessed by several people of whom one was a highly experienced fire brigade officer. Though possibly the most remarkable and reliably witnessed occurrence of possible SHC in modern times, this case is always ignored by the sceptics. It is so obviously *not* amenable to any of the usual excuses, i.e. carelessly dropped cigarettes, open coal fire, gas stove, electric fire, etc.

Apart from the physical impossibility of alcohol bursting through an abdomen and igniting with no source of ignition and maintaining an impossible pressure for an equally impossible length of time, we also have to face the fact that the amount of alcohol in a human stomach could never have done the damage to the flooring and stairs that was in fact caused. Six square feet of flooring and stairs was quite heavily charred. The mahogany newel post was charred for a length of two feet or so and to a depth of three quarters of an inch. If alcohol-soaked material normally burned to that extent then there would be an awful lot of charred and inedible Christmas puddings after the flaming brandy treatment.

From the official fire brigade photographs of Bailey's corpse, lying on the first-floor landing and stairs, it would

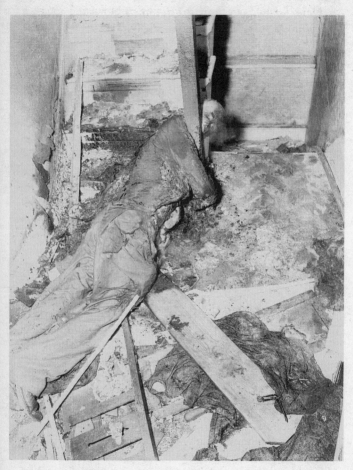

Death scene of the tramp Bailey, showing burn damage to the stairs.

seem likely that he was about to mount the stairs to the second floor when the tragedy struck him. As the roaring flames burst through his abdomen he probably grabbed at the wall for support with his left hand and instinctively clasped his open right hand to his flaming abdomen.

Jack Stacey had to use a pry bar to force Bailey's jaws apart to release him from the charred mahogany newel post. He assumed that Bailey died in agony because his teeth were clenched so tightly on the newel post. That does not have to be the case. The photo shows clearly that Bailey's head and face were subjected to a substantial amount of heat. If his open mouth was in contact with the corner of the post then the ligaments and tendons would contract strongly with the heat so closing his jaws tightly on to the intervening newel post. This is a more likely scenario.

My investigations into cases of people falling victim to SHC have led me to believe that they do not move once the flames erupt. In all probability they do not move for some time before the actual eruption, hence the title of this book, *The Entrancing Flame*.

Jack Stacey further stated that he had to put a reel hose into the abdominal cavity to extinguish the flames and that they did not extinguish easily. That Bailey was alive when he started burning is not in dispute. The pathologist gave the cause of death as 'asphyxia due to inhalation of fire fumes'. Here we have one of the most bizarre causes of death imaginable. The man suffocated on the fumes of his own combustion.

There are more than a few fire officers who are convinced of the fact of SHC, however, Jack Stacey is not one of them. He will have no truck with such 'nonsense'. He is the archetypal bluff Yorkshireman and he doesn't believe in mysteries. Bailey was an alcoholic, addicted to meths drinking and had drunk too much of it. The meths had erupted through his abdomen and somehow exploded into flame. It was an

The eviscerated tramp Bailey, showing the apparently missing right hand.

unusual death from Jack Stacey's view but not worthy of all the fuss that has been made of it over the years.

Whenever the sceptics among the scientists conduct experiments to prove the validity of the 'wick effect' the case of Bailey is studiously avoided. Though the BBC 'Newsnight' programme featured the case of Bailey and featured Jack Stacey narrating his personal involvement, no forensic sceptic chose to attempt to explain away Bailey's death as being a result of the 'wick effect' or any other effect.

Every schoolboy knows that candle wicks do not burn downward with audible blue flames. Stacey related how the flames emanating from Bailey's abdomen were scorching the landing and stairs underneath the corpse. The burn damage to the floor, stairs and newel post is plain to see. It is obvious that no 'wick effect' caused that amount of charring to the mahogany newel post. The official fire report states: 'about 6 sq. ft. of timber flooring on landing on first floor slightly damaged by fire'.

The Bailey case is an anomaly which is ignored because it cannot be made to fit within the constraints of the 'wick effect' theory. Most other cases of SHC do bear some similarities to 'wick effect' cases and can be 'procrusteanated'[1] to fit, albeit uncomfortably.

Note

1 See Chapter 12, 'The Procrustean Stretch'.

CHAPTER TEN

Anomalous Phenomena

Anomalies are all too often dismissed as aberrant data of no importance. When the accepted rules state that such and such should always add up to a certain result, and in the main they do, the occasional anomaly is not considered to be of any real importance. After all, 'it is the exception that proves the rule'. How often have we heard that homily trotted out when someone is confronted by an apparent anomaly? The phrase as it is understood today is not even logical. How can that which breaks the rule prove the rule to hold good? The answer is that it cannot and the homily, though comforting in the face of an anomaly, is meaningless. This was not always so. When the homily was coined the word 'prove' had an entirely different meaning to its present-day one. It was used in the sense of 'testing'. Thus, 'it is the exception that *tests* the rule'. Anomalies should not be shrugged off. They have purpose and, if carefully considered and examined, will often lead us to a different conclusion to that we would otherwise arrive at – possibly a much more accurate conclusion.

In Chapter 16 on Ashton and Soudaine, I will show how several anomalies were remarked upon but then brushed aside. By so doing valuable clues to the existence of SHC were ignored.

The remains of the socks and trouser bottoms of Henry Thomas, the remains of Annie Webb's stockings and the remains of Ashton's socks, trouser bottoms and shoes were all anomalies which were ignored. When I finally realised the significance of those unburned items of clothing they were no longer anomalous. They became perfectly explicable when considered as aspects of SHC. I feel sure that most anomalies are the direct result of the tightly defined specialities that exist in the sciences. Some facts do not fit comfortably within an artificially prescribed discipline. They overlap two or more separate disciplines which perhaps should not be so separated. This compartmentalising places an artificial restriction on the acquisition and understanding of knowledge. That it is so compartmentalised is a direct result of the limits of our brains or minds to comprehend the whole picture. We need more unspecialised overviewers of knowledge (as proposed by the physicist Irwin Shrodinger in his essay, 'What is Life?') who, while they will not fully understand each discipline, will be able to make connections between different disciplines that could provide even greater leaps of knowledge. I ask all seekers of truth to embrace the anomaly – it may be trying to tell you something.

Though not all scientists believe in the 'wick effect', they are not about to embrace the SHC hypothesis without proof. I applaud such an attitude. What I deplore is the atmosphere that prevents such scientists speaking up and voicing their doubts about the 'wick effect' without being subjected to a witch hunt by their less open-minded colleagues. I have spoken to, and corresponded with, numerous scientists, coroners and pathologists who have confided in me that they are not able to accept the 'wick effect' as a complete answer to the phenomenon. Many have said that they believe I am right when I suspect there is more to be discovered. I have letters from such people explicitly stating their disbelief in the 'wick effect'. I will not name them in this book and cause them possible embarrassment at the hands of their colleagues and peers.

Having been faced with a situation that had all the appearances of SHC (the death scene of Henry Thomas) I had no course but to embrace the possibility of SHC. I must stress the word 'possibility'. Being open-minded I was quite prepared to recognise any positive proof of the 'wick effect' However, it transpired that the explanations put forward by the sceptics in support of the 'wick effect' were inherently unlikely and SHC seemed to be by far the more reasonable prospect. It became more and more like a viable hypothesis with every so-called explanation that flew in the face of reason. I later saw 'experiments' conducted, not with the intention of discovering the truth, but specifically aimed at proving the 'wick effect' hypothesis (BBC 'Newsnight' and 'QED' programmes in 1986 and 1989, and the Arthur C. Clarke programme, 'The Burning Question', 1994–5).

To date I have no personal knowledge of any scientist carrying out any experiments to test the SHC hypothesis. Neither have I come across any literature describing any such experiments. Every so-called experiment that has been carried out has been so done for the sole reason of supporting the 'wick effect'. Sceptical scientists have castigated me for not being convinced of the 'wick effect' mechanism by the 'evidence' of experiments which have all failed miserably. Such failed experiments are then quickly passed over with a few assertions that the experiment would have succeeded if there had been more time or more heat. Though termed 'experiments' at the time they were made, when I point out that they failed miserably these 'experiments' suddenly become 'demonstrations' made merely to illustrate a point. Test tubes and steel skewers have been used as the stiffening core of a fat candle instead of bone and when the fact was queried the answer has been that bones are saturated in fat and will burn quite readily[1]. Full accounts of these and other 'experiments' are given in later chapters.

Earlier in this book I mentioned Dr Ron Westrum. He gave me great encouragement in investigating SHC in the face of solid opposition from the Establishment. His particular field of study is the reaction of society in general and scientists in particular to anomalous events. I can best describe him by quoting his CV from *Knowledge: Creation, Diffusion, Utilisation* (vol. 3, no. 3, March 1982) as follows:

> *Ron Westrum is Associate Professor of sociology at Eastern Michigan University and Associate Director of the Centre for Scientific Anomalies Research there. He is Associate Editor of the centre's publication,* Zetetic Scholar, *and is also Editor of the* Social Psychology of Science Newsletter. *He is interested in a broad range of issues in the sociology of knowledge and has published several articles on social knowledge of anomalous events.*

One of Professor Westrum's most striking examples of a hidden event is the battered child syndrome which is now accepted worldwide as fact. In actual fact it took 100 years, from the first remarking of the syndrome in 1860 until 1961, for the matter to receive official acceptance. As is usual in these events it was not the expert paediatricians who discovered the BCS. It was a lowly radiographer, John Caffey, who had for some years noticed, on his X-ray photos of children, evidence of many past injuries in the form of broken arms, legs and ribs. He wrote a paper on the subject in 1946 and again eleven years later. His articles were published in a radiological journal and were not picked up by paediatricians in general. He also promoted his ideas on the subject in teaching seminars and at conferences. In the mid-1950s notice began to be taken when further articles on the subject were published by others in the *Journal of the American Medical Association*. Still the medical profession did not recognise the BCS. Many paediatricians would not believe that non-psychotic parents could treat their children in this fashion. Also, most believed that it was only isolated incidents anyway.

Around 1961 a survey of hospitals and district attorneys revealed a total of 749 cases. The results were published under the title, 'The Battered Child Syndrome', in the *Journal of the American Medical Association*. Such a furore was created in the national and professional magazines, journals and newspapers, that within a few years laws were passed in all fifty states requiring the reporting of apparent cases of BCS. The number of cases reported grew steadily year by year until by 1976 over 500,000 cases were being reported annually. These are only the *reported* cases. In 1967 it was thought that the real number of abused children in the USA was somewhere between two and a half and four million. This appalling treatment of children by their parents had always occurred. It was just not *seen*.

Another favourite example of Ron Westrum's is the 'ball lightning' saga. Ball lightning has for hundreds of years cropped up from time to time and was firmly believed to be just another item in the catalogue of fanciful paranormal phenomena. Reported sightings of ball lightning were dismissed by the experts as being in all probability either hallucination or the result of the retina of the eye of the 'observer' retaining an image after seeing a flash of normal lightning. The phenomenon defies several 'laws' of physics and so is still to this very day not scientifically possible.

As late as 1979 the existence of ball lightning was denied on the grounds that 1,500 observers had taken part in a survey of thunderstorms conducted by the British Electrical Research Association. Not one of the observers had mentioned seeing ball lightning. However, a query revealed that the survey did not specifically mention ball lightning. So the survey's relevance to the question of ball lightning is somewhat suspect.

Specific ball lightning surveys brought surprising results. One survey (Aryl, 1966) showed that about 4 per cent of the respondents had seen it. As it can only be seen over a short distance it was considered that ball lightning occurred about as often as normal lightning. The phenomenon of ball lightning is now generally accepted as fact by meteorologists (but still not by all). However, it is still just as physically impossible as it ever was. How it behaves is known, how it manages to behave thus is unknown. In fact it is a much more mysterious phenomenon than SHC which will probably prove much easier to explain in terms of normal science once it is recognised there is a phenomenon to investigate.

Seeing is not merely a mechanical act. No two people ever see the same thing in exactly the same way. Seeing is largely a psychological process inextricably bound up with our prejudices, training, knowledge, mood, etc. Untrained eyes and minds do not see the same things as trained eyes and minds. Any untrained person being shown an open corpse on the mortuary table would only see a revolting mass of flesh and blood. They may recognise the odd organ such as the heart or liver, kidneys etc. They would see nothing of the attachment of muscles to bones, nothing of the fascia separating the various muscles. They would see nothing of antagonistic muscles and see how they work in opposition to create movement and even allow us to stand or sit still without collapsing in a heap. No two people can ever see the same thing or situation and gain exactly the same impression or knowledge from what they saw.

Let us consider for a moment Sir Francis Bacon (1562–1626), statesman and philosopher and considered to be the father of modern science. Imagine that he were walking in dense forest and came across a time-warp giving him a glimpse of action in this present day. He sees a drag-racing driver as he is disappearing into the bowels of his monstrous drag-racing machine. He then sees that machine roar off in an ear-shattering crescendo of noise and disappear in clouds of smoke and methanol vapour. The time-warp closes and Sir Francis Bacon is once again alone in the sixteenth-century forest. Now for the sixty-four dollar question. What did Sir Francis see? How would he describe what he had just seen? There is no way that he would be able to say that he had just watched a man climb into a machine and drive off in it. He has no concept of self-propelled machines. He has to interpret what he saw in the light of his state of knowledge, which, at that time would most likely have been greater than that possessed by most other living men. If his religion was strongest then he would have seen a sinner being dragged off to hell by the devil in a cloud of hellfire and brimstone. On the other hand were mythological beasts to figure largely in his imagination then no doubt he would have seen a man being carried off and devoured by a fire-breathing dragon.

I am just as guilty of not seeing what is there as the next person. When it comes to SHC I look with a certain amount of knowledge and a certain amount of conviction. Therefore I see what a sceptic, wholly convinced of the 'wick effect' and equally armoured in his 'knowledge' that SHC is a myth, does not and cannot see. As an example of how the lack of knowledge restricts the ability to see that which is in plain view, I draw the reader's attention to the photograph of the tramp Bailey (see page 79).

When I first acquired the photo I noticed that he seemed not to have a right hand. I knew that this picture was famous and had been studied by many SHC researchers and sceptics. There had never been (to my knowledge) any published comment on the missing hand. I fell into the same trap as the forensic scientists. They say that if SHC did occur then it would be known to them. Others before had investigated the phenomenon to no avail. There is nothing to see out of the ordinary so they do not see anything extraordinary. I did not clearly see that Bailey's right hand was indeed no more. I half persuaded myself that it was due to the camera angle. After all, if his hand was missing it would have been mentioned before. I held that view for eight years, until I was suddenly and unexpectedly given reason to suspect that the hand had possibly been destroyed in the flames emanating from his abdomen. (See the case of Jeannie Saffin in Chapter 19.)

Before I had even checked the photo I could see clearly in my mind that the hand was indeed missing. It appeared to have been burnt off. When I checked with several other people who had been equally familiar with the photo over the years they admitted either to a vague curiosity about the apparently missing hand or else had never noticed it was missing.

This further demonstrates that we tend to see that which we expect to see. Though I pride myself on often seeing that which escapes the notice of others I allowed myself not to see what was in plain sight . . . *seeing* carries the connotation of understanding. There is a world of difference between merely looking and seeing. When we finally get to understand something that has puzzled us, our enlightenment is often expressed with the words 'I see' meaning 'I now understand'.

SHC will, sooner or later, be perfectly explicable by physics and chemistry. It is no use denying the phenomenon merely because it is extremely difficult or because there are so few cases it is not worth the effort. I have reason to believe that there are, in fact, many cases of SHC incinerations in Britain alone each year. They are mostly passed off as the result of carelessly dropped cigarettes. My reasons for this estimation will be given later.

When sceptical scientists use the words, 'There is no scientific proof', those are weasel words; they are copping out. What they really mean is, they are as yet unable to find the scientific proof that will prove or disprove the argument. Scientific proof is always available but throughout the history of man there have been many occasions when some phenomenon or other has been ascribed to supernatural causes or dismissed as hallucination until science developed sufficiently to provide an understanding of the 'impossible' phenomenon. Science still has a long way to go before it can claim to have all the answers. It is slowly dawning on some scientists, especially mathematicians in the field of 'fuzzy logic', that the old scientific method of investigation is not necessarily suited to the investigation of all phenomena. It is a fact that some phenomena do not lend themselves to investigation by the 'scientific method'. The 'scientific method' requires that an experiment must be replicable by anyone and must yield the same results every time. A little thought on the part of the reader will soon cause him or her to realise that SHC is one such unaccommodating phenomenon. Once a person has combusted and been reduced to ash there is no way to replicate the event. It would be more honest for scientists to say, 'We do not as yet know of any scientific proof', instead of categorically claiming that there is no scientific proof. This would apply especially when there is no 'scientific proof' that the phenomenon does *not* exist. As Ron Westrum is fond of saying, 'In the rear-view mirror of history, we can easily distinguish the meteorites from the mermaids.'

We can easily laugh at Lavoisier and co. for their naivety in so readily dismissing so many reports of stones falling from the sky. To us, in this modern space-age, meteorites are common knowledge even to children. It is true that hindsight gives us 20/20 vision and so we should not be so ready to ridicule anything that does not fit within the present confines of our knowledge. Proper investigation of such phenomena can lead to further advances in our knowledge of the universe. It will also, on occasion, prove the myth to be just that – an empty myth based on superstition and ignorance.

Let us have no more of sceptics pontificating on the impossibility of any disputed phenomena and dismissing the matter out of hand with the words, 'There is no scientific proof', especially when, as in the case of ball lightning there has been no scientific search for the scientific proof. In the event of such a search being made and failing to reveal the necessary proof such a fruitless search should still not be considered as proof positive that the investigated phenomenon does not exist. Such a conclusion can only be justly arrived at when scientific proof is available that proves the conclusion. The absence of proof of existence is not proof of non-existence. Such absence of proof has two possible explanations. 1. The phenomenon being investigated does not exist, hence the dearth of scientific evidence to prove its existence. 2. The phenomenon does exist but the proof, for the moment, eludes us because we don't know where to look or are unable to recognise it.

I have come across several instances where clues to the validation of the SHC hypothesis have been missed or deliberately ignored, after initial puzzlement, because they do not fit in with the 'wick effect' hypothesis. The clues are mainly to do with the speed of the combustion. The 'wick effect' necessitates an uninterrupted burning period of between twenty-four to forty-eight hours to complete combustion without forced oxygenation. On several occasions clues to the incineration period being much shorter have been overlooked or ignored.

Because anomalous phenomena are being ignored by the people who should be investigating them such phenomena are seldom to be found reported in the professional journals of those same people. When, on occasion, they are stirred to make some sort of investigation into a particular phenomenon then they find that there are so very few reports that they conclude there cannot really be any substance to the phenomenon. A typical example is shown in the next chapter. Professor Gee, in 1965, while citing a case reported on by Dr Gavin Thurston in *Medical-Legal Journal*, 1961, comments, ' ... this appears to be the only recorded case in this country [Britain] during the present century.' In actual fact there have been hundreds of cases reported worldwide this century in the press and in journals that specialise in recording events of a strange and anomalous nature. This is (like the Battered Child Syndrome) in spite of the fact that cases of SHC are hidden. They are seldom reported at the time as such. Of those that are reported only a minuscule fraction are commented on by anyone in the Establishment, such as coroners or pathologists.

So when a sceptic decides to look up the literature on the subject and finds little or nothing he mostly assumes that if there were any reported occurrences of the phenomenon then the experts, of which he is one, would be aware of them. Ron Westrum lists two fallacies which cause the most problems in preventing sceptics from looking into the problems. They are as follows: 1. If anomalous events are observed, they will usually be reported. 2. If they are reported, the relevant 'experts' will be aware of the reports.

We already know that experts are not all that keen to report events that may draw ridicule down upon them and thus harm their reputation and promotion chances. When they look in the literature for reports of the events they find there are none or so few as to cast doubt on the existence of the phenomenon. So another instance of the phenomenon goes unrecorded.

I hope that by now I have given the reader some insight into the reasons that dictate the sceptical scientist's mind-set with regard to allegedly paranormal or even supernatural phenomena. I regard the paranormal in the same manner that I regard anomalous events. They are all normal manifestations and occurrences within the physical laws of the universe within which we live. I just believe, with some justification, that we do not as yet understand our universe, either the whole or its parts. As we acquire more and more knowledge so the list of paranormal/supernatural/anomalous events grows ever smaller. I fully expect the apparent phenomenon of SHC to be brought within the realms of the 'normal' within the not too distant future.

Note

1 Professor Gee's demonstration on 'Newsnight'.

CHAPTER ELEVEN

Preternatural Combustion – The Facts

> *'What's in a name? That which we call a rose*
> *By any other name would smell as sweet.'*
> *Romeo and Juliet* W. SHAKESPEARE

In this chapter the facts of preternatural combustion or PC, more commonly known as the 'candle or wick effect', will be examined in detail. We will see how blind acceptance of a theory can lead normally discriminating people into the most ridiculous errors of judgement. It is possible to successfully counter all the anti–SHC arguments without resorting to the supernatural. That scientists should avoid the subject of SHC like the plague is perfectly understandable. It is extremely unlikely that SHC will ever be successfully demonstrated. Who would volunteer? 'Anyone for combustion?' The odds on the likelihood of anyone combusting in the presence of a committee of the Royal Society must be truly astronomical. Should such an unlikely event occur, it is doubtful that even the scientists would stand back and objectively observe the process to its conclusion. Having themselves interrupted the process of incineration they would, in all probability, deny that the occurrence was evidence of SHC because there was still only anecdotal and not scientific evidence of the phenomenon.

Hidden in the fantastical body of SHC literature are many accounts of genuine occurrences of SHC. There are also a lesser number of instances where people have been grossly incinerated by the normal processes of combustion. Such cases are examples of a phenomenon known as preternatural combustion. (Dictionary definition of 'preternatural' – 1. Exceeding what is natural or regular; extraordinary. 2. Lying beyond or outside normal experience; supernatural.) These cases have often been mistaken for SHC. A small number of PC cases have been examined by experts who, having proved the natural causes of the combustion, have promptly declared all cases of SHC to be as easily explicable. It is a common logical fallacy to extend an argument to cover subjects that, though similar in some respects are not the same.

Extensive research has convinced me that there are no writers on the subject who have dealt with an occurrence of SHC or who have even seen the aftermath of such an occurrence, which would enable them to accurately distinguish between fact and fantasy. Consequently there is a proliferation of books perpetuating the most preposterous flights of fancy. We are inundated with compendiums of strange events, including SHC, wherein all kinds of weird theories are put forward in explanation of the SHC phenomenon. No reasonable person can possibly accept such ridiculous assertions as fact. Understandably, no scientist wishes to be associated with these lunatic theories.

My task is to separate SHC from the realms of the supernatural and purely fanciful. Once it is established that such a phenomenon exists then some progress will have been made towards understanding it. SHC is a natural phenomenon and will, eventually, be scientifically explicable. Apparent contravention of the accepted physical laws does not prove the impossibility of SHC. I am far from certain that SHC contravenes the laws of physics in the same way that ball lightning appears to. An atmosphere must be created in which scientists can examine the subject of SHC both dispassionately and without fear of ridicule.

One of the most notable protagonists in the SHC controversy is Professor Gee. His paper on the subject, entitled 'A Case of Spontaneous Combustion', was published in *Medicine, Science and the Law* (vol. 5, 1965). He states in the opening paragraph:

> *Belief in the occurrence of spontaneous combustion of the human body is of respectable antiquity. More recently opinion has swung away from the quasi-supernatural views of earlier years, to regard such cases as due* to unusual degrees of flammability of the human body *in certain circumstances, distinguishing the condition with the name* preternatural combustion.

The term 'spontaneous combustion' is used only once in the whole article, as quoted in the above paragraph. The term 'candle effect' is mentioned *en passant*, as having been coined by Dr Firth of the Home Office Forensic Laboratory Service. The single mention of these two phrases has fuelled the controversy for the past thirty years.

The whole of Professor Gee's article is devoted to a detailed investigation of the remains of an eighty-five-year-old lady who fell dead onto the hearth of an open coal fire. From the evidence of his opening paragraph Professor Gee did not consider the normal body to be anything like a candle. He agreed with the conclusions of Dr Gavin Thurston, H.M. Coroner, who stated that a human body could burn in certain, specific circumstances.

Professor Gee stated in his paper that the lady was ' . . . grossly incinerated, apart from the right foot which lay beyond the damaged floorboards. Both arms and the left leg had been almost completely destroyed.' He also describes how he conducted 'a few simple experiments', in which he burned some human fat, wrapped in cloth, to demonstrate the 'candle effect'. Professor Gee effectively demonstrated the difficulty of burning a human 'candle'. He stated that he had to apply the flame of a Bunsen to the fat candle for a full minute to start it burning. (A Bunsen burner is a type of gas blowlamp, commonly used in laboratories.) The prolonged application of the Bunsen flame was necessitated by the high water content of the human fat. Sufficient water had first to be driven off before the then 'clarified' fat became sufficiently flammable.

To quote Professor Gee:

> *One end [of the fat candle] was ignited by a Bunsen flame, the fat catching fire after about a minute. Although the Bunsen was removed at this point, combustion of the fat proceeded slowly along the length of the roll, with a smoky yellow flame and much production of soot, the entire roll being consumed after about one hour. (my italics).*

He further stated that the burning was carried out in the forced draught of an extractor fan which obviously ensured a more than adequate supply of oxygen to fuel the flame. The flame temperature was rather low and the burning incomplete as indicated by 'much production of soot'. Professor Gee also stated that melted human fat will burn at about 250°C. This is human fat without the water – rather like clarified butter which the Tibetans use with wicks for lamps.

In short, after the prolonged application of a gas torch, the professor set fire to a few ounces of human fat, wrapped in several layers of cloth. These few ounces of fat then took 'about one hour' to burn away in a forced draught. Had an appropriate amount of flesh, bone and blood been involved, I very much doubt that the burning would have proceeded to completion quite so satisfactorily.

The professor described his experimental candle as consisting of, 'a test tube, to provide firmness, enveloped in a layer of human fat, the whole enclosed by several layers of thin cloth'. Surely a bone would have provided the necessary firmness? It would also have demonstrated whether such a human candle (albeit all fat and no lean) could destroy bone. Professor Gee's own account of the experiment convincingly demonstrates the extreme difficulty of burning to ash a complete human body with all the flesh and bone plus about ten gallons of water. Such an occurrence is virtually impossible with a normal air supply and an external source of flame – let alone in a sealed room with an atmosphere so oxygen-depleted that a wax candle cannot burn (as in the cases of Henry Thomas and Annie Webb). SHC mostly results in the total destruction of the torso. 'Total' means *total*, nothing less. Not a single organ survives, neither do the bones, except for the odd fragment. Having described the corpse of the lady as 'grossly incinerated', Professor Gee then writes, 'The coronary and internal carotid arteries showed atheromatous disease. No soot particles were present in the trachea. Blood from the right foot contained no carboxyhaemoglobin' (the blood was free of carbon monoxide). These findings show that the victim was dead before she burned. SHC seldom leaves any trachea (windpipe) or coronary arteries to examine. As quoted earlier, 'Both arms and the left leg had been almost completely destroyed'. Already the description differs markedly from the typical SHC case. It is obvious that there is more damage to the extremities and limbs than to the torso. SHC is more prone to destroy the torso completely while leaving extremities untouched – provided they are not in contact with the torso during the incineration.

The professor was correct in his conclusion that the case was *not* one of SHC. The body lay in a fireplace and was ignited by a fiercely burning coal fire. It lay in the updraught of the chimney which provided a more than adequate supply of oxygen to assist the combustion.

Professor Gee carried out his experiment to test the validity of the conclusions arrived at by Dr Thurston, with regard to 'preternatural or spontaneous combustion'. Dr Thurston's conclusions were: 1. That under certain conditions a body will burn in its own fat with little or no damage to surrounding objects. 2. The combustion is not spontaneous, but started by an external source of heat. 3. This has occurred where the body has been in the draught up a chimney from a lighted fire. Oxygenation is good and the pull of the flue prevents outward spread of the fire.

So, there has to be an 'external source of fire' to maintain burning at least until the body is well and truly burning in the updraught of a chimney where oxygenation is good'.

So how can all the alleged instances of SHC be dismissed as the 'wick effect' by assuming that the victim was ignited by coming into contact with a 'viable source of ignition' while brushing against a lighted gas stove with an undisturbed kettle partially covering the gas flame? Or by a spark from a lighted fire or radiant heat from an electric or gas fire when there is no physical evidence to show that the victim was ever in contact with such 'viable sources'?

About a year before dealing with the Henry Thomas combustion, I attended at the death of another elderly man. He had carried a bucket of coal in from the coal shed and had made up the kitchen fire rather generously. While kneeling before the grate he suffered a massive heart attack and fell headfirst into the fire. Thus he was found some time later. Though his head was badly burned, and melted fat had run on to the hearth, there was no sign of any tendency on the part of the corpse to burn like a candle. The conditions of this case were exactly the same as those investigated by Professor Gee but the result was entirely different. This backs up Professor Gee's use of the word 'preternatural' in as much as it shows that a human corpse does not have a natural tendency to burn away even when lying on a well-stoked fire in a strong updraught. Those conditions alone, it would seem, are not sufficient to guarantee the reduction of the corpse to ash.

Professor Gee reports surprisingly that, at the time of writing (1965), he could only find one other reported instance of preternatural/spontaneous combustion in the literature this century. The two cases in my county both occurred in 1980. The Southampton and Folkestone cases (see Chapter 18) occurred in December 1987 and January 1988. No doubt there have been many more. The two in my county did not come to light until 1986 and then only as a result of inquiries by the BBC television producer, Bill Treharne Jones (see Chapter 5). In the case of ball lightning there were never any official reports of its occurrence until meteorologists were specifically asked to report observations of the phenomenon. No doubt the same lack of official interest militates against the reporting of many more cases of SHC.

Professor Gee's paper is constantly quoted by those opposed to SHC. He is regarded as the ultimate authority on the subject. In actual fact he examined a case that appeared, at first sight, to be SHC and he proved conclusively that it was an instance of the 'wick effect' (preternatural combustion). His conclusions have, ever since, been used to explain away cases that are manifestly totally different from the case on which he reported. It all derives from his unfortunate choice of title for his paper – 'A Case of Spontaneous Combustion.'

The fiercest and most bitter arguments can often rage over a controversy that is primarily a question of semantics. It makes no difference whether a rose is called a rose or a pansy or anything else. The scent of the flower is in no way dependent upon its name. The name makes no difference to any discussion of the quality of its perfume. However, let's assume that someone, engaged in a discussion of the relative merits of the scents of different flowers, mistakenly associates the name 'rose' with a nettle. A heated argument could easily arise about the scent of the 'rose'. No matter how heated or protracted the argument neither party would be able to convince the other that their assessment of the scent of the 'roses' was correct. The impasse exists until both parties correctly identify their 'roses' and then agreement naturally follows. The argument was over a problem which did not exist, as is so often the case with arguments.

People die because of such misunderstandings and countries have gone to war over such trivia. It pays to define all terms correctly whenever an argument arises. The term 'spontaneous human combustion' has been unwittingly hijacked by Professor Gee and pressed into service as descriptive of a case of 'preternatural combustion'.

The Greek philosopher and teacher Socrates insisted that every term used in an argument should first be rigorously defined and agreed by the opposing parties before argument was allowed to commence. Too many of Socrates' contemporaries considered him a pain in the neck. They cured the ache with a hemlock cocktail. Politics (invented in ancient Athens) became instantly more colourful, interesting and dangerous.

The argumentative Sophists could once again indulge in their favourite sport of winning arguments by fair means or foul without 'kill-joy' Socrates blowing the whistle on them and screaming 'foul'. Socrates took all the fun out of argument. By the time every term had been laboriously and boringly defined, it usually transpired that there was no disagreement to argue over. Even worse, the problem was often painlessly and inadvertently resolved in the process of defining the premises. Such behaviour resulted in a very peaceful but totally mind-numbing lifestyle for the argumentative Greeks. So they invited Socrates for one last drink – an offer he was unable to refuse.

Were Socrates around today to ensure that the terms were properly defined, the 'wick effect/SHC' argument would never have got off the ground. The facts of the 'candle effect' and the known facts of SHC cannot be brought into agreement because the two phenomena are entirely different.

The case Professor Gee investigated was first thought to be an incident of SHC. He examined the case and quite properly concluded that it was not SHC but preternatural combustion of a body in the presence of an adequately oxygenated external source of combustion. Had the professor entitled his paper 'A Case of Preternatural Combustion' the whole controversy may have been resolved. The term 'wick effect' has since become inextricably linked to SHC. Few people have actually read Gee's paper including the vast majority of scientists. Most experts in the field of combustion have heard of the two phrases.

Some know that Professor Gee carried out experiments while others just know that 'scientific experiments' have been carried out at some time by some person of note. They also 'know' that the whole matter has been satisfactorily resolved and the phenomenon of SHC is in fact entirely explicable in terms of the 'wick effect'. They have no idea that the 'wick effect' only describes the partial burning of an unusually flammable corpse in conditions of high oxygenation. Secure in their 'knowledge' they do not even consider facts which should stop them in their tracks.

One fact, which should give any first year chemistry or physics student pause for thought is, how can a human 'candle' burn in conditions which will not support the burning of an ordinary candle? It seems that the very 'knowing' is sufficient to close the eyes of people who should be more than usually observant.

We are all subject to prejudice. After nine years of research into SHC I must confess to being more than a little prejudiced against sceptics who dismiss the subject of SHC as the result of overheated imaginations of people of poor intellect. In my police work it was entirely necessary to suspend my natural prejudices in order to approach a situation with an open mind. If a police officer approaches an inquiry with a preconceived notion he is liable to see only those facts that fit his preconceptions. Such an attitude can result in a lost conviction or, even worse, an unjust conviction. Since my first experience of SHC I am constantly amazed how scientists, of all people, can be blind to concrete facts which relate to anomalous phenomena. It seems they cannot see that which they do not believe.

It is a common human trait to name everything whether or not we understand that which we name. To have named something gives us a power over that something. Hence the witches of old (and no doubt the witches of today) convinced themselves that they had power over demons by the mere fact of knowing their names. Even in this enlightened age most people are reassured to a certain extent once the doctor has put a name to their previously unknown dreaded symptoms.

By giving opponents of SHC a name ('wick effect') to apply to the phenomenon, which in itself explained away the very phenomenon, Professor Gee has made it possible for the phenomenon to be easily dismissed. Should any lay person raise the question of SHC he is promptly informed that the phenomenon has been thoroughly investigated by the acknowledged authority, Professor Gee. He is further informed, in no uncertain terms, that so-called spontaneous combustion has been proven to be entirely explicable in terms of present-day physics and is in fact due to the 'wick effect'.

This sounds most erudite and authoritative to the uninitiated. It certainly has been very effective in silencing most claims to the existence of SHC. Thus the professional experts silence the awkward questions of the laity. As George Bernard Shaw said, 'All professions are conspiracies against the laity.' (*The Doctor's Dilemma*, 1906.)

I will quote some facts given me by two experts in the fields of crematoria construction and pathology. Firstly Dr G.S. Andrews, retired pathologist, who worked for many years in Gwent County and carried out the post-mortem examination of the sparse remains of both Henry Thomas and Annie Webb. He does *not* subscribe to the SHC theory. However, he describes the condition of about six people presumed to have burned to death *per year* as the direct result of a carelessly dropped cigarette, 'In each case I feel the deceased has set fire to themselves or the fire has started in their bodies. It is not a question of the fire starting around them. They start a conflagration within themselves.' I then asked if any of the cases he had examined of lonely individuals being found burned to death in armchairs or beds had displayed unusually severe damage to the abdomen when there was not a great deal of damage to the surroundings. He replied, to my amazement, 'I don't know about a lot of burning elsewhere but a lot of them have the abdomen more or less completely destroyed.'

Such damage to the abdominal area entirely supports my contention that a great many more cases of SHC occur which escape notice because the fire brigade extinguish the fires before the bodies can consume themselves. Dr Andrews also said that he had dealt with about six cases of complete incineration, such as the Thomas and Webb cases, in thirty-eight years as a Home Office Pathologist.

My second expert is Clive Chamberlain, Managing Director (in 1989) of Evans International Ltd, manufacturers of furnaces including crematoria. Bearing in mind that pathologists (and myself) consistently report the total destruction of torsos including the bones, Clive Chamberlain states:

Bones do not crumble to dust as a result of combustion. They calcite. In other words they go to calcium oxide instead of calcium carbonate. But they do retain a honeycomb texture which is relatively easy to crush. You certainly would have something retaining the general shape of a bone. If you tell me that there isn't any then my scepticism is extreme. In fact all the remains from a cremation have to be crushed in a kind of spin dryer with steel balls in it.

When I quoted Professor Gee's experiment with human fat wrapped around a test tube, Clive Chamberlain commented,

'I think it best if I stay out of pathology and he stays out of cremation.'

Two non-academic, practical experts have stated categoric, verifiable facts relating to their specific fields of expertise. They have not ventured into some other field on which they are not qualified to comment. The pathologist states categorically (in his post mortem reports on Henry Thomas and Annie Webb) that bones are reduced to ash – which I can personally verify. The crematoria expert states with equal force that bones cannot be so reduced by cremation.

The two statements are mutually exclusive. Both cannot be true. Yet they are. The obvious solution to the seeming paradox is that the victim's bones are consumed by a process which is far more intense and effective than a crematorium. I would not dream of disbelieving either Dr Andrews or Clive Chamberlain – they both speak the truth. In spite of some of my earlier comments on experts I recognise and respect genuine experts who stick to their field of expertise. It is the expert in one narrow field who presumes to speak with authority about matters in a different field in which he has no expertise that draws my criticism. An example of such an overstretched 'expert' would be one whose field of research concerns the combustibility of materials used in the construction industry pontificating on conditions resulting in the destruction of human bodies, especially when he has never even seen such an occurrence or even the aftermath of such an occurrence.

I proposed, in my first article published in *New Scientist*, that the water in the body could, by some as yet unknown mechanism, break down to its constituent gases of hydrogen and oxygen. Hydrogen, burning in oxygen, produces a colourless flame. That is pure hydrogen burning in pure oxygen. Whatever is consumed by such a flame will cause the flame to burn in an assortment of colours such as blue. This accords with sightings of burning victims, e.g. the tramp Bailey. Such a form of combustion would answer the paradox of the combustion of a body in a low oxygen atmosphere and would also overcome the problem of the large amount of water in the body which inhibits normal combustion.

Destruction of the body by hydrogen and oxygen would produce, as a waste product, the same amount of water as was consumed in the combustion. This water would be produced as superheated steam. The expansion of this steam would be so great that it would be forced up the chimney at a great rate, leaving very little to condense on the cold outside window panes. The terrific heat in the confined room would heat all surfaces so that there would be no noticeable condensation on those surfaces. This solution also perfectly accords with the principle of 'Occam's Razor', which argues that the best solution is the simplest one using the known facts.

Coincidentally, early in 1989, the BBC programme, 'Tomorrow's World', demonstrated a newly invented portable steel cutting and welding apparatus. It can easily be picked up with one hand. It is fuelled by water. One litre of water produces 2,000 litres of hydrogen and oxygen per hour. The welding/cutting torch burns the combination of hydrogen and oxygen. Such heat – about twice the heat of a crematorium – can easily destroy bones. So my hypothesis is not quite so untenable

No doubt there will be objections to my hypothesis for all sorts of seemingly practical reasons. However, I am reminded of Einstein and Rutherford. In 1933, Rutherford succeeded in splitting the atom and in so doing validated part of Einstein's theory, specifically, $E=MC^2$. Einstein and Rutherford said that the splitting of the atom was only of academic interest and could never be put to practical use. A monumental boner to say the least. This was a mere twelve years before Japan was atom-bombed into submission. We have lived for the past fifty years under the threat of a final all-out nuclear holocaust. The danger is far from over. Chernobyl demonstrated that it is not necessarily the military nuclear devices that we have to fear. The whole world could end as the result of what the acknowledged experts considered to be merely an academic curiosity. It does not always pay to let the experts have the final say.

A normal candle with a wick in the centre burns slowly and evenly with very little wasted wax. A candle with the wick wrapped around the outside would melt and the molten wax would flow away from the burning wick. Within a minute or so a standard-sized candle so constructed would have completely melted and the molten wax would have flowed away from the burning wick which would soon go out. The greater part of the wax would thus remain unburnt. I have experimented with beef fat wrapped in cloth and burned as a fat candle. Most of the fat was soon melted by the encompassing flames and ran away from the burning external wick. Thus the greater part of the fuel value of the fat was not utilised. This is what happens to a great deal of the body fat in cases of SHC. Far from the fat providing the heat source sufficient to destroy flesh and bone it is melted by the destructive heat source and flows away. The carpet and rug was saturated to quite an extent around the body of Henry Thomas. The fat-soaked carpet made an ideal 'candle' yet it did not burn at all. The carpet was only burned where it was in contact with the burning body. The fire did not spread beyond the periphery of the burning corpse. This argues that the source of the fire was within the body and not external to it. Fire officers and a scenes of crime officer also stated that the floors were swimming in melted body fat at the scenes of the deaths of two other victims – Alfred Ashton and Barry Soudaine (see Chapter 16).

CHAPTER TWELVE

The Procrustean Stretch

It is a common fallacy to stretch the facts of a known incident to cover other incidents which, though similar, are entirely different. SHC sceptics, even highly qualified scientists, are constantly indulging in such behaviour. Once a pseudo-SHC case is found to have a logical explanation, they eagerly insist that all cases of SHC are equally explicable if only the necessary time and resources were available to enable them all to be thoroughly investigated. I have already stated that there are instances of SHC and instances of PC (preternatural combustion, alias the 'wick or candle effect'). Ignorance of the true state of affairs causes both phenomena to be categorised as one and the same. Every time a case of PC is correctly diagnosed, and the cause of ignition found, the sceptical investigators claim another successful debunking of the 'SHC myth'. The circumstances and facts of such successfully investigated PC cases are subjected to the Procrustean rack and stretched in an endeavour to force them to fit the unsolvable SHC cases.

I will state, in fairness to my sceptical opponents, that they are mainly unaware of the fact that there are at least two entirely distinct, though superficially similar, phenomena. Being completely satisfied that there is only one phenomenon to deal with it is not entirely unexpected that they should act as they do. For the most part their actions are entirely honest in that they are convinced of the correctness of their behaviour. Admittedly there are some scientists who are not entirely convinced by the 'wick effect' explanation in all cases. But that's life. There is always someone who will not go with the flow.

I have never heard of any scientist who has spent any time in actually investigating the SHC phenomenon (with the exception of Professor Gee – and he only thought he was investigating a case of SHC). Every so often one or more of them will venture an opinion on the subject (usually in answer to people such as I publishing an article or appearing on TV describing apparent instances of SHC). Even more rarely some will be persuaded to demonstrate how the 'wick effect' works, confident that such a demonstration will convince the misguided that the 'wick effect' is being mistakenly confused with SHC.

The journal *Fire* dated May 1986 contained an article entitled, 'Spontaneous human combustion – more open-minded research is the answer'. The article was a joint effort by Alan Beard and Dougal Drysdale, both of the Unit of Fire Safety Engineering, University of Edinburgh. (Dr Dougal Drysdale figures largely in Chapter 15, QED). The article questions whether or not there is such a phenomenon as SHC and concludes rather definitely that there is not. It can all be properly explained in terms of everyday science (with which I wholeheartedly agree) and always results from a normal, external source of ignition (with which I equally wholeheartedly disagree).

Beard and Drysdale state that determining whether or not the phenomenon exists is largely dependent on what information is available. They then quote one of the very few cases that has a rational explanation. The story goes thus: an unnamed man was leaving his place of work (unstipulated) when he burst into flames upon lighting a cigarette. This case of 'SHC' was quickly resolved when it was revealed that the unfortunate victim was in the habit of using an airline to blow off the dust from his clothes prior to leaving his place of work. On that occasion it transpired that he had used an oxygen line by mistake. His oxygen-impregnated clothes had naturally burst into flames when the cigarette was lit either by match or lighter. Case solved.

This case is beloved of the sceptics and is constantly quoted to show that there is always a rational explanation of 'supposed SHC' if only one looks long and hard enough. It has to be constantly quoted by them because there are so few cases that can be explained away so satisfactorily. This case was obviously *not* an instance of SHC. It was taken from the annals of the 'investigations' by Nickell and Fischer, officers of CSICOP. The Committee for the Scientific Investigation of Claims for the Paranormal is an American organisation which is the brain-child of one Paul Kurtz. As the organisation claims to be scientific in its investigations of claims of the paranormal it is not unreasonable to expect them to apply scientific methods to check any reported paranormal phenomenon and publish the results – whether they were pro or con the investigated phenomenon.

In quoting the oxygen-line case above Drysdale and Beard give the impression that the reason for the true cause of ignition remaining undiscovered in other cases is entirely due to the lack of effort put into finding such a source. This is a fallacy. In all of the cases examined in this book the utmost effort was made by the investigating authorities to find a valid source of ignition. In all the cases they failed. In one or two of the cases they placed the blame on some perfectly innocent coal fire or gas fire.

It is of interest that these unsubstantiated claims as to the source of ignition are seldom if ever made by the investigating firemen or police officers. In many cases one finds that the investigating officers are convinced that the cause is SHC. The fire and police officers encountering instances of SHC seldom, if ever, mention SHC in their reports or at the inquests – purely in deference to their continuing promotion prospects. The unsubstantiated hypotheses are always put forward by the forensic experts and such sceptics as members of CSICOP.

The French psychologist and statistician, Michel Gauquelin, together with his wife, Françoise, set out to prove statistically that the evidence for astrology was unsatisfactory. To their surprise they found in some respects that the position of the planets at birth can have some influence on the personality. These findings squared with the people that were at the top of their professions or famous athletes. There was a statistically significant preponderance of famous soldiers and athletes born under the influence of Mars and scientists under Saturn, etc.

Professor Hans Eysenck, a famous psychologist, who has shown that psychiatric analysis therapy is, for the most part, a waste of time and money, was sceptical of the Gauquelins' findings. He decided, with his wife's help, to check the Gauquelins' work. If they were correct then the same method should differentiate between introverts and extroverts. Introverts would tend to be born under Saturn while extroverts would tend to be born under Mars or Jupiter. He did not expect to find that this would be the case. He was as surprised as they were to find that the Gauquelins were correct. Eysenck was completely honest and said, 'To find some solid fact in the astrological field was surprising'. He also said that the discovery was 'not entirely welcome – we like to find our preconceptions confirmed'. It is to be regretted that not all scientists are as honest as Gauquelin and Eysenck. Neither of them were in favour of astrology, yet each was too much the scientist to suppress their unwelcome findings. Gauquelin and Eysenck both took the trouble to investigate something that they were both convinced did not exist. As some sceptics would say, they took the trouble to investigate a negative.

As a matter of interest it is no longer possible to carry out such a study, as the number of natural births in the Western world has declined considerably. Many women do not give birth these days at the moment decided by nature. Births are brought on or delayed to fit in with the schedule of the hospitals in which the babies are born. In America, where suing for medical malpractice is practically a national sport, obstetricians are opting more and more for the caesarean delivery rather than allow mother or child to suffer as a result of prolonged labour. For some reason the planetary influence does not appear in non-natural births. The reason for this anomaly could be that it is not the moment of birth that is influenced by the position of the planets but the moment that birth should naturally occur. Possibly the correlation between planet positions and birth would hold if, instead of using the actual non-natural birth time, the time and date of the natural birth time could be calculated. If such a study were carried out then it might be proven that the influence is indeed on the unborn child as it approaches birth. It might even be that the influence is at a much earlier stage in the life of the embryo — possibly even at conception.

Ron Westrum supplied me with a number of sources of information and writings on the subject of SHC. One such article was written by a Danish burns surgeon, Mogens Thomsen, MD, PhD. It was printed in *Burns* (vol. 5, no. 1). Thomsen rehashes numerous old cases of alleged SHC with varying comments as a prelude to the final case which he recounts in some detail, claiming to have found the definitive answer to all the speculation about SHC that has taken place over the preceding centuries. He begins by stating, 'In the year 1847, however, an event took place which should put an end to the belief in this strange phenomenon for good.' More than 100 years had passed since this 'definitive' case had occurred without it having made any real contribution to the controversy. Still Thomsen continued the tale.

In the year mentioned, Count Gorlitz, living in the region of Darmstadt, arrived home after dining out and was unable to find his wife. Eventually her private rooms were broken into and her body was found in a partially incinerated condition. The rooms were in a complete state of disorder. A door was broken and windows smashed. A writing desk mirror was smashed and nearby candles melted. The Countess's head was terribly burned as was most of her torso. Burned remains of combustible materials (unspecified) were littered about the partly burned desk. The corpse was lying close by. It was assumed to be a case of SHC by some experts but opinions differed.

Some three years later the Countess's servant, a man named Stauff, was accused of her murder, tried and convicted. He was sentenced to life imprisonment. He later admitted that he had in fact murdered the Countess. On the day of the deed he had gone to her room, which he found unoccupied, and was tempted by the sight of jewellery and money in the open drawers of the writing desk. The Countess caught him in the act of stealing and a struggle ensued in which he strangled her. To cover up his crime he heaped the combustibles on the desk by her body and set fire to them. No instance of SHC – merely a case of murder and an attempt to cover up the crime. The only mystery to me is why anyone should have seriously considered SHC at all. The room was in complete disorder with doors and windows smashed. This should have indicated that a struggle took place and should have pointed to the likelihood of murder.

The case was yet another mistaken instance of preternatural combustion. We already know that Dupuytren was postulating preternatural combustion in 1830. Had he advanced an opinion on this case then he would undoubtedly have been correct. The confusion between SHC and PC will continue until the individual cases are properly investigated and segregated in the light of subsequent discoveries. That there are scientifically recognisable differences I shall prove at the end of this book.

Dr Thomsen has fallen into a common logical trap. He has found one case that was mistakenly classified as SHC and was later proven to the satisfaction of all to be entirely explicable as an attempt to cover up a murder. He then, with absolutely no justification, declares by implication that all apparent cases of SHC are equally explicable. Such cases need only to be investigated with sufficient diligence. How can the solving of the murder of the Countess Gorlitz account for people being seen to burst spontaneously into flames? Especially when the victims have not been dry cleaning their clothes with the aid of an oxygen-line.

Using Thomsen's line of reasoning one could say that all cases of suicide must be murder because on more than one occasion apparent suicides have been proven to be murder. All Thomsen has proved is that Countess Gorlitz was murdered by her servant, Stauff, who nearly got away with murder because of the gullibility of some experts.

A quite detailed account of the case of Countess Gorlitz, and many others, can be found in Blackwood's *Edinburgh Magazine* dated April 1861, in a definitive article by George Henry Lewes. One-time friend and later opponent of Charles Dickens, Lewes published several letters which passed between him and Dickens after Dickens' publication of the description of the death of Krook in his novel, *Bleak House*. Lewes was incensed that Dickens had propagated the 'myth' of spontaneous combustion. In his article, Lewes recounts several instances of SHC as reported by various witnesses, all of whom he dismisses as not worthy of belief. His main reason for refusing to believe such witnesses is much the same as that of Lavoisier. He did not believe them because that to which they attested was unbelievable. That is a pretty good example of circular reasoning. I quote Lewes: 'In these accounts it is usually stated that the body entirely disappears down to a greasy stain on the floor and some remains of bones. *Everyone knows this to be impossible* [my italics]. Allowing for the fact that Lewes has slightly exaggerated his description of 'these accounts' he has described exactly the scene that I and many others have witnessed. There are many photographs extant depicting precisely that sort of scene despite Lewes's claim that, 'Everyone knows this to be impossible'. So much for the impossibility of the occurrence.

Note

1 *The Paranormal – An Encyclopedia of Psychic Phenomena*, Brian Inglis, Paladin, 1986 (pp. 260–61).

CHAPTER THIRTEEN

Miscellany

I remember reading as a child an apocryphal story relating how the Chinese first discovered the art of cooking. A soon-to-be-culinary Chinese farmer kept a pig in a shed and one day the shed burned down with inevitable consequences for the pig. The farmer and his family, who must until then have eaten the pigs raw, discovered that roast pig was so much more tasty. From then on, whenever they wanted roast pig for dinner, they just burned down another shed complete with pig. Anatomically, pigs are considered to be much like humans in many ways. It seems they even have a very similar flavour when roasted. No doubt they also burn or do not burn in similar fashion. If pigs burned as easily as the sceptics would have us believe that humans can, we could possibly still be eating raw pork ... barbecued pork spare ribs are all very well but ashes are something else.

Humans, like pigs, are extremely difficult to destroy by fire. When I attended the Fortean Unconvention 94, the major mouthpiece for CSICOP, Joe Nickell, gave his explanation of the death of Dr J. Irving Bentley who was incinerated on 5 December 1966 at his home in Pennsylvania, USA. This case is one of the American classics of SHC. The famous picture shows a hole in a wooden bathroom floor beside a bath. Tilted at an angle across the hole is a walking frame. The hole measures approximately two feet by eighteen inches. Lying at the edge of the hole, furthest from the bath, is a male human foot and a short length of lower leg. The Zimmer frame is made of aluminium and has rubber caps on each of the four feet. Though only inches above the hole the rubber feet are still intact. Below the hole can be seen a wooden joist burned halfway through.

Nickell's 'scientific' explanation is that the doctor set fire to his dressing gown by carelessly dropping sparks of tobacco on to it from his pipe. Nickell's reason for this assumption is that the partially burned remains of the dressing gown, which was found in the bath, bore numerous small burn marks of the kind that result from sparks of tobacco burning the material briefly before dying out. I would have thought that when a garment displays many smoulder holes, all allegedly as a result of dropped tobacco sparks, such a display tends to prove that the garment is very difficult to set on fire in this manner.

There is no record that Nickell, or any other person, tested the remains of Dr Bentley's dressing gown in order to ascertain whether or not it was remotely possible for it to catch fire from the sparks of a pipe. I have tried very hard to cause different types of material to burst into flames by placing lighted cigarettes on them, but to no avail. Though the materials will either melt or smoulder they could not be induced to burst into flame even in a stiff breeze. They could only be made to smoulder faster. (In Chapter 21 – Static Flash Fires neither a Home Office chemist nor the famous Shirley Institute were able to make a smouldering cotton catering jacket burst into flame. I will also later describe my own unsuccessful attempts to make smouldering material burst into flame.)

Nickell insisted that the doctor made his way to the bathroom, having set his dressing gown alight, where he tore it off and threw it in the bath, where it was subsequently found partly burned. The doctor is then supposed to have burned away to ashes by the normal process of combustion. Nickell insists that the burned floorboards and joist provided the necessary fuel to destroy the body and reduce it to ashes. Now he is really putting the cart before the horse. In scientific terms he is putting effect before cause and that is one principle upon which all scientists (with the possible exceptions of quantum physicists) are agreed: the scientific method requires above all else that effect must follow cause. If the burning gown was removed then what set the floor on fire? How could the doctor's body catch fire from such a momentary fire as a partially burned dressing gown? There was no evidence that Dr Bentley was wearing any clothes under the dressing gown of sufficient bulk and quantity to have sustained the 'wick effect'. The doctor had to set the floorboards on fire before they in turn could consume him. No mean feat.

In the normal course of combustion, bodies do not burn holes through wooden floors. In fact the reverse is the case. Fire officers are forever coming across human bodies lying on the only surviving portions of floorboards in rooms which have been gutted by fire. All the rest of the floorboards have burned away, leaving only the much sturdier joists, except where human bodies have been found on the boards. The bodies have prevented the flames from consuming the boards under them and the remaining portions of the floorboards are in the shape of the bodies which prevented them from burning. The effect is somewhat like that of the chalked outline of a murder victim which is so beloved of the producers of TV crime programmes. This is as it should be. This is normal. In the normal, natural, everyday world with which we are all familiar, human bodies smother flames they do not fuel them.

In 1986, I went to the crematorium at Cwmbran, Gwent, to view the cremation process at first hand. Strangely enough, crematoria managers are quite happy to show anyone the cremation process. They seem anxious to show the public that the incineration of their loved ones is conducted with the best possible taste. As I recall, it was a freezing cold day in early spring with the March winds driving icy sleet in near horizontal blasts, which made the warmth of the crematorium most welcome. I watched the process intermittently from the moment the coffin was inserted into the firing chamber through to the final production of the hour glass type 'ashes' we are familiar with. They are more like a dark grey basalt sand than ashes.

I will not dwell on the physical changes the corpse undergoes in the process of being reduced to ashes. The complete process, as viewed through the window into the chamber, is at certain stages somewhat gruesome. After an hour or so the corpse I observed had been reduced to a fragmented skull and various pieces of thigh bones, vertebrae and pelvic bones, etc. These were raked out and some more breakage occurred in the process showing that the medium grey calcined bones were quite brittle. These bone fragments were then placed into the cremulator. The cremulator is a machine which resembles a somewhat large spin drier and it contains a number of large steel balls. The calcined bone fragments were placed in the machine and the power switched on. It spins at high speed, just like the spin drier it so much resembles, and after a short spin the sand-like ashes pour out of the bottom, either to be presented to the relatives or to be scattered on the nearby garden of remembrance.

This process of reducing one human corpse to ash, when starting from cold, takes approximately thirty cubic metres of gas and 600 cubic metres of pre-heated forced air per hour. A crematorium, using forced draught, oxidises (burns) a corpse at 900°C. To achieve the same effect, without the forced draught, requires a temperature of 1600°C for many hours. Some sceptics have maintained that the only reason forced draught is used at a temperature of 900°C is to reduce the production of smoke billowing from the chimney which would upset the mourning relatives. As efficiency and cost reduction are the two main bywords of any operation these days I would suspect that those are the criteria responsible for the operation at lower temperatures and in much shorter times. The increased forced draught costs nothing above the cost of the actual plant – air is still free. Gas is very costly and to raise the temperature to 1600°C for several times as long would increase the costs enormously. Such an operation would also require a lot more crematoria to offset the much slower throughput of corpses.

I described the calcined bones of Henry Thomas as being as white as blackboard chalk. The 'ashes' resulting from the cremation of corpses is a medium grey and nothing like the ashes I found. Thomas's bones had obviously been subjected to a far greater heat than that produced by a crematorium. When it comes to calcining human thigh bones to whiter-than-white ash the 'wick effect' is a total non-starter.

Dr Wilton M. Krogman, PhD, was a genuine American expert on the destruction of bodies by fire. For some strange reasons, that I have yet to ascertain, he spent quite some time in the 1930s destroying human bodies by fire. It is reported that he performed these tasks using wood, coal and kerosene (paraffin). Whatever the reasons for his experiments, he was, on occasion, consulted by the FBI about the destruction of human corpses by fire.

Dr Krogman visited the scene of the incineration of Mary Reeser, the most famous of all American cases of SHC. Mrs Reeser, aged sixty-seven was reduced so completely to ashes, while sitting in an armchair in her apartment in St Petersburg, Florida, on 1 July 1951, that only one foot and its slipper remained. The apartment, which was of wooden construction, and the furniture was undamaged except for the chair Mrs Reeser had been sitting in. It too had been completely reduced to ash except for the steel springs. In nearly all other cases of SHC the skull survives. It is always blackened and devoid of flesh and the brain is sometimes reported as having been grossly heat shrunken. There was no trace of Mary Reeser's skull. There is no mystery involved in the disappearance of her skull. As she was sitting in an armchair at the time she and the chair incinerated it is more than likely that her skull dropped down on to her flaming torso and was consumed in the process. Normally the incinerating corpses finish up in a horizontal position so the skull does not receive additional incineration from the torso.

Dr Krogman was one forensic scientist with real hands-on, practical experience in the burning of human corpses. He did not expound the 'wick effect'. Having viewed the scene and asked his questions, he said:

> I cannot conceive of such complete cremation without more burning of the apartment itself. In fact the apartment and everything in it should have been consumed. . . . I regard it as the most amazing thing I have ever seen. As I review it, the short hairs on my neck bristle with vague fear. Were I living in the Middle Ages, I'd mutter something about black magic.[1]

Dr Krogman did not support the SHC hypothesis (at least not publicly). Like many sceptics of things supposedly paranormal, having made a statement accepting the possibility of a paranormal event while still off guard, he later recanted and attempted to rationalise his experience. He put forward a theory to the effect that Mrs Reeser had been burned to ashes elsewhere by someone with access to crematorium-type equipment or materials. The resulting ashes and remaining foot were then carried back to the apartment, where the mystery assailant added the finishing touches, like heat-buckled plastic objects and a door-knob that was still hot in the morning.[2] At least Dr Krogman did not try to write off Mary Reeser's incineration as another example of the 'wick effect'. He had far too much experience and knowledge to even consider the 'wick effect' as a solution to the mystery.

Among other documents that Professor Ron Westrum sent me was a copy of a letter to him written by Dr Krogman who wrote, among other things, that he did not believe in the 'wick effect'. I wrote to Dr Krogman in an attempt to get his direct comments on what he actually thought and said about the Mary Reeser case. I was not completely at ease with his reported statements regarding a murderer removing Mrs Reeser from the scene and cremating her elsewhere before returning the remains to her apartment. I have to bear in mind that although Dr Krogman was no adherent to the 'wick effect' hypothesis, there is no reason to suppose that he embraced the SHC hypothesis. He could, for all I know, have been as violently opposed to the SHC hypothesis as the most rabid of sceptics. If he was a dyed-in-the-wool sceptic then his alleged statement is perfectly understandable. Unfortunately he died a couple of months before I sent the letter.

Professor Westrum also supplied me with a copy of an interview he had with Mr Fulton Butts, Evergreen Cemetery, Detroit, USA. Mr Butts handles over 800 cremations per year, and at that time (July 1982) had performed that service for four years. He had, up to that time, incinerated in excess of 3,000 bodies and could rightly be called an expert in the process. Dr Westrum acquainted Mr Butts with the general details of alleged cases of SHC. He said, 'I discussed with him . . . the reports of SHC and the bearing that his own experience has on the evaluation of the phenomenon. His general reaction was: "From my experience in the crematory, I can't see it happening".' Mr Butts seems to be a man short on words and long on sense.

During the course of my police service I attended at the scene of several house fires where people had died. It is not all that often that bodies in house fires are severely fire damaged. Mostly the fire brigade are in attendance soon after the fire is discovered and the fire is quickly brought under control.

People die in house fires mostly from the inhalation of smoke from the burning furnishings. The cause of death in such situations used to be mainly carbon monoxide poisoning. Since the introduction of various man-made materials in modern upholstery far more toxic fumes are given off and in vast quantities. These fumes are so lethal that only a couple of breaths are needed before the inhaler is unconscious and then dead. Such lethal materials are now banned in the construction of household furniture but there is still a lot of such furniture in homes.

Bodies are mostly recovered from house fires bearing little fire damage. More often than not the victims die in their sleep from the fumes. On the rare occasion that a house is completely gutted, bodies are usually recovered more or less intact. If the body has been subjected to prolonged exposure to fire then the extremities are liable to be destroyed. The torso, however, remains whole.

I was once called out late at night to attend at the scene of the crash of a light aircraft on Tredegar Mountain in Gwent. The plane had burst into flames on impact and the pilot was trapped by his feet and so burned to death. The fire, fuelled by high octane aviation spirit and strong mountain winds, burned itself out before the fire brigade could get up the mountain with their equipment.

As I struggled up the mountain to the crash scene I passed a row of houses on the outskirts of the town. Looking down on to the town I caught the appetising smell of roast pork which made me suddenly salivate with hunger. My appetite was soon spoiled when I realised that the wind was blowing off the mountain from the crash scene. I now know why Caribbean cannibals are supposed to have called their victims 'long pig'.

Having got to the scene I found that the corpse of the pilot had been removed from the wreck. The damage to the corpse was entirely consistent with having been subjected to prolonged and fierce burning. The torso was entire though the abdomen had split open revealing the entrails. The arms and legs were drawn up into the classic 'monkey position'. This means that all the limbs were fully flexed due to the heat contraction of the tendons. The hands and feet were missing. The entire corpse was burned black. This is how human corpses are supposed to behave when subjected to extremely fierce fire. The extremities are destroyed and the torso remains. Parts of the aluminium fuselage had melted in the extreme heat. In cases of SHC the exact opposite occurs. Extremities are often completely untouched while the torso is totally destroyed. The extremities that are burned are so burned because they came within the immediate proximity of the burning torso. It matters not whether the extremities are clothed or bare, the result is always the same – spread out from the torso they survive; in contact with the torso they are incinerated.

When I attended the Fortean Unconvention at London University in June 1994, I shared the platform with Joe Nickell of CSICOP, Jenny Randles, co-author of *Spontaneous Human Combustion*, and Ron Bentley, retired London Fire Brigade fire officer now in charge of security at the Houses of Parliament. A member of the audience asked what was the main difference between the normal burning of a corpse and SHC. I explained the difference as I have just stated above. Ron Bentley gave an extremely apt simile. He said that the effects of SHC on a body was as strange and unusual as if you were driving a wreck of a car along a road and were involved in a collision and your wreck was suddenly transformed to a brand-new condition. We all know such an occurrence to be entirely impossible. To people who are used to seeing the effects of fire on the human body then the mechanism that reduces the torso of a human to ashes on a living-room floor is equally impossible. The only real difference between an instance of SHC and the reverse car wreck is that SHC does happen.

In 1731, the Countess Di Bandi of Casena, Italy, became a victim of SHC. Hers is one of the earliest recorded instances of SHC. I have no doubt that in those times there was an occasional instance of SHC among the lower orders. However, it is only in recent times that the trials and tribulations of the ordinary working classes have been of any concern to the reading and writing classes. Literary interest did not manifest itself in the doings of the common man until the lower classes themselves became literate. Medieval literature only chronicled the lives and adventures of royalty, the nobility and clerics. An occasional combusting peasant would hardly impinge on the consciousness of the ruling classes. Such an event would no doubt be dismissed as just another instance of a drunken peasant getting too near the fire in his close hovel.

The Countess, aged about sixty, had retired for the night, her maid having assisted her in the arduous preparations for sleep. The same maid found her mistress's sparse remains in the bed chamber the following morning. The bedclothes were thrown back and on the floor, several feet from the bed, was a pile of ashes. At the edge of the ashes lay the Countess's stockinged legs (just like Annie Webb's) and between the legs lay her blackened skull, where it had apparently rolled after becoming detached from her neck at some stage of her incineration. She appeared to have burned while sitting upright on the floor. The rest of the room was untouched by fire and in the same condition as the rooms of any modern instance of SHC. An oil lamp stood upright on the floor near the ashes but the terrific heat had evaporated the oil completely. Several candles had also melted and the wax had apparently evaporated away, leaving only the unburned wicks.

Castles and mansions of the early eighteenth century no doubt suffered from draughts and the lack of central heating. I could well imagine that a lady of her years, sleeping alone, would have heavy drapes hung at the doors and windows to reduce the draughts. The effect of such drapes could well have been to reduce the influx of air so that once the Countess began to burn the atmosphere would have soon been depleted of oxygen. The same conditions would thus have been created in her bedroom as obtained in the sealed rooms of Annie Webb and Henry Thomas.

No possible source of ignition could be found to account for the incineration of the Countess. It seemed that she had awoken in the night and had thrown back the clothes and got out of bed before being struck down by the incinerating flames. She seems to have retained control of her movements long enough to sit down and to set the lighted oil lamp down upright upon the floor beside her. Had she fallen with the oil lamp in her hand it is unlikely that it would have landed upright. The most mystifying part of the incident is how a lady of her high rank managed to get out of her bed unassisted by her maid.

Note

1 *Incredible Phenomena*, edited by Peter Brooksmith, Orbis, 1984.
2 Ibid.

CHAPTER FOURTEEN

Of Dinosaurs and Fossils

In January 1989, I went to the BBC 'QED' offices in London. The 'QED' team filmed an interview with me on the subject of SHC. On the day before the programme was to be shown I was asked to appear on BBC Breakfast Television being interviewed by Jeremy Paxman on the subject of SHC. I said I had no intention of going live on TV to face some scientists skilled in TV debate without knowing what the questions would be.

I was assured that the producer would meet me at my hotel in the evening and I would be thoroughly acquainted with the questions to be asked. When I arrived at Paddington railway station in the early evening I was met by a chauffeured car and taken to my hotel where I waited all evening. No one contacted me. I phoned the studios late in the evening and was told that things were very hectic for some unspecified reason and that the producer would call me later. He called around 10.30p.m. still under 'terrific pressure', again unspecified. He assured me that a car would be sent to collect me in the morning and deliver me to the studio in plenty of time for me to be apprised of the programme's content and I would be able to run through the questions before going on air. Come

the morning a chauffeured car duly arrived and I was transported to the BBC 'Breakfast TV' studio. Immediately on
arrival I was shown into the hospitality room and introduced
to Dr Dougal Drysdale BSc, PhD, FIFireE, of the Unit of Fire
Safety Engineering at the University of Edinburgh. The intro-
ductions were barely over when we were escorted to the
studio floor. En route I briefly met with the producer, still
protesting that he had been unable to speak with me because
he was rushed off his feet.

While walking to the studio set I managed to elicit from
Drysdale that he had no experience of any fire deaths such as
the ones I showed him photos of. He said his work dealt with
fire hazards relating to materials used in industry. He did mention that he had burned a piece of animal fat. When I queried
the relevance of such an action in relation to the complete
combustion of a human body with its high water content, he
replied, 'There is a lot of water in fat'.

On camera, I was asked by Jeremy Paxman to describe the
incident of SHC that I had dealt with as a scenes of crime
officer. I briefly did so. When asked to comment on my story
Dr Drysdale replied, 'Well, I think first of all we have to recognise that there's no evidence that it was spontaneous
combustion. No one has actually observed one of these
instances occurring from the moment of ignition right
through to death and the final remains. We've only got the
final remains to go on.' I was flabbergasted. This was the first I
knew that Drysdale disagreed with the SHC hypothesis. I do
not spend my days deep in discussion of the subject of SHC.
As a matter of fact it is seldom that I get the chance to discuss
anything of consequence. I am therefore not skilled in the art
of discussion. My ability to reason and deduce are best exer-
cised in a literary form. I need time to think and martial my
arguments. Before I realised what was happening we were off
the set and out of the door on our respective ways. Had I a
few minutes in which to gather my thoughts I would have

demonstrated the fallacy in Dr Drysdale's comments.

In view of the vast amount of knowledge relating to dinosaurs and many other extinct species, which has been accumulated solely by examination of their extremely sparse fossilised 'final remains', I thought Drysdale could have chosen his words more carefully. There are numerous reports of living people having been seen to burst into flames. The witnesses have allowed their humane concern for the suffering of a fellow human to override their scientific objectivity. They have always doused the flames in some fashion or other. The victims seldom survived more than a few days.

In November 1994 palaeontologists claimed to have found another of our distant relatives. He is a man they have named Charles. Charles was allegedly an upright walking man with heavy musculature and about six feet tall. He lived around 500,000 years ago. No one watched Charles being born, live his life, die and eventually disintegrate and finally be reduced by the ravages of half a million years to two small pieces of bone. The palaeontologists have built from those two pieces of bone greatly enhanced reputations. Their discovery will generate many learned papers, discourses and books. All this from two scraps of bone.

Yet again, in July 1995, four small bones, locked in a drawer of a museum for years and thought to be footbones of an ancient baboon, are now declared to be footbones of 'Littlefoot', a creature that seemingly existed some three and a half million years ago. It is alleged to be an intermediate creature between the apes and man, a partial missing link. Great excitement in the scientific world.

Yet all the bones reduced to ash, untouched extremities and blue flames witnessed coming from bodies, both live and dead, is nowhere near sufficient proof of even the possibility of SHC. It seems to me that there is a clear case of double standards operating in the scientific world.

I have no experience of a person erupting into flames. I

consider myself more than a little privileged to have observed such an event at one remove. I have, however, interviewed retired fireman Jack Stacey about the still-burning unfortunate, Bailey. We are obliged to take eye-witness accounts of individuals spontaneously combusting on faith. If the witness is a credible person, having no reason to lie, then his or her account must be accepted as true and should be properly investigated in order to find confirmatory physical evidence. The evidence of eye-witnesses is accepted in both civil and criminal courts. Such evidence should at least be worthy of consideration.

There is already confirmatory physical evidence in such cases. It consists of the remains of the people alleged to have combusted. Instances of SHC do at least result in tangible remains. We are not being asked to rely entirely on the accounts of the witnesses as in cases of alleged visitations of aliens, etc., where the whole 'evidence' consists entirely of the testimony of 'witnesses' with nothing of a material nature to show as confirmation.

We cannot possibly demand that we each have personal knowledge of every event before believing it. The one great advantage humans have over other animals is our ability to learn and to pass on knowledge to others. Thus each generation advances. Otherwise the sum total of man's knowledge would be limited to that which he could personally experience in his lifetime. Each succeeding generation would be doomed to make the same mistakes in order to acquire the same limited amount of knowledge. We would still be running around like 'Charles', living short, sharp and brutish lives. And we would be few in numbers. (The world in general and many species of creatures, both extinct and extant, would be far better off were that the case.)

The acceptance of second-hand knowledge becomes hazardous when one accepts blindly, without even considering whether or not the knowledge accords with common sense. If the 'knowledge' being imparted seems unreasonable then one should demand more proof or test the statements being made to ascertain their validity or otherwise. Such a line of action is certainly required when the same, seemingly ridiculous claims, continue to be made from time to time by different people in different places. The advocates of the 'wick effect' have fallen into the opposite trap of blind acceptance. There are far too many anomalous facts that do not fit comfortably into the 'wick effect' scenario. If they bothered to apply the yardstick of reason to these anomalies and investigate them instead of merely brushing them aside with barely a thought as minor inconsistencies, 'the exception that proves the rule', etc, they would easily avoid this trap.

CHAPTER FIFTEEN

Quod Erat Demonstrandum

> 'Be prepared to give up every preconceived
> notion . . . or you shall learn nothing.'
>
> T.H. HUXLEY

> 'Weigh not so much what men assert as what
> they can prove.'
>
> SIR PHILIP SYDNEY

> 'The great tragedy of science – the slaying of a
> beautiful hypothesis by an ugly fact.'
>
> T.H. HUXLEY

Before I agreed to do the 'QED' programme, Theresa Hunt, the programme producer and director assured me that she was conducting a serious scientific study of the phenomenon of SHC. At first I refused to do the programme. I had not been overjoyed at the somewhat theatrical treatment of the subject by the BBC 'Newsnight' team in 1986. Neither was I pleased at the editing which left me 'believing in the paranormal', having cut out my denial that paranormal events are supernatural. I was especially displeased to see some clinical psychologist airing his views to the effect that people such as I have a need to believe in magic. I have always stated that I believe the phenomenon of SHC to be entirely natural. Yet the 'Newsnight' film made me appear a convert to the supernatural.

During the course of more than half an hour of continuous filming, with no retakes, I recounted the cases of Henry Thomas, Annie Webb and the tramp, Bailey. I stressed that all three were alive when they started to burn and I further stressed the fact that, in the case of Thomas and Webb, their torsos had been completely reduced to ash in rooms which were virtually devoid of oxygen. I made it patently clear that the water-laden torsos were reduced to ash under conditions such that an ordinary candle could not have remained alight. I stated on camera that, in the cases of both Thomas and Webb, burning furniture ceased to burn once the oxygen level dropped. I also stressed, at various times, that I did not subscribe to any belief in the 'supernatural'. I stated that I was sure the phenomenon was entirely natural but *not*, by any stretch of the imagination, due to the so-called 'candle or wick effect', or preternatural combustion. I also told of Dr Ron Westrum's work regarding the behaviour of scientists when faced with anomalous phenomena. I had given Theresa Hunt the name and address of Professor Westrum at Eastern Michigan University, USA. I noticed his name and phone number on her office notice board.

I returned to Wales looking forward to viewing the programme that would at last kill the myth of the 'candle effect' and possibly galvanise the authorities into recognising the possibility of SHC. If only pathologists, fire officers, scenes of crime officers and coroners could be alerted to report any cases that might possibly be attributed to SHC then we could well find a sudden surge in such reportings. As Professor Westrum related, the battered baby syndrome was not seen to exist until the correct mind-set was created thus enabling people to accept that such a terrible tragedy did actually occur.

Back home in Gwent, I settled down to watch the 'QED' programme. There was a general introduction to the subject and all the old chestnuts were aired (I hoped for the last time).

When it came to the turn of ball lightning as a possible culprit, I was more than a little intrigued to see top electronics expert, Professor Jenison of Kent University, earnestly explaining the behaviour of ball lightning as though it was, and always had been, a phenomenon which was understood perfectly. The reader may recall how, as late as 1973, ball lightning was still thought, by some authorities, to result purely from hallucination on the part of the observers. I noted that Professor Jenison did not mention that ball lightning perversely fails to conform to the known laws of physics. In fact it completely defies the first law of motion: 'Every body remains at rest or in uniform motion unless it is acted upon by other forces.' Ball lightning seems able to move at will, without being affected by the force of gravity. It can also stop, start and change direction in apparent direct contravention of the laws of motion. It is a prime example of anomalous phenomena which seems to play havoc with the rationality of too many scientists. About a third of the programme was taken up by sensational irrelevancies – such as burning haystacks, will-o'-the-wisps and excerpts from BBC productions of *Bleak House*. This struck me as strange for a supposedly scientific inquiry. The rest of the programme, to my further and utter amazement, was devoted to establishing the validity of the 'wick or candle effect'.

Dr Dougal Drysdale demonstrated how easily the 'candle effect' could reduce a complete human torso to ash. He proceeded to wrap some 'animal fat' in a piece of cotton material to simulate a human candle with an external wick. The piece of fat that he proceeded to wrap up was about six inches long and an inch wide in the round. Once the fat had been completely obscured by the cloth roll, which overlapped the fat by an inch on either side, the camera zoomed in for a close-up of the fat roll. Suddenly we were looking at an entirely different piece of fat. Whereas the first piece of fat had been overlapped by the piece of cloth by an inch on either side, the second piece of fat was now protruding about one and a half inches on the one side. It was not stated what sort of animal fat it was. It is clear on the film that the fat was the sort that comes cooked a rich golden colour from an oven – a process, I might add, that just happens to drive off the water. The sudden change in the shape, size and colour of the fat passed without comment by Drysdale or the narrator. (Professor Gee's human fat candle, complete with natural water content, required the application of a Bunsen burner for a full minute before igniting.) The whole fat candle apparently burned away quite quickly – because time-lapse photography was used. No mention was made that the complete combustion of a mere few ounces of fat actually took two hours. (Dr Drysdale later informed me of the time taken to burn the fat.)

I later burned a piece of beef fat myself. I was unable to get the wet type of beef fat to burn at all so I used the hard, virtually waterless, suet-type fat. I wrapped six ounces in some cloth and set fire to it in a basin. It burned readily and took forty-five minutes to burn away completely. In the process of burning a lot of melted fat ran away from the burning 'candle'. As the melted fat was contained within the basin it was all eventually soaked up by the wick and burned. This was my second attempt. The first candle I burned in a flat dish similar to that used by Drysdale. So much fat ran away from the melting 'candle' that most of the rendered fat remained unburned. Having the wick outside the candle resulted in the very quick rendering of the beef tallow to liquid which flowed away from the flame and so remained unburned. The fact is that a lot of the fat in the human victims of SHC is similarly rendered down and flows away from the body. The rug and carpet under the remains of Henry Thomas were saturated in body fat. This greatly reduces the amount of fat available to fuel the 'wick effect'. The length of time taken by such small amounts of fat without the far less flammable adjuncts of blood, muscles and bone, to burn away suggests strongly that the 'wick effect' is a process that takes days rather than hours to complete.

Drysdale's 'candle' seemed to burn without any great loss of excess liquid fat. The dish containing his candle appeared to remain practically clean of excess fat. Later in the programme, Dr Drysdale attempted to demonstrate how bone could be reduced to ash at low temperature by the all-consuming 'candle effect'. He took an unspecified animal bone which appeared to my untutored eye to be the thigh bone of a pig. Though both animal and human bones normally come clothed in large amounts of flesh, blood and fat, Drysdale consigned the bone, completely stripped of flesh, to the bowels of a muffle furnace which was already up and running at a temperature in excess of 500°C.

Prior to placing the bone in the furnace, Drysdale explained:

> *In a crematorium you need high temperatures – round about 1,300°C or even higher – to reduce the body to ash in a relatively short period of time. But it is a misconception to think you need those temperatures within a living room to reduce a body in the same way . . . At relatively low temperatures at about 500°C, given enough time, the bone will eventually come down to something approaching a powder.*

After eight hours at a temperature slightly above 500°C, the bone was removed from the furnace. It was still recognisably a bone and medium grey in colour (as maintained by Clive Chamberlain, the manufacturer of crematoria). Drysdale then assured us that 'over a period of twelve hours or so it is quite likely that the bone will smoulder slowly enough to reduce it to a powder.' This was not demonstrated.

I need to remind readers at this juncture that experts such as crematoria superintendents and manufacturers of crematoria specify operating temperatures of 800°C to 900°C. When

Drysdale specifies cremation temperatures in excess of 1,300°C I feel he must be confusing a crematorium with a blast furnace. The melting point of steel is around 1,500°C. I fail to see how Drysdale can equate the possible reduction of a bare bone (yet to be successfully demonstrated) in the constant radiated heat of a muffle furnace with the possible burning of flesh-covered human bones in a candle-type flame.

Drysdale's demonstrations can be summed up as follows: about 1lb of *pre-cooked* animal fat (compared with human fat it was highly flammable), wrapped in cotton, was burned in a well-ventilated laboratory; a pig bone (stripped of its protective fat, flesh and blood) was incinerated for eight hours in a furnace at a temperature twice that established for the burning of human fat). This results in an obvious failure to reduce the bone to ash. Drysdale then confidently asserts that a further four hours of such incineration would no doubt produce the desired effect. He sums up by claiming that the so-called spontaneous human combustion phenomenon can easily be explained away by his demonstration of the 'candle effect'.

By this stage in the proceedings, I was expecting someone to remark upon the absolute failure of the demonstrations to have shown anything other than the growing improbability of the 'candle effect' reducing a complete human corpse to ash under any conditions, let alone those of reduced oxygen.

In the course of filming my interview for the programme I emphasised that I believed the phenomenon of SHC to be both entirely natural and scientifically explicable, but not by the 'candle effect'. When describing the cases of Thomas, Webb and Bailey, I stressed that all three were *alive* when they started burning. I supplied Theresa Hunt with the pathologists' reports and police statements which proved my claims. I described my own theory about hydrogen and oxygen. All of this film was edited out.

David X. Halliday was also featured on the show giving his considered scientific opinion as to the cause of ignition in the cases of Ashton and Soudaine. Halliday said that in every case of this type that he examined, he found a perfectly good ignition source present in the premises, be it an electric fire or a gas hob. This was often coupled with evidence that the victim has either ignited his or her own clothing or objects have been ignited in the immediate vicinity of where they collapsed. He added that the two cases the QED people told him of were very similar to the types of fire that he had examined in the past. He then said it was clear from the photographs there were viable ignition sources present, even on first inspection. In the one case he drew attention to an electric fire next to the hole in the floor (Ashton). In the second case (Soudaine) he noted that a gas hob was present right next to the victim.

This opinion does not explain the case of the tramp, Bailey. The fire brigade photos of the scene of Bailey's demise are excellent, but unfortunately for Halliday and his colleagues there was no possible 'viable source' to be found anywhere in the house or on the body of Bailey. Though I had supplied Theresa Hunt with the Bailey photos and the evidence showing he suffocated on the fumes of his combustion, neither Drysdale nor Halliday were called upon to venture an opinion as to how Bailey came to be ignited. Neither was there an 'obvious viable source of ignition' in the Henry Thomas case. I had already pointed out the inexplicable element of the forensic scientists' opinion that Thomas had fallen into the open fire headfirst and, having ignited his head, then sat down in his armchair with legs stretched out in front of the TV set to burn to ash. Halliday was not asked to express an opinion on the Annie Webb case where it was supposed that she had fallen on to the gas fire without leaving a trace of her contact with the fire, itself a forensic impossibility. His comments were restricted to the two cases that I had not yet investigated. Having since investigated them (the cases of Ashton and Soudaine) I have found that yet again there was not a scrap of physical evidence that either victim had come into contact with the viable source of ignition, i.e. the one-bar electric fire, which was most likely not even switched on, and a gas stove burner partially obscured by a half-full simmering kettle.

Halliday stated that he often finds these 'viable sources' of ignition coupled with evidence of the victim's clothing having caught fire from the sources. In the two cases on which he gave his opinion there was not the least shred of evidence to support the claim that either the victims or their clothing had been in contact with the sources. In actual fact, in the next chapter you will learn that the investigating scenes of crime officer specifically stated that he could find no evidence of Soudaine having caught his clothes on fire on the gas hob. In the case of Ashton and the electric fire there is more than a strong suspicion that the fire was not even switched on. There is certainly no proof that it was switched on. It is stretching the bounds of credulity to assume that a person can be reduced to ashes by a one-bar electric fire even when it can be proved to have been switched on. When there is no proof to that effect and it is highly probable that it was not switched on then it seems rash to assume a person could be reduced to ash by the agency of such a fire.

In an obvious attempt to counter my claim that bodies cannot burn away like candles in rooms so deficient in oxygen that burning furniture soon ceased to burn, the services of Stan Ames of the Fire Research Station were enlisted. Ames first attempted to explain away the curious fact that plastic cabinets and control knobs, many feet from burning corpses, melted out of shape while paper and other flammable materials, mere inches from the incineration, were not even scorched. He demonstrated, by means of a computer model and actual filmed tests, how a raging maelstrom of super-hot flame and gases, from fiercely burning polyurethane-filled furniture, quickly rises to and spreads across the whole ceiling. As the layer of gases is fed by the roaring blaze so it deepens and descends into the room until it is so close above a television set that the set is melted by the radiant heat – seconds before the set is *completely destroyed* by the intense heat.

If ever there was a clear example of taking a sledgehammer to crack a nut, this was it. In the filmed test one saw the lampshade disappear in a momentary flash as it was engulfed by the fireball in its furious progress across the ceiling. The instantaneous destructive power of the fireball was truly awesome. The dramatic effect of the presentation was lost, however, on anyone whose mind stayed on the original objective. This objective was to demonstrate how plastic objects came to be melted when *no other* fire damage was caused. Ames' demonstration, based on his computer programme being fed the melting point of Ashton's TV cabinet, showed a room wherein everything was being totally annihilated. Photographs of scenes of Ashton's incineration were shown prior to the demo. They clearly showed that no damage was caused to polystyrene-tiled ceilings or net curtains. They were not even scorched. What was the point in Ames demonstrating the power of his rampaging, out-of-control fire monster? It is one of the more mystifying aspects of SHC that it can cause damage, normally requiring masses of flames, without burning anything other than the victim and the objects in contact with the burning body.

Admittedly, Ames did demonstrate how a plastic TV set could be melted out of shape without being in contact with flames just a few seconds before the whole room was gutted.

In the case of Henry Thomas, I described how the plastic lampshade had softened with the rising heat and oozed down over the light bulb to fall to the floor. Or rather it fell on top of Thomas's shoes. The shade had never been subjected to anything remotely resembling the Ames' scenario. But Ames saved the best till last. To demonstrate how a body can continue to burn in conditions too deficient of oxygen to support the continued burning of furniture he gave us another demo.

Totally missing the point that the furnishings at the scenes of SHC, which had originally been burning quite fiercely, had been totally extinguished (by lack of oxygen) with not so much as a single spark remaining, he set up a fire chamber to demonstrate how a body can be totally consumed by slow, flameless combustion over a period of six hours. Not having a human body readily to hand he used an equivalent substitute – a modern stuffed armchair, which is, in contrast to a human body, highly flammable. A dead pig I could have gone along with, a dead sheep even, but an overstuffed armchair?

The chair was apparently set alight with no trouble. Everyone retired from the chamber. Through a viewing port we saw the chair briefly flaming away quite fiercely. The soothing dulcet tones of the narrator, Anna Massey, solemnly assured us that, 'The most important feature of this experiment is to demonstrate that the smouldering process could sustain itself long enough to reduce the body to ash, or, in this case, the armchair to its springs.' Keep in mind she said the chair would be reduced to its springs – that's a firm promise.

Anticlimax is the word that somehow springs (no pun intended) readily to mind. The door swung open to reveal to the audience what was meant to be the naked chair springs. Instead, we were confronted by the complete chair – only slightly damaged by fire. It would have been as good as new after an hour's work by a competent upholsterer. A good half of the surface covering was totally undamaged. The framework, the readily combustible *wooden* framework, appeared undamaged. At this juncture I really did expect Ames to throw up his hands and admit defeat. But with barely a moment's hesitation, and apparently in all seriousness, he continued unabashed, 'So! Really, this is broadly what we expected to find. It can all be explained in terms of ordinary physics and chemistry.'

Ames had failed to demonstrate how a chair can be reduced

to its springs in conditions of low oxygen and, having failed with the totally irrelevant chair, was claiming successfully to have demonstrated how a human body can so be reduced to ash.

Had the demo been a complete success it would still not have verified the scientists' hypothesis. Ames was supposedly attempting to show how a body can smoulder to ash in conditions of low oxygen such as I described in Chapter 14. Dry, fibrous material can smoulder for many hours without flame in an oxygen-depleted atmosphere something below 16 per cent oxygen. But a candle cannot smoulder. When a candle burns it does so by the heat of the flame melting the wax which, as a liquid, is then drawn up the fibrous wick by capillary action. As the liquid wax reaches the flame it becomes gaseous and can now burn. When the flame is extinguished, for whatever reason, the tip of the wick, which is virtually devoid of wax, smoulders for a few seconds and burns away to delicate ash. The red glow of the flameless burning works its way down the wick until it reaches the portion that is soaked in molten wax. At this relatively low temperature the molten wax acts like water and promptly douses the charring wick. So, a candle cannot smoulder for more than a few seconds. Why then do experts, who subscribe to the theory that humans can burn away like inside-out candles, try to prove by means of a chair that bodies can smoulder away in a manner which is totally impossible for a candle?

My earlier comments on the limited fields of expertise of scientists fully explains the paradox. The problem was split into two halves. Each half was given to a specialist who concentrated solely on his particular problem, albeit unsuccessfully. This procedure resulted in incompatible attempts to solve the problem. Their desired solutions could only be applicable to the problem of SHC if a human body could behave like a candle and a dry fibrous armchair at the same time. In the subatomic world of particle physics, quanta (packets of energy) can be observed as both waves and particles. We are operating in the macro world and quantum mechanics hardly apply to candles and stuffed chairs.

After Ames' demonstration with the chair, still clothed in its 'too, too solid flesh', I felt certain this must be the end. The narrator would announce that the champions of the 'candle effect' had failed miserably in their endeavours, thus, once again leaving the question open. But instead the narrator's soothing, mellifluous tones summed up thus:

> *So it seems that nearly every aspect of these mysterious fire deaths can now be explained. Some form of ignition causes the body to burn. The heat dries out the body so that condensation forms on the windows. Once the body is dry, the fat melts and orange fatty deposits build up on surfaces like the light bulb. It would seem the mystery is finally over.*

'The heat dries out the body . . .', 'Once the body is dry . . .' – what is this mysterious heat source that dries out the body so that it can burn? Vaporising ten gallons of water in a small sealed room would result in more than condensation on the window. Anyone who has allowed a kettle to boil dry and vaporised a pint or so of water in the kitchen will know what I mean.

So, there is no mystery. All that is required is an unspecified source of ignition to first dry out the body and then it will burn. David X. Halliday of the Metropolitan Police Fire Investigation Unit then made an appearance. He earnestly stated, 'With some people the existence of spontaneous human combustion is a matter of faith and no evidence in the world is going to convince them otherwise.' He continues, 'As a scientist I am quite satisfied that spontaneous human combustion does not exist.' I was the only person on the programme who was pro SHC.

On 16 May 1989, I spoke by telephone with Dr Dougal

Drysdale at Edinburgh University. We had a long conversation in which I endeavoured to obtain clarification of several points raised in the 'QED' programme. I asked him why he had chosen the temperature of 500°C in the attempt to destroy the bone. He replied, 'We originally did the experiment at 500°C for twelve hours – actually it was fourteen hours and at the end of fourteen hours the bone was quite friable [can easily be crumbled or pulverised]. Now I reckon if we could have carried out the experiment at 700°C then after eight hours, the bone would have been very nearly rendered down to powder. The point I was trying to make was that at low temperature, given enough time, the bone can be reduced to powder.'

I then asked what his field of work was. He said that his work involved assessing fire hazard. I said, 'For materials used in construction is it, like that?' He replied, 'Yes, that's right.'

I then asked Drysdale where he obtained his figures of 1,300°C or even higher for the operating temperatures of crematoria. He answered, 'I think I got that from, um, I can't recall now.' I told him that I had the figure of 800 to 900°C from a crematorium superintendent. He said, 'That's a figure that's floating around in my head. It's one that I picked up along the way.'

Drysdale also told me that he was at the Fire Research Station with Stan Ames and that is where he carried out his fat-burning demonstration. I commented on the unwillingness of the armchair to oblige Ames by smouldering to ash. He replied, 'That chair – that test didn't perform the way it should have performed.'

I then asked what type of animal fat he had used. He said, 'It stank to high heaven. It was beef.' I then asked how long the piece of fat, wrapped in cotton, took to burn away. He replied, 'A long time, probably about two hours. I'll tell you one thing, I did that experiment in Edinburgh with some animal fat from the butchers. It worked extremely well. I tried it twice. Very easy to ignite and it burned for a long time. They produced this piece of stinking animal fat down at the Fire Research Station and we couldn't light the bloody thing. It was terrible.' I then asked him if that was why the film showed a sudden change of the piece of fat when he was rolling the fat up. He answered, 'That's right, that's right, yes.'

I asked him why human fat was not used instead of animal as it was human combustion that was being investigated. He said, 'Yes, well, ethically it might be a little tricky.' I then reminded him that Professor Gee had used human fat wrapped around a test tube for firmness. I said it would have been more realistic if Gee had used a bone for firmness. We could then have seen what effect, if any, it would have had on the bone which is presumed to be reduced to ash in a human candle flame. I also referred to the fact that it took a whole minute's application of a Bunsen burner flame for Gee to get the human fat burning. To this Drysdale replied enigmatically, 'Yes, but there's beef fat and there's beef fat.' He continued, 'We've tried wrapping – taking a bone with fat on it and wrapping cloth around it. It [the fat] burns away but we haven't managed to produce the destruction of the bone yet. We've got a lot of work here. I'm sure it's a matter of finding the right conditions.'

I later contacted Clive Chamberlain of Evans International Ltd of Leeds (crematoria manufacturers). I asked him to what use would a furnace be put which operated at temperatures in excess of 1,300°C. He said it would most likely be used in the melting of metals. He also said it would be impossible for any crematorium to operate at such temperatures – it would collapse.

QED – quod erat demonstrandum – means 'which was to be demonstrated'. Whatever was demonstrated by the 'QED' team and their experts, it was not that living humans are large versions of twopenny candles.

The exercise, which was supposed to scientifically examine

the phenomenon of SHC did no such thing. No proper consideration appeared to be given to the scientifically verifiable facts of the three victims being alive at the commencement of their incineration. If one living person apparently allows himself or herself to burn to death without resistance then that is remarkable in the extreme. That living people should consistently remain unmoving while being burned alive should cause even the most sceptical among us to question the orthodox theory. (This is more fully explained in chapters 17, 18 and 19). The case of the tramp Bailey, which is impossible to dismiss as an example of the 'wick effect', was not featured in the programme. Surely a more interesting programme would have resulted from merely revealing the incontrovertible facts without making any unfounded claims regarding SHC. The bare facts, as they stand without comment, are fascinating.

The power of television programmes such as 'QED' is truly awesome. It seems to me that by far the majority of people do not see what is actually shown on their TV screens. What they see is completely modified by what they expect to see. In some cases, such as the 'QED' programme, the viewers are told what they are going to see before being shown the result. Consequently large numbers of people are convinced that the failed experiments actually demonstrated the hypotheses that were postulated beforehand. Such is the power of suggestion. When the piece of fat was substituted I was convinced there would be uproar by critics and viewers. To date (six years after the programme) I have yet to find one other person that noticed the fat switch. When I show the video I made of the show, having previously pointed out the fat switch, it is immediately obvious to everyone. Not one person fails to see the switch. Yet when they are not told few, if any (none to my knowledge), spot the switch. Such is the power of suggestion. In spite of the result of Ames' experiment with the chair many people are convinced of the slow-burning effect on a human body in conditions of low oxygen. On occasion, when the subject of SHC comes up in conversation and I reveal that I am actively investigating the phenomenon, I am subjected to the galling experience of being informed that the matter of SHC has been resolved. It is no longer a mystery. It was all explained on 'QED' some years ago and is entirely due to an unusual method of slow-burning without oxygen.

Television somehow causes many people to switch off their critical faculty. They seem to just absorb whatever comes out of the box. No wonder that soap viewers attack certain soap actors in the street and castigate them for being nasty to some other soap character. Possibly watching too much television causes some people to become detached from reality. Reality for them is unquestionably what appears on TV.

CHAPTER SIXTEEN

Ashton and Soudaine

In December 1987, Barry Soudaine, aged between forty-five and forty-seven, was living in a flat over a bakery owned and operated by Reg Gower in Folkestone, Kent. Soudaine was a lonely alcoholic. His girlfriend, who had been living with him, had died of cancer and, since her death, he had totally neglected his health. Reg Gower told me that Barry 'never bought any food and spent all his money on drink'. He said that on many occasions he had found Barry 'absolutely paralytic'.

While the main part of the flat was situated over the shop, the kitchen was on the ground floor at the rear of the bakery. Barry was last seen alive by Reg Gower at about 6p.m. on Sunday 27 December 1987. Reg Gower was going out for the evening with his wife. For once Barry seemed to be reasonably sober as he entered his flat. When Mr and Mrs Gower returned that night at about 10p.m. they saw that the lights were on in Barry's flat. Just over twelve hours later, at 10.45a.m., Reg Gower went to his shop. Immediately he entered he smelled burning. He checked his bakehouse and found nothing untoward.

Gower entered the kitchen which is a narrow, oblong-shaped room, both sides of which are fitted with kitchen units.

A gas cooker stands in the right-hand rear corner. The smell was bad in there and looking towards the rear of the kitchen he saw a charred mass. On closer examination he could see that this was all that remained of Barry. He recognised the distinctive training shoes that Barry had bought from his stepson. He also recognised the remains of the corduroy trousers which Soudaine had been wearing.

Reg Gower observed, 'There was no smoke or fire in the room but the gas ring at the front of the cooker was blazing. The kettle was half on the ring.' This statement is of some significance which will be explained later. Reg Gower then left the kitchen and informed the police of the tragedy. His statement was taken down by Detective Sergeant S. Harris.

The scenes of crime officer attending at the scene was Detective Sergeant Nigel William Cruttenden. D.S. Cruttenden had then been involved in fire scene investigations for over eight years and had spent three of those eight years at the Home Office Forensic Science Laboratory as a liaison officer. He stated that the only fire damage to the kitchen was a slightly melted plastic air vent a few inches up the wall close to the remains and slight charring to a base unit at floor level. The damage to the base unit was probably caused by one of the arms burning off the body and falling against the unit.

In spite of his extensive fire and forensic laboratory experience, Cruttenden was clearly surprised, if not shocked, at what he saw. In his statement to the coroner he stated that he was unable to explain how a body could suffer such gross fire damage while the kitchen and furnishings were virtually undamaged. Even a plastic brush and dustpan which were only six inches from the incinerated body were undamaged by heat and a nearby tea towel showed no sign of scorching. Polystyrene ceiling tiles had not melted.

Cruttenden verified what Gower had said regarding the kettle and the gas stove. He said that one of the front rings of the cooker was alight. He also said that a kettle was on the hob and positioned between the two front rings. Most significantly he also said, 'The kettle had not boiled dry and it was still about half full.' He then made a further equally significant comment, 'On closer examination of the hob there was [sic] no remnants of clothing or ash to suggest any burning.'

Cruttenden's evidence to H.M. Coroner was different to what he said when he appeared on the 'QED' programme where he stated, 'Having ruled out murder and suicide and SHC, the only thing left for the death of Barry Soudaine was that he'd had a heart attack, caught himself on fire by the lighted gas stove, fell to the floor and then burned like a candle from above downwards.' Let us examine Cruttenden's unsubstantiated 'assumptions' one by one.

1. '. . . he'd had a Heart attack . . . ' There was no evidence of heart attack. The pathologist's report to the Coroner mentions fire products in the lumen of the larynx and upper part of the remaining trachea. There was also debris occluding the laryngeal lumen. The pathologist (Michael John Heath, MB BS DMJ (Clin et Path) Forensic Pathologist and Lecturer in Forensic Medicine at the London Hospital Medical College) stated in the conclusion to his report that flecks of carbon over the surface of the tongue and also in the laryngeal lumen were evidence that Soudaine had inhaled the products of combustion. Dead men do not inhale. Soudaine was alive when he began to burn.

2. '. . . caught himself on fire by the lighted gas-stove . . . ' This statement appears to be at odds with his statement of evidence wherein he specifically stated that he was unable to find any such evidence. Cruttenden's claim that Soudaine 'caught himself on fire by the lighted gas stove' thus appears to be unsupported by his own evidence to the coroner.

3. '. . . and then burned like a candle from above downwards . . . ' Soudaine was face down when he burned. The front and sides of his chest were completely destroyed as

were the contents. The thoracic vertebrae were burned sufficiently to expose the thoracic vertebral canal. All of which
means that he burned upwards from beneath.

When he made his original statement to the coroner,
Cruttenden found it inexplicable that so much damage could
have occurred to the body and so little to nearby vulnerable
objects, such as a plastic brush and dustpan and polystyrene
tiles. This was hardly mentioned on the 'QED' programme.

How and why did he so readily rule out SHC? What
knowledge has he of SHC that allows him to rule it out? In
order to rule out SHC it would be necessary for Cruttenden
to know the criteria which need to be present to support the
SHC hypothesis. He would then need to show that those
vital criteria were not present. He ruled out SHC solely
because forensic scientists insist (without proof) that the phenomenon does not occur.

The one major difference between SHC and occurrences
of the 'wick effect' is the time factor. It is strongly suspected
that SHC is a fast process taking possibly less than an hour.
The 'wick effect' is claimed to take around fourteen hours,
although the likelihood is that it takes about twenty-four
hours and possibly more.

The investigators missed two opportunities to narrow down
the time factor in this case. In the first instance, Detective
Sergeant Harris, in taking Reg Gower's statement, noted the
fact that Gower had observed the flat lights to be on at 10p.m.
the previous evening. No mention was made as to whether
the lights were still on at 10.45a.m. when Gower discovered
both the remains of Soudaine and the half-full kettle still on
the lighted gas stove.

If the lights were out when Gower arrived on the scene
that would have suggested that Soudaine had got up in the
daylight and put the kettle on for a cup of tea. He would
hardly have fumbled his way down the stairs in the dark when

there was no other person in the flat for him to disturb by putting on the lights. Then we have the half-full kettle on the 'blazing' gas stove. Cruttenden remarked on the fact that the kettle was still half full and that it was placed between the two front rings. I spoke to Reg Gower about this and he told me that the kettle had been placed so that it would continue to simmer on the boil. How full does a person fill a kettle to make tea for one? My wife and I seldom fill our kettle more than half full to make tea for two. Had the kettle been full then how long would it take to boil down to half full when in the position it was found with the one ring 'blazing'? Why did Cruttenden not carry out a couple of simple tests with the kettle? He could then have established a maximum and a minimum time for the incineration of Barry Soudaine.

At the time I spoke to Reg Gower I had not noticed the ambiguity in his official statement relating to the flat lights still being on or not. By the time it did occur to me Reg had already died. His widow was adamant that the shock of finding Soudaine's incinerated remains brought about his premature death. She said that he was never the same man after the event which constantly troubled his mind.

Is it likely that a man should suffer a heart attack and fall on to a lighted gas stove and set himself on fire without leaving a trace and without knocking off the kettle? I think not. At the inquest into the death of Barry Soudaine, H.M. Coroner Brian Smith (a most enlightened and unbiased man) said, 'There are questions which have not been answered nor will they be answered.' Though the condition of the body made it impossible for the pathologist to accurately determine the cause of death, his findings did indicate that Soudaine was breathing for part of the time he was incinerating unless, by some amazing coincidence, he had somehow breathed in fire products of some other fire immediately prior to his death and subsequent incineration. It is highly likely that Soudaine was alive at the start of his incineration. Brian Smith was certainly doubtful that Soudaine had accidentally set himself ablaze by falling against the gas hob. He was not satisfied that death was accidental – he returned an open verdict, the only proper verdict under the circumstances and one of the very few such verdicts in modern alleged SHC cases.

Just over one year after Soudaine's demise, there occurred another classic example of SHC in the Southampton area. This incident was also featured on the 'QED' programme and once again the facts were presented in a way which fitted the 'wick effect' theory.

On a January day in 1988, the sparse remains of Alfred Ashton were discovered on the ground floor of his house in Southampton. A fire brigade investigating officer, ADO Roger Penney, attended the scene after firemen had ensured the premises were safe. His job was to investigate the cause of the fire and complete a report. He found a hole burned through the wooden floor and the lower portion of Ashton's legs were found at one edge of the hole. The position of the lower legs showed that Ashton had burned face down. When Penney was interviewed on the 'QED' programme about this case he said, 'I noticed that the trousers, shoes and socks were not damaged at all. The cut-off point, where the body had smouldered, was a clean cut.' His reference to the body having smouldered is really just a figure of speech as there is no evidence to show that the body had smouldered. However, the significance of his remark lies in the description of the remaining clothing on the lower limbs of Alfred Ashton. Penney found the fact of the survival of the clothes in an undamaged condition below the burn line worthy of comment. It is a common factor in cases of SHC that clothing does survive on the unburned extremities.

A foot or so from one edge of the hole, above and to the right of the legs stood an old-fashioned single-coil electric fire capable of generating one kilowatt of heat. This type of fire is not fitted with a reflector so the amount of radiant heat is considerably less than that given out by a more modern one fitted with a highly polished reflector. A lot of the heat is absorbed by the comparatively large ceramic block on which the tungsten coil is mounted. Consequently, about half of the heat is given off into the air above by the process of convection. Such a fire would have to be within a very few inches of a piece of newspaper before it could cause the paper to ignite. (In the 'QED' reconstruction of the Ashton case a modern reflecting electric fire was shown.) The rest of Alfred Ashton, in the form of ashes, had fallen through the hole in the floor.

Penny examined the electric fire and found that it was not fitted with a switch. It was plugged into a wall socket, the switch of which was in the 'off' position. He was unable to ascertain whether or not any person, including firemen, had switched the fire off since the incineration of Ashton. He thought it unlikely that anyone had switched the fire off at the wall because the cable supplying the wall plug had been burned through. Thus the socket was dead. Firemen do not interfere with evidence unnecessarily so why should one switch off a fire that was not capable of burning?

There was typically little damage to the room apart from smoke damage. A nylon anorak-type coat, hanging on a chair within a foot of the hole, showed slight signs of heat damage. The plastic cabinet of a portable TV set some distance away was melted and distorted. The wooden floor only burned where it was in contact with the burning body. Terrific heat had been generated hence the melted TV set but the consuming flames were restricted to the corpse and the materials that were in contact with the body, i.e. the wooden floorboards and clothing. As in the case of Henry Thomas, the burn line on the trousers coincided precisely with the limit of the burned portions of the legs.

Yet again Ashton was alive when he started burning. The pathologist gave the cause of death as 'burning'. His comments relative to the body were to the effect that the whole body, including the bones had been destroyed leaving only the lower legs.

ADO Roger Penney also stated on the 'QED' programme that, though he had initially considered SHC as a possible cause, he had finally concluded that the true cause was indeed the innocuous one-bar electric fire – even though there was no proof that it had been switched on.

As a sequel to this incident I record the fact that I later interviewed Roger Penney just prior to his retirement. He told me that he was convinced that the electric fire played no part in the incineration of Alfred Ashton. He was always of the opinion that the cause might well have been SHC. As a career fire officer he did not wish to jeopardise his career by publicly stating a belief in the possibility of SHC. Now that he is retired Roger Penney is not concerned about adverse criticism.

It was this incident, involving the melted TV cabinet, that Stan Ames of the Fire Research Station, endeavoured to explain away with his super-hot fireball which destroyed everything in its path.

When I wrote to the Hampshire coroner, R.N. Mackean, asking for copies of the death report and depositions he was unco-operative, expressing his opinion that he did not consider me a properly interested person to whom the details of the Ashton case should be supplied. I also spoke, by telephone, to the Hampshire police officer who was the coroner's officer who was equally unco-operative.

It is about time we had a Freedom of Information Act in this country as they have at present in the USA. Coroners' reports, along with a great deal of other information, are locked away for many years before they become available to the public. In the case of coroners' reports the time-span is seventy years. No doubt the biblical life-span was deliberately chosen so that anything untoward would not become public knowledge during the lifetime of the officials to whom such revelation would be embarrassing. Coroners do have the right to release information if they consider the person requesting the information to be a properly interested person. To date, R.N. Mackean is the only coroner who considers me not to be a properly interested person. He obviously considered Theresa Hunt, the 'QED' producer, to be such a properly interested person because the programme had access to the inquest report and photographs. The inquest report on the death of Alfred Ashton was shown on the programme. Cause of death was recorded as 'unknown'.

CHAPTER SEVENTEEN

Trances

In October 1994, I appeared live on the TV show, 'Schofield's Quest'. Each week Philip Schofield hosts the show in which viewers are asked to phone and write in with information about whatever mystery or 'Quest' is featured that week. Needless to say, on the week that I appeared one of the mysteries was that of SHC. I briefly stated the circumstances of my experience of the death of Henry Thomas. The fact that I was in the process of writing a book on the subject was mentioned and anyone with any knowledge of any incidents of SHC was asked to respond. The programme was put together by Michael Hurll TV Ltd, and Heidi Hannell (researcher for Michael Hurll TV Ltd) forwarded to me all the responses to the 'Quest'.

Due to the fact that the 'Quest' is a family show and is screened well before the 9p.m. watershed, I was unable to go into any gruesome details. I would like to have asked anyone with knowledge of persons allegedly burning to death as the direct result of a carelessly dropped cigarette to respond. As most instances of SHC are explained away, not many people are aware that such instances have actually occurred. However, the response was sufficient in that practically the whole of the rest of this book results from the responses to that programme. I am greatly in the debt of Philip Schofield, Heidi Hannell and Michael Hurll TV Ltd.

One of the letters so received was sent by Mike Stubbins, of Pocklington, Yorkshire. His letter read as follows:

> *Dear Sir,*
> *When we found Wilf he said he felt no pain and appeared to be in a trance or shock. He was wearing a jacket and his shirt was buttoned at the wrist. Neither showed signs of burn although his arm was burned up to the elbow. Unfortunately he died 18 months after the event but could never remember what had happened. All the other information is enclosed. I hope this will be of some assistance.*
> *Yours faithfully*
> *Mike Stubbins*

The 'information' enclosed was a cutting from the *Pocklington Post* of an article by Nicola Townend, dated 25 April 1991. The article featured a picture of a seemingly sprightly elderly man named Wilfred Gowthorpe. The picture revealed that his heavily bandaged left hand was minus the small and ring fingers. My experiences of the press to date are such that I require solid corroboration before I accept any newspaper report as correct in all aspects. I contacted Mike Stubbins and took statements from both him and his wife Sandra in accordance with the normal practice of obtaining evidence. Having obtained the statements I have to admit that Nicola Townend did a first-class job of reporting the facts. I cannot fault her. The statements of Mike and Sandra Stubbins are reproduced below:-

Statement of Sandra Stubbins, aged 42 years

It was in January 1991, we were decorating the house at the time. Wilf Gowthorpe aged 71 years, was staying with us in the daytime and he was helping too, he was more like an uncle to us. At night he went to his own flat. He was basically a lonely man. I went out for half an hour and Wilf said he would clean up. I returned after about half an hour and Wilf was in a corner of the kitchen. The paste bucket and brush, which he was going to clean, were in the sink and the cold water tap was running. I was a home help at the time and I thought that he had suffered a stroke. I phoned for the doctor immediately.

He came straight away, it was Dr Dunham. He examined Wilf and said, 'What has he done to his hand?' I said, 'I don't know'. 'Oh!' he said, 'it's hospital straight away.' Both fingers were amputated at hospital. They said they were so charred if they had not been amputated they would have broke off on their own. He was in hospital for about five months. His arm was burned right up to his elbow. How could he have done that? His shirt sleeve was buttoned at the wrist and his jacket sleeve came down to his wrist. Neither his shirt sleeve nor his jacket sleeve were burned. At the hospital they were asking me how he could have done it. I had felt the kettle, in case he had scalded himself, but it was cold and I checked all the electric plugs but was told that he couldn't have electrocuted himself because he would have blown all the fuses and blackened the plug. He couldn't remember anything about what happened. He seemed to be in a trance. It was a cold day but Wilf was soaked in sweat. His clothes were wet through from perspiring, except his left coat sleeve and his shirt sleeve, they were dry.

It wasn't as if he'd had his hand in water. When I phoned the doctor I also phoned my husband and he arrived just before the doctor. I called for an ambulance and we went to the hospital with Wilf but he couldn't remember anything about what had happened to him. He kept saying for ages afterwards, 'What happened to me, what did I do?'

The smell was terrible. I have never smelled anything like it. It was foul. It did not smell anything like a piece of meat burning, it was really horrible. It still smelled horrible in the hospital after they had amputated his second finger. It was awful. I searched the kitchen floor and surfaces but could find no sign of any burning or dripped fat or blood. When I left him he was about to wash out the paste bucket. When I returned he was in the corner as if in a trance and the bucket and brush were in the sink and the tap was running. Whatever happened would seem to have happened just after I left.

Wilf never married. He had lived with us for sixteen or seventeen years during the day. As I said, in the evenings he stayed at his little flat. He had a little dog. He watched TV.

S Stubbins
3 December 1994

Statement of George Michael Stubbins, aged 54 years

It was one day in January 1991. I was at work when my wife telephoned to say that she thought Wilf had suffered a stroke. I rushed home and when I went into the kitchen I saw Wilf leant in corner against work-top. He was like in a trance or shock, whichever, I don't know as I've never seen shock. But I would describe him as being in a trance. You couldn't get anything out of him. He wouldn't speak except for a bit of a grunt. I asked him what was wrong but you couldn't get anything out of him, it was like he was in a trance.

Doctor came at that point. He tried talking to him but could get no answer. We tried to get him to sit down and pulled him away from work-tops and then doctor said, 'What have you done to your hand Wilf?' It was the first time anybody had seen that. His left hand was very badly burned. We left it to the doctor and tried to find how Wilf had burnt himself. We checked every source of heat. There was no electric on. The gas had not been turned on. There was no heat at all there. The central heating had just come on — that was warm. All electric switches were turned off. A paste bucket that he had been cleaning up was in the sink and the cold water was running full bore.

*Wilfred Gowthorpe, SHC
survivor?*
Copyright *Pocklington
Post*

   *What I find so strange was that his shirt sleeves were but-
toned up and his jacket sleeves came down to his wrists yet his
left arm was burnt right up to his elbow. His little finger and
ring finger of his left hand were badly burned and were amputated. His other two fingers were quite badly burned and he had
to have skin grafts on his arm and two remaining fingers. The
weird thing was that his thumb was not damaged at all. He
couldn't have caught hold of anything hot enough to burn two
fingers to cinders without damaging his thumb.*
   *I asked at the hospital if he could have electrocuted himself
but they said that to do that kind of damage it would have
killed him long since. He was in hospital for about fifteen weeks
altogether. When he came out of hospital he was the same as he
always was except he could never remember what had happened to him. As far as he was concerned, he was cleaning up
and that was it, he couldn't remember any more than that. At
the time he was not even showing any signs of being in pain
although the burns were terrible.*

                                             *G.M. Stubbins
                                             4 December 1994*

At a later date when I spoke with Sandra Stubbins she told me that Wilf felt no pain until he had been in the hospital for some hours. Strangely enough when he first came to his senses he kept laughing and asking what had happened to him. He had no idea how he came by his injuries. The last thing he remembered, prior to regaining consciousness in hospital, was going to the sink with the paste bucket to wash it out. For the next eighteen months, until he died of a heart attack, he constantly asked what had happened to him. He was never able to recall any part of the events that caused him the loss of half of his left hand.

It would appear that this case is one in which actual flames do not figure. When a man's hand and arm are so badly burned *inside* his shirt and jacket sleeve that two fingers need to be amputated and his arm, up to his elbow, requires skin grafts necessitating fifteen weeks' treatment in hospital, it can be no ordinary fire or heat source that can contrive such damage without burning his shirt and jacket sleeve. There are always the knowledgeable sceptics who insist that the injuries must have arisen from severe scalding because that is the only method they know wherein flesh can be seriously heat damaged without burning the covering clothes. But we are not talking here about mere heat-damaged flesh. At atmospheric pressure water can only heat up to 100°C. It then vaporises. Temperatures far in excess of 100°C are necessary to burn fingers to such a degree that they are in danger of dropping off. Even super-heated steam does not blacken and char flesh. We all know the difference between boiled and grilled flesh.

Though there seems not to have been any flame involved in this case, the heat source, whatever it was, must have been pretty fierce. The damage to Wilf Gowthorpe's hand and arm took place in less than thirty minutes. At the start of the thirty-minute period he was perfectly normal and about to wash out a paste bucket. Whatever caused his injuries occurred soon after Sandra left the house. The bucket, which he was about to clean, was still in the sink with the cold water tap running at full bore when Sandra returned. Obviously Wilf had not had a chance to clean out the bucket before he became entranced. The burning may have been instantaneous or may have taken longer but it was certainly over in less than thirty minutes. This was no case of long, slow burning as posited in the cases of the 'wick effect'. In addition the victim was very much alive.

This case threw a metaphorical spanner into the works of my theory. There were no flames roaring from the abdomen. Indeed it is patently obvious that, in the incineration of Wilf Gowthorpe's hand and arm, there were no external flames involved. There have, in the past, been more than a few claims that SHC victims have burned inside their clothes without burning the clothes or, in some cases, bedclothes. Such instances have been much more rare than the more standard type of SHC case with which I have dealt up to now. I have ignored such happenings because they did not fit into the criteria that I laid down at the beginning of this book, namely that I would only investigate modern cases of which I had either personal knowledge or for which I could obtain the official police and coroners' reports together with official witness statements. The Gowthorpe case fits the criteria in that it is modern and I have been able to interview the actual witnesses first hand. I am satisfied that the facts are as stated.

I stated earlier in the book that I feel there are at least three different manifestations of the phenomenon of SHC. This flameless burning of extremities is the second of the three types. Were it the only modern instance I would have ignored it. I did in fact ignore it, fascinating though I found the case, until a couple of months after I had obtained the information when I suddenly recalled a case that I had read of some ten years previous. The same case was repeatedly brought up at the Fortean Unconvention 94 at London University by Joe Nickell, the officer of CSICOP

The version that I read had been written up by someone

who was extremely antagonistic towards the concept of SHC (as is Joe Nickell) and had intimated that the victim had been endeavouring to cheat an insurance company with a false claim relating to the loss of a hand due to scalding in steam from a mobile home shower unit. The victim's name was Jack Angel. I was unable to trace the original article that I had read but was very glad to find the case fully reported by the famous American investigator of SHC and all manner of paranormal phenomena, Larry E. Arnold. He is the Director of ParaScience International Inc. On reading the results of Arnold's investigation of the Jack Angel case I found that he was a much maligned man with regard to the so-called false insurance claims. More importantly his case exactly mirrors that of Wilf Gowthorpe except that the facts are even more fascinating.

Jack Angel was a travelling salesman in the garment industry and travelled around the USA in his mobile home which he had adapted to serve as a mobile showroom for the garments he traded in. In November 1974, Angel arrived at Savannah, Georgia. He parked his mobile home in the car park of a motel. Some time that day he got into his pyjamas and went to bed in his mobile home. He awoke *four days later*. His right hand was completely charred black. He had a hole in his chest which he described as 'this big explosion in my chest'. He was also burned between his groin, on both his legs and one ankle and up and down his back in spots. As was the case with Wilf Gowthorpe he felt no pain.

Having got out of bed he showered and dressed and then went into the cocktail lounge of the motel. Just imagine, here is a man who has awoken with serious burns to his body and his right hand is burned black. He is so insensitive to any pain that he showers and dresses and then repairs to a nearby cocktail lounge. Angel said that he was staggering as though drunk and still only half-conscious of his injuries.

The normal consequence of receiving such terrible injuries

would have the victim in such agony that he could not possibly endure a shower, either hot, cold or medium. The mere fact that he was able to act as he did is proof enough that these burns were not your every day run-of-the-mill-type of burns. Whoever heard of anyone suffering such burns without pain, apart from Wilf Gowthorpe? When a waitress remarked on his condition he said, 'Yeah, looks like I got burned'. Though aware of his injuries he still felt no pain. Shortly after he collapsed and was taken to hospital where he awoke to find a doctor peeling skin off his arm with tweezers.

Around midnight that same day Angel finally became fully conscious and at the same time experienced 'excruciating pain'. Yet again this case parallels that of Wilf Gowthorpe. Gowthorpe came around to some extent in the hospital hours after being admitted and, unlike Angel, was subject to inexplicable bouts of laughing before he fully recovered his senses. He was then aware of great pain for the first time. Angel said that a doctor at the hospital told him that he had burned internally and not externally. Angel's right hand and part of his lower forearm were subsequently amputated.

At his request, Angel's wife examined his motor home and found that the bed sheets showed no sign of burning. She was unable to find any sign of anything having burned in the motor home. The controversy over insurance claims etc., arose when a firm of lawyers contacted Angel and offered to sue the manufacturers of the motor home for three million dollars on a contingency basis. This meant that Angel would not have to finance the case. The lawyers would finance the proceedings and hopefully recoup their outlay and fees from the award if any.

The lawyers, being natural pragmatists, assumed that Angel must have received his injuries as the direct result of some malfunctioning equipment in the mobile home. They had the home turned over to a prestigious engineering and technology firm to be inspected from top to bottom in order to find the cause of Angel's injuries. The vehicle was stripped down to its wheelbase and component parts in an endeavour to find the cause of Angel's hopefully litigious injuries. For a while their hopes were pinned on the shower heater but that proved not to be the culprit. When it was suggested that he had been burned by steam, Jack Angel dismissed the possibility out of hand, insisting that he had been burned from the inside and not outside. As he said, burning by steam is still external burning and he was adamant that a doctor at the hospital had told him he had burned from the inside. In fact nothing that was in the mobile home or was part of it could be found to have caused Angel's horrendous injuries.

After two and a half years the suit was dropped one week before it was due to be heard in court. So Angel had not made any attempt to make a fraudulent claim. Lawyers had tried, on his behalf, to prove liability on the part of the mobile home manufacturers. They had, quite reasonably, assumed that as Angel received his injuries in the mobile home then the cause of his injuries must exist within the home. It followed that anything in the home capable of causing such horrific injuries must result in a substantial damages award by the court.

If Angel's injuries were not due to SHC then the experts that stripped his mobile home should have been able to find the cause. They were unable to find even the slightest clue to a possible cause. This case certainly refutes the claims of CSI-COP and other sceptics to the effect that the causes of alleged SHC incinerations can always be found if only sufficient effort is made to find them. In addition to there being no clue to the cause, the injuries were most bizarre in themselves. The burning was such that the only explanation any of the doctors could give was that the burning was internal. If the burning was internal then that must by definition rule out any external source of burning.

Angel never made any claims as to how he came by his

injuries. All he knew was that he fell asleep and then awoke four days later with terrible, unexplainable burns to his body. He somehow managed to acquire these injuries without causing damage to his pyjamas or the sheets of the bed on which he had lain for four days in an apparent trance.

The parallels with the case of Wilf Gowthorpe are clear. Both men received serious burns to their hands necessitating amputation. In both cases the burning was clearly internal. The clothing covering the injured limbs showed no signs of burning in either case. Neither Gowthorpe nor Angel could ever remember what had happened to them. (It would seem that both had been in a trance when they received their terrible injuries and so were never able to recall what happened to them.) At the instigation of his lawyers, Angel was put under hypnosis by a psychologist and regressed back to the time when he received his injuries. He still could not recall anything relating to his injuries. When a person suffers a shock sufficient to block their memory of the event that memory can usually be recovered by hypnotic regression. If a person is in a trance when an event occurs that person is unaware of what is happening. There is therefore no event in their memory, subconscious or otherwise, for them to recall. One might as well expect a patient having undergone an operation under total anaesthetic to recall the details.

When I dealt with the case of Henry Thomas, which was my introduction to the phenomenon of SHC, I felt that he had been in a trance at the commencement of his incineration and had at least remained so until no longer able to move. This feeling was strengthened with each succeeding case that I researched. The obvious fact of the victims not moving while burning has usually been explained away by sceptics as the direct consequence of the victim being stupefied with alcohol. They would have to be extremely stupefied for them not to move when burning to death. It is hard to imagine a more agonising end than death by burning.

In his article relating the story of Jack Angel, Larry Arnold confirms my belief that victims of SHC are in a trance at the time of their incineration. He said that Angel's lack of pain was, 'confirmation of our belief founded upon other SHC events that this pyrophenomenon circumvents or disengages the body's neurosensory system'. It is plain to any serious investigator of the SHC phenomenon that the victims do not react to pain and in the two cases of Gowthorpe and Angel we have absolute confirmation of that fact. The 'circumvention of the body's neurosensory system' seems to last until the survivors come completely to their senses. They appear to be in a deep trance while burning and in a somewhat lighter trance for some time after when they regain a certain amount of consciousness while still in an anaesthetised state which lasts until they regain full consciousness, at which point they suddenly find themselves in the grip of excruciating pain.

Sandra Stubbins said that Wilf suffered until the day he died. She thought it may have been better for Wilf had he not survived the experience. Jack Angel elected to have his hand and lower arm amputated in order to save himself months of painful reconstructive surgery and skin grafting possibly to no effect. Wilf spent fifteen weeks in hospital undergoing painful skin grafts which did not take to his hand although the grafts to his arm were successful.

Sandra Stubbins was insistent that when she returned home to find Wilf Gowthorpe in an apparent trance there was a pervasive stench in the room which she could not identify. She was positive that the stench was connected with whatever had happened to Wilf. It bothered me somewhat that her husband could not recall having noticed any untoward smell. Then I realised that he had arrived home only after being summoned by Sandra on the telephone after she had called the doctor. The time lapse and the opening of the door could have dissipated the smell by the time Mike got home. As Sandra remarked in her statement the stench was certainly not that of burning flesh. If Wilf had burned his hand in any normal manner then the resultant smell should have been one of burned flesh. There was no mention of any unusual smells in the motor home of Jack Angel after his partial incineration. It would be surprising if anyone had noticed any such untoward smell after four days or so had elapsed.

When I attended the death scene of Henry Thomas the prevailing smell reminded me of an old-time bakehouse. However, those who first entered the sealed room some three hours before, remarked on the stench that greeted them. By the time I entered the room it had been well-ventilated. The same stench, over-ridden by mains gas, was noted at the scene of the incineration of Annie Webb. This same indescribable stench is also remarked upon by the witness to the incineration of Jeannie Saffin. Twelve years after the event he cannot forget the stench (see Chapter 19).

CHAPTER EIGHTEEN

Atomic Flames

One of the first people to respond to my appearance on the 'Schofield's Quest' programme was Peter Sadler of Marton, Blackpool. Peter completed an apprenticeship in electrical engineering in 1942 and spent all his working life in engineering of various sorts. He spent 18 years in research and development on radar, atomic energy, crystallographic X-ray development for research labs and universities. He was also the founder and managing director of Genevac Ltd which specialised in the design and manufacture of high vacuum components for use in the atomic energy industry. He is now retired and, like myself, is busily enquiring into anything and everything that takes his fancy, including SHC.

Peter sent four pages of information and speculation on the subject of biochemistry. He focused on tiny organelles within each of the many billions of cells of the body called mitochondria (they occur in the cells of all living creatures). These organelles number up to as many as 2,000 per body cell. Mitochondria provide the energy and heat requirements of the body by a sub-cellular atomic process, part of which consists of combining hydrogen and oxygen atoms which result in an explosive release of energy and the creation of molecules of water. This is part of the respiration process of every single cell in the body. Thousands of mitochondria in every single body cell are producing countless mini explosions per second.

Peter Sadler also stated that as part of the process of obtaining energy from food molecules, a voltage of 0.225 volts is generated across the inner membrane of the mitochondria. Nearly a quarter of a volt of electricity is generated in each of thousands of trillions of mitochondria. As I absorbed this fascinating information I immediately saw that I had in all probability been attacking the problem from the wrong angle.

I had for some years postulated a situation wherein the water in the human body, by some as yet unknown process of electrolysis, was broken down into its constituent gases of hydrogen and oxygen. The gases would be somehow ignited by static electricity. I had also recently learned that vegetable plankton (phytoplankton) photosynthesise sugars from the breakdown of oxygen and hydrogen. The hydrogen is converted into sugars with the aid of chlorophyll and the oxygen is discarded as a waste product. Plankton are responsible for the production of more bio-oxygen (atmospheric oxygen) than all the rain-forests in the world. I was in the process of trying to find out whether any form of animal life could also separate hydrogen and oxygen when I received the letter from Peter Sadler. While I had been looking for a process that separated water into hydrogen and oxygen there already existed a process within the mitochondria that produced water from the explosive combination of already separate hydrogen and oxygen. In a few more weeks I would have arrived at mitochondria as a natural progression through my reading of biology. However, Peter Sadler provided me with a shortcut to the information. In the light of the known facts of the function of mitochondria, it seems highly likely that the process of combustion is triggered by too much hydrogen and oxygen coming together at one time in a single defective mitochondrion. The resulting explosion could then conceivably set off a chain reaction throughout the body.

Peter Sadler argues that the voltage of the mitochondria adds up to 45,000 volts per centimetre (I assume cubic centimetre). He suggests that a defective mitochondrion with a thinner inner membrane could break down under the load of the voltage and the hydrogen/oxygen explosions would proliferate at an exponential rate throughout the body and reduce the torso to ash without flame. The process would be fast. I am inclined to agree with him about the flameless incineration in such circumstances. This would seem to be the process which resulted in the partial, apparently flameless incineration of both Wilf Gowthorpe and Jack Angel. However, we do have the reports of witnesses who have observed the flames roaring from the abdomens of SHC victims. (See Chapter 9 detailing the partial incineration of the tramp, Bailey). Possibly the separation of the hydrogen and oxygen, as per my original theory, is the cause of the outwardly flammable cases of SHC. Highly flammable gas in quantity has to fuel the overtly burning cases. Jack Stacey (the fireman) reported that the flames were 'issuing at force' from the abdomen of the dead Bailey. Jack Saffin, Jeannie's father, told his other daughter, Kathleen, that he had never heard flames roar like those that were consuming Jeannie (see Chapter 19).

I made my own inquiries into the mechanisms of mitochondria and found that everything Peter stated about the organisms was quite true. The mitochondria perform about forty different processes in part of the cellular respiration process known as the Krebs cycle (the full workings of the cellular respiration process are still not fully understood). During my quest for knowledge in the biochemical field I found that the mitochondria-stuffed body cells also contain lysosomes which are sacs containing large numbers of digestive enzymes. The various enzymes are capable of digesting just about every type of material of which the body is composed. Their normal function is to digest food for use in the cells. They also digest dead cells and dead white blood cells that have done their duty in overcoming invading foreign bodies. Should the lyso-some sac be ruptured then its contents are quite happy to digest their host cell.

These biochemical details are relevant to SHC. The classic pattern of SHC burning results in the torso being reduced to ashes with the odd extremity untouched. Mid-calf of the leg is about the common limit to the downward destruction. The upward destruction mostly results in a blackened skull which sometimes contains a dried and grossly heat-shrunken brain. I had often wondered what it was about the brain that pre-vented it from burning in these circumstances. I surmised that the fuel source was the torso, wherein the hydrogen/oxygen conversion and burning process commenced and spread out-wards. The fuel seemed to run out after it spread out equally in both directions up and down the body for a certain distance which coincided with the head and the general area of the knee. The distance from the abdomen to the top of the head and from the abdomen to the knee are roughly the same.

What I learned of the activity of lysosomes triggered a memory from many years past regarding the effect of oxygen deprivation on the brain. Deprived of oxygen for approxi-mately four minutes, irreversible processes occur within the brain causing irreparable damage. What also happens when the brain cells are deprived of oxygen for four minutes or so (depending on body temperature) is that the lysosomes in the brain cells seemingly commit suicide and break open, thus dis-charging all their enzymes into the cells to digest them. It is for this reason that the process is irreversible, a partially digested brain is never going to function properly again.

There have been cases of people being drowned in ice-cold conditions who have been revived after an hour or more. This is because the body temperature was quickly reduced to such a low level that the whole cell respiration process was slowed down to such an extent that the oxygen present within the cells was sufficient for the extremely lowered metabolic rate.

All chemical actions and reactions are slowed down by a lowering of the temperature of the chemicals involved in the process. By the same token the process is speeded up by raising the temperature. So when a person drowns in near-freezing conditions the oxygen in the brain cells is used up at a greatly reduced rate and the lysosomes are not triggered into committing suicide. Anyone experiencing such a cold-induced state of suspended animation stands a chance of being successfully revived.

It seems that the brain-cell lysosomes are much quicker off the mark to self-destruct than those in other types of body cells. Possibly it has something to do with the fact that the brain uses up nearly as much oxygen as the rest of the body when resting. The brain has a naturally high metabolic rate. Once the oxygen supply is cut off and circulation stops then the cells have to rely on whatever oxygen they already contain to carry on the respiration process. The brain uses up oxygen much faster than other organs thus causing the lysosomes within its cells to self-destruct soonest. Although a person becomes brain-dead through lack of oxygen, other parts of the body die at varying rates and according to the ambient temperature. This phenomenon is ably demonstrated by the mere fact of organ transplants. If the cells of the heart, liver, lungs, kidneys, etc., were to self-destruct at the same rate as those of the brain then there would be no organ transplants. Neither would severed limbs be reattached hours after accidental amputation. Do you see where I am heading?

Once we are dead, for whatever reason, the individual cells of our bodies carry on their normal functions as long as they have the energy to do so. If the mitochondria are responsible for the incineration of living humans then they can only continue to explode in a chain reaction as long as they are alive and contain both hydrogen and oxygen. Once the victim's heart is stopped by the incineration process, the supply of oxygen from the air and hydrogen from food (transported by the blood supply) cease. If the incineration is the direct action of mitochondria then such action can only continue while the host cells and the mitochondria are alive. Thus the brain is merely heat-shrunken by relatively external flames, instead of being incinerated from within itself, because all the mitochondria would have been digested by the self-destructive activity of the lysosomes.

The flesh of the skull and the neck would also be incinerated by the mitochondria exploding in the chain reaction. By the time the reaction reached roughly to the knees the lapse of time and the increased chemical activity (due to the increase in heat from the expanding incineration) would have brought about the demise of the mitochondria in the remaining lower legs. Thus the incineration would come to an abrupt halt.

This scenario fits in perfectly with the fact that trouser legs have been burned so cleanly and then ceased to burn and have shown no sign of being soaked with melted fat as they would have if the fuel source was the melted fat as in cases of 'wick effect'. The failure of the incineration to proceed much beyond the knee area seems to be independent of whether or not the lower legs are bare or clothed, in stockings or trousers. All of these items of clothing are supposed to act as wicks but for some strange reason do not do so below a certain point. This is also regardless of how fat or lean the legs of the victims are. Proponents of the 'wick effect' have explained away the mid-calf boundary as being a result of insufficient fat fuel. The fact is that the mid-calf limit holds whether the legs are fat or thin, clothed or bare. This does not fit in with the fat wick theory. The victims do not wear clothing covering their necks and heads so how can the 'wick effect' destroy the substantial amount of flesh and bone comprising the neck and the flesh of the head? There is no material to char and form a basis for a wick. Hair on the head burns away in seconds and leaves no char for use as a wick. Suitable charred material is an essential ingredient for the operation of the 'wick effect'.

In his book, *Chaos*, James Gleick describes an aspect of the new science of Chaos Theory which he refers to as 'sensitive dependence on initial conditions'. As a barely audible sound can be electronically amplified to an eardrum-bursting level so the merest disturbance of the air by the wings of a butterfly could eventually be amplified by the weather systems of the planet into a destructive storm a month later on the opposite side of the hemisphere. The example is somewhat exaggerated to demonstrate the principle of Chaos Theory.

In the light of chaos theory it now seems feasible that the exploding mitochondria could be triggered by a microwave or cosmic ray striking a defective mitochondrion. (I do not believe that such is the case but it is worthy of consideration.) Our bodies are constantly being bombarded by such rays which mostly pass clean through us without causing us any inconvenience. If the 'butterfly effect' seems a little too far fetched then let us consider a much more probable scenario which I will call the 'rat effect'. In the recent abnormal flooding which occurred in Holland (winter, 1994–5) it was feared for a while that a dyke would give way. Consequently thousands of people and animals were evacuated out of harm's way. It was stated by one expert that all that was required to burst the dyke was for the increasing pressure of the rising waters to force through an existing rat-hole in the dyke unnoticed. The pressure of water rushing through the rat-hole breach could soon widen the hole to such an extent that the volume of water then released would sweep away the dyke. The end result of such a 'rat effect' without the prior evacuation could have been far more calamitous than any butterfly-generated storm systems in New York.

I have, over the years of researching SHC, become more and more convinced that the trigger of SHC is psychic. I use the word 'psychic' not in the sense of psychic mediums or any other paranormal sense. In the absence of being able to examine the phenomenon of SHC by the accepted scientific method one is obliged to utilise the same ploy as psychologists in gathering data. One needs to collect statistical evidence by finding relevant facts that are common to all or most cases of SHC. The American investigator of SHC and all things paranormal, Larry E. Arnold, has also stated that he believes there is a psychic element involved in triggering the phenomenon.

A psychic trigger would explain why only humans are subject to the phenomenon. As far as we know only humans are capable of rational (and not-so-rational) thought and thus capable of creating the state of mind that could trigger off such a catastrophe, albeit unintentionally. Every single one of the victims whose cases are featured in this book were lone and lonely people (with the exception of the cases of static flash – see Chapter 21). That is a total of ten people in all, seven in the UK and three in the USA. Everyone of those individuals (with one notable exception which will be dealt with in the next chapter) lived alone. Several attempts have been made in the past to categorise victims of SHC. Some of the categorisations have been as follows: old people, fat people, alcoholics. Of the victims listed in this book some were old, some fat, some were alcoholics, but none were all three. The only single factor they had in common was loneliness or at least living alone. I cannot prove that they were all lonely. Being alone does not necessarily equate with loneliness. I have been able to ascertain the mental state of five of the victims – they were all lonely people. Regarding the mental state of the other five, I have no evidence one way or the other.

When ten people of varying ages, sex and social standing all succumb to the phenomenon of SHC and all have one thing in common, i.e. 'aloneness' then that is statistically significant. In fact when it comes to statistical significance the score is a perfect 100 per cent.

Practically day by day more evidence is coming to light of the power of the mind over functions of the body that were until recently considered to be entirely autonomous. There must be some sort of mind/body interface whereby our desire to move is converted into physical movement. The actual method by which the non-corporeal mind interfaces with the body is not yet understood. What better level could be found wherein the mind could affect matter than at the sub-atomic level of the mitochondria?

I may well be totally wrong regarding the explosive chain reaction of the mitochondria. In all probability biochemists will swear that such a process is impossible, despite the fact that they do not yet fully understand the workings of human cells. I am happy to accept that the process is seemingly impossible in the light of our present level of knowledge. However, until every single aspect of cellular biochemistry is fully under-stood then who can say what is or is not possible? Who knows what will be possible in the light of future knowledge? Humans, for the most part, learn by analogy. For many cen-turies the men of medicine fumbled along in their arrogant fashion convinced they knew it all – bleeding people to death to release the adverse 'humours' which they 'knew' were caus-ing the illness. They assumed that the heart was the furnace that heated the body, it was also the seat of our emotions. They observed it moving apparently of its own volition and con-cluded it had a life of its own. They had to wait until long after the pump was invented, with which to pump out the bilges of ships, before they finally realised that the heart was a self-regulating pump. That knowledge alone was insufficient to stop them bleeding their unfortunate patients to death for many years to come. Medical men are still meddling with matters in which they have insufficient knowledge, which probably explains why, during a month-long strike by doctors in Israel in 1973, the mortality rate dropped by 40 per cent. The same phenomenon was observed in similar doctors' strikes in Columbia and Los Angeles in 1976.[1]

The mere fact that a phenomenon is totally inexplicable and apparently defies the laws of physics is no reason for denying the existence of that phenomenon. Until we developed the science of mechanics, and developed theories about the levers and pulleys we had already invented, we could not understand how our limbs and joints operated. Until we developed an understanding (even now far from perfect) of electricity and electrical circuits we had no idea how our brains functioned. We still have a lot to learn about the brain and electricity. Now that we have powerful computers we also understand more of the workings of the brain when we view the brain as analogous to the computer. What further inventions will we have to create before we are able to fully understand the functions of the brain?

The living cell explosion theory fits the SHC scenario perfectly well without any stretching or cropping.

Note

1 *Body Power*, Dr Vernon Coleman, Thames & Hudson, 1984.

CHAPTER NINETEEN

The Entrancing of Jeannie Saffin

Jeannie Saffin was still a child when she died aged sixty-one. Brain damaged at birth by a bungled forceps delivery, mentally she remained a child all her life. In September 1982, Jeannie was living at the family home in Edmonton, London, with her father Jack (since deceased) and a brother. Until a year previous she had never been out of the company of her mother upon whom Jeannie doted. Jeannie's mother became senile in the last years of her life. But Jeannie's love for her mother remained undiminished and she stayed constantly in her company until the day her mother died.

In the year following the death of her mother, Jeannie constantly pined for her. Though she lived with her father and a younger brother she was extremely emotionally attached to her mother. She did not understand the concept of death. All she knew was that her beloved mother was no longer with her. Her younger sister Kathleen and Kathleen's husband, Donald Carroll, lived close by and were frequent visitors yet Jeannie was locked in a lonely, desolate world of her own constantly pining for her mother. The witness statements of Donald and Kathleen Carroll are reproduced as follows:

Statement of Donald Edward Carroll aged 61 years

It was in September 1982. I was round at my father-in-law, Jack Saffin's place, doing a bit of decorating for him. My sister-in-law, Jeannie Saffin, was sitting on a chair in the kitchen. She was mentally retarded and always sat with her hands in her lap. Her mental age was about five or six years. She could not read or write but she could talk. When her mother was alive you sometimes had a job to stop her talking. She was sitting on some newspapers which Dad had thrown on the chair. He was sitting at the kitchen table, writing out a bet or something like that. I was decorating in the hallway just outside the kitchen. The kitchen door to the hallway was open.

I had been upstairs for something and was just coming down to go home for some food when I heard Dad shout out, 'Jeannie's burning!' I ran into the kitchen and saw Jeannie standing near the sink with flames coming out of her mouth and her midriff. Dad was at the sink with a cup and he was throwing cups of water over Jeannie. I grabbed a large saucepan full of water and threw it over her and the flames went out. As soon as she stopped burning I ran down the hall to the phone and dialled 999 for an ambulance. Jeannie was trying to pull her clothes off but I stopped her.

The ambulance men were very quick in arriving. When they came in they threw a bucket of some solution over Jeannie. I asked them why they had done that when we had already stopped the flames. They said it was to stop her clothes from sticking to her. Jeannie was still on her feet but she was not saying anything and she did not seem to be in any pain.

When we went to see her in Mount Vernon Burns Hospital she was bandaged from her head to below her knees. There were lots of people in the Mount Vernon with bad burns from oil rig fires and that. They were all lying naked on their beds with just a cover that laced up above them but no bandages. Jeannie was the only one bandaged up like that. The nurses said it took them six to seven hours to change her dressings. I could see into Jeannie's mouth and the inside of her mouth was burnt.

When I went to the inquest there was the coroner and a couple of other people sitting there. They asked me a few questions. They were talking among themselves. I heard one of them mention human combustion and someone laughed. I blew my top and went for them. I said, 'How can you say that when I was there and I saw it. You weren't there.' The coroner said, 'I sympathise with you but I cannot put down spontaneous human combustion because there is no such thing. I will have to put down, misadventure or an open verdict. I think it was put down as an open verdict. [The verdict was in fact misadventure.]

It was definitely SHC. There was no way that she could have caught fire. She was terrified of fire and would not touch matches. It was a hot and very humid day and there was nothing alight in the kitchen except the pilot light on the grill. Even if there was some way she could have caught fire how could she have been burning more than her clothes? I can't remember seeing her clothes on fire except for seeing the flames coming from her midriff, they must have burned her clothes. Her red nylon cardigan was melting but it was not in flames. Her hair did not burn either – she had gingery hair. There was no clothing ash on the floor. Her clothes did not burn much at all. When I went into the kitchen the flames were coming from her mouth like a dragon and they were making a roaring noise. I am deaf. So much so that I am in receipt of a pension from the War Office. I became deaf as a result of my service in Malaya as a National Serviceman. Even so, I heard the sound of the flames coming from Jeannie. At the time I didn't have time to think how strange it was, all I could think of was, 'Oh my God! Let's put the fire out'. But I keep thinking about it and every now and again it comes up and you get a bit upset about it. It's very hard to explain over the phone.

When I heard this idiot on 'Schofield's Quest' phone in about exploding cows it was like he was making fun of the problem. I *thought if I could get on the phone to the show with him I could put the facts to him and let him swallow them. There were so many people on the phone that I got Kath to write in to the show, but nothing come of it — only you.*

It was a hot day and there was no fire or anything else burning in that kitchen that could have set fire to Jeannie. I would think it took less than a minute to put the flames out. My father-in-law burned his hands quite badly trying to put out the flames. Jeannie's burns were really, really horrible.

The flames kept coming from her mouth and her abdomen until I extinguished them with the water. Jeannie never made a move while all this was going on. The smell from the burning was absolutely horrible. I have never been able to get that smell out of my mind. It was like gases mixed. The chair and the papers she was sitting on were untouched by fire. The flames were coming from her middle and her mouth. It was obvious that the flames were coming from inside her. From her knees down she was untouched. The rest of her was terrible.

Jeannie was very slim. She wasn't big, average I would say for a female. She was on the slim side but not skinny. Another thing about her was that she could never sit in the sun — she would come up in big blisters.

I would like you to be able to get some notice taken of this. There was someone in the coroner's court who was laughing at me when I said it was SHC. I've had others laughing since. Not around here in Edmonton — people around here know what happened and they don't think it's funny. It annoys me when I hear these people talk about candles and exploding cows. If they had seen what I saw of Jeannie they would think differently. She took about a week to die.

D.E. Carroll
20 November 1994

Statement of Kathleen Carroll aged 58 years

My sister, Jeannie Saffin, was about sixty-one years old in September 1982, when she died. She was mentally defective from birth and had always lived at home with Mum and Dad. She was devoted to Mum and had never been out of her company until Mum died in 1981. Jeannie missed Mum terribly and constantly fretted over her loss until she too died.

My husband Don was round at Dad's doing a bit of decorating for him. He told me how Jeannie went up in flames while she was sitting on some newspapers on a chair in the kitchen. Dad was in the kitchen as well. She just sat there and didn't move. They had to pull her out of the chair and put the fire out. She was terribly burned. Her head was all swelled up like a football. The strange thing is that the newspapers she was sitting on weren't damaged. It was a very hot and humid day and there was no fire on or anything to set her on fire. Besides she was burning from the inside.

She was taken to Mount Vernon Burns Hospital. She was burned all over. She had about 70 per cent burns. She lived for about a week. It used to take the nurses hours to change her dressings. The doctors and nurses kept coming up to us and asking how she got burned like that. They couldn't understand how she could get burned the way she did. In between going to the hospital we got some books from the library about spontaneous human combustion. The policeman and the firemen both said it was SHC. I saw the pictures in the books where just the lower legs were left beside a pile of ashes. On one occasion, when we visited Jeannie, I lifted the bottom of the sheet and saw that she was bandaged down to below her knees. From there down to her feet was untouched. It was just like the pictures in the SHC books. One of them mentioned that SHC might be a form of 'psychic suicide'.

K.A. Carroll
20 November 1994

When I spoke to Don Carroll on the phone, twelve years after he had witnessed Jeannie's horrific partial incineration, he still had difficulty talking about the event. On a couple of occasions he had to hand over to his wife while he composed himself. As he said, 'I keep thinking about it and every now and again it comes up.'

It is one thing to research these cases from witness statements, pathologists' reports and fire reports, but it is an entirely different matter to interview a person who has actually watched a loved one erupt into flame. Though I have become largely inured to the suffering of people during my police service I was greatly touched by Don Carroll's story. I particularly felt for him as he recounted his experience in the coroner's court. Imagine, a man giving evidence at the inquest on the death of his sister-in-law. He has to recount how he witnessed one of the most horrific, nightmarish events that any person could possibly experience, and he is laughed at. The coroner, while expressing his sympathy, insists he cannot record a verdict of death by spontaneous human combustion *because there is no such thing.* The man has seen the flames roaring from both her abdomen and her mouth, 'like a dragon'. He has heard the unearthly sound of the flames. All the while Jeannie maintains her stance without screaming or crying out in any way.

Don insists that he and Jeannie's father extinguished the flames in just under a minute. I suppose he must be correct in his estimation of the time. Jeannie could hardly have survived such an incineration for much longer, yet survive it she did for eight days. I know from experience that in moments of crisis, to those involved, time seems to slow down. In the short time that it took for the flames to be extinguished, the flesh of her fingers (which were directly in line with the flames apparently bursting from her abdomen) was destroyed. Her fingers were reduced to blackened bones. Don Carroll told me this when we were talking some time after the statement was taken. Having experienced such a horror he then had to endure ridicule and denial of what he had seen and experienced. Is he supposed to think that he and Jack Saffin both hallucinated or imagined what they saw?

In this present-day know-it-all scientific age, a woman can erupt into flame in the full view of witnesses and her body be ravaged with flames while sitting on newspapers in a chair and neither the papers nor the chair suffer any fire damage, and the facts will be denied in a coroner's court because such things cannot be. If Jeannie Saffin did not receive her injuries by SHC then how did she receive them? A uniformed police officer attended the scene from the local station. The police officer, Constable Leigh Marsden, later brought some cuttings relating to SHC and gave them to Kathleen Carroll. Constable Marsden was in no doubt that Jeannie was a victim of SHC.

As an ex-police officer I find it very strange that no investigation into the cause of Jeannie's death was ever carried out by the CID. Are the Metropolitan Police not concerned about middle-aged ladies being burned to death in their homes when there is no logical explanation? Whenever a person dies, other than by natural causes certified by the family doctor, an investigation into the cause of death is made by a police officer designated to investigate on behalf of the coroner. I have carried out such duties on many occasions when I was on uniformed duties. If the coroner's officer is not entirely satisfied that the cause of death was accidental or natural causes then the CID are called in to investigate. As a matter of course the CID usually look in on the incident first to ensure that it is not a case for their talents. The coroner's officer does not decide the result of the case. He presents his findings to the coroner who either issues a death certificate in a straightforward natural death case or holds an inquest.

Jeannie Saffin's death resulted in an inquest. It was opened on 28 September 1982 and then adjourned until 3 December 1982, by the Coroner, Dr John Burton. Dr Burton kindly furnished me with the documents relating to the inquest.

Jeannie's family, specifically Kathleen and Don Carroll, had requested that I should investigate the death of Jeannie because they had never been informed of the actual cause of her death or how she was supposed by the authorities to have burned as she did.

Dr Burton obviously adjourned the original inquest until inquiries could be made as to how Jeannie Saffin came to sustain the burns that eventually killed her. The pathologist had given the cause of death as bronchopneumonia due to burns. The hospital notes of her treatment at Mount Vernon start at 7p.m. the day she burned. This was the time she arrived on transfer from North Middlesex Hospital. The notes commence: 'Approximately 4p.m. today thought to have burned herself? How? Found by ambulancemen in kitchen, wearing nylon clothes, not on fire. Not in smoke-filled room.'

The part about burning herself was pure speculation. The rest of the sentence gives some indication of the bizarre nature of Jeannie Saffin's burning. The question mark and the word 'how' certainly express puzzlement. The ambulancemen may have misreported how she came to be burned but they were trained technicians and perfectly capable of reporting what they actually saw. They reported that she was wearing nylon clothes which were not burned. No wonder nurses and doctors kept asking the Carrolls how Jeannie came by her terrible injuries. Remarking upon the fact of there being no smoke in the room shows even more puzzlement about the source of her burns. As her clothes were unburned they obviously thought that there should have been signs of something having burned in the kitchen to have caused her injuries. A reasonable supposition if we are to rule out SHC. A woman is received into hospital with 30 to 40 per cent full-depth burns to her face, hands and various parts of her body yet her clothes are, for the most part, unburned. Her nylon cardigan is melted not burned. Her hair is unburned. Had there been evidence of furniture burning in the kitchen and smoke damage to the walls and ceiling it would still have been a mystery how she came to be burned *inside unburned clothes*. The report also states that she was not in pain. Is this normal? Remember, neither Jack Angel nor Wilf Gowthorpe felt any pain until some time after their partial incineration.

She was sufficiently conscious to open her eyes when spoken to but only moved in response to painful stimuli e.g. a needle prick. She showed no response to spoken commands. Bearing in mind Jeannie's mental state we cannot read too much into her lack of response to verbal commands given by strangers.

Her injuries were listed as follows: mainly full thickness burns of face (meaning that the skin was completely destroyed exposing the underlying fat). Burns to the neck, shoulders, chest, left arm, abdomen, thighs and left buttock – mixed full thickness and deep dermal with superficial patches on abdomen. Hands – mainly full thickness burns, both surfaces. Total 30 per cent. In a letter to the coroner's officer, a locum registrar in plastic surgery, stated that Jeannie's injuries had resulted from a flame burn. He said that the depth of the burns was so thick that she must have been in contact with the flames for some considerable time. He also stated that she was not unusually fat. Don Carroll stated that she was slim and the pathologist described the body as 'that of an elderly lady, slimly built'. The pathologist also estimated the total body burns as 30 to 40 per cent.

On 20 September 1982, Jeannie was still 'only responding to pain'. The notes also mentioned that her hands were 'both very deeply burned'. Paradoxically Jeannie suffered the worst burns to her face and hands – the two parts of her body not covered by clothing. What sort of external flames could burn all the skin from her face and not burn her hair? Jeannie was certified dead at 8.10a.m. on 23 September 1982 nearly eight days after she erupted into flames.

I mentioned earlier that the only single factor common to

all the victims dealt with in this book was 'aloneness'. At first sight Jeannie Saffin seemed not to fit in this category. After all she lived with her father and brother and was constantly visited by other members of the family. Even though she was never physically alone she may well have been the loneliest person of them all – locked in her child's mind, pining for her beloved mother who had left her. One can be lonely in a crowd as many a single person, having moved to London or some other large city, has found out. Loneliness is a state of mind. Jeannie had, for sixty of her sixty-one years lived constantly in the company of her mother to whom she was absolutely devoted. Mrs Saffin died a year before Jeannie's tragic death. In the last few days of her life she was even more withdrawn and had slept a lot and eaten little. When her brother was told of Jeannie's incineration his immediate, instinctive response was, 'She brought it on herself'. The family are certain that her state of mind somehow triggered her incineration. They are not the first to suggest that SHC is a form of unintentional psychic suicide.

CHAPTER TWENTY

The Investigation –
Past and Present

*'Any fact is better established by two or three
good testimonies, than by a thousand arguments.'*

C.P. SCOTT

In response to the coroner's request for information relating to
the cause of Jeannie's death, Police Constable Leigh Marsden
of Edmonton Police Station went to Jeannie's home on
Saturday 2 October 1982. He examined the kitchen and interviewed both Jack Saffin and Don Carroll. As is usual in police
statements only the observable facts are included. There is no
speculation just bald facts. PC Marsden stated that the wooden
Windsor chair, in which Jeannie had been sitting when she
caught fire, was situated in a corner of the kitchen about two
inches from two adjacent walls forming a corner. He said the
chair was unmarked and showed no evidence of burns. He
also noted that the two walls were unmarked. As the walls
were only two inches from the chair they were also only a
matter of inches from Jeannie's body when she was sitting in
the chair. He noted that the nearest source of a naked flame
was a small pilot light on the overhead grill of a gas cooker
some four to five feet away from the chair. He also noted that
the pilot light was situated under the grill hood and was thus
unable to set anyone alight even if they were in contact with
the cooker. Leigh Marsden also noted that the nearest gas
point and electrical point were both sited next to the cooker

and some four to five feet from the chair. He makes no comment as to how Jeannie may have come to ignite. The fact that it was impossible for her to have caught fire by accident is implicit in his statement.

On Monday 13 February 1995, through the good offices of the Metropolitan Police press office, I spoke with Leigh Marsden. Some twelve or more years after the event Leigh Marsden still remembers the incident. When PC Marsden went to the hospital he was told that a death certificate would be issued as Jeannie had been in their care for a week. (The death certificate was in fact issued by the coroner, J.D.K. Burton. It was issued on 3 December 1982, the date of the second inquest into the death of Jeannie Saffin.) As a matter of course, Leigh was asked to call round and ascertain that the circumstances of her death did not involve any criminal activity.

Leigh Marsden was satisfied that the cause of the death of Jeannie Saffin had to be Spontaneous Human Combustion. On returning to his station he informed the CID that there were no criminal circumstances and expressed his opinion that the cause was indeed SHC.

That was the end of the case as far as his involvement goes. He was not called to give evidence at the inquest into Jeannie Saffin's death. As an afterthought Leigh mentioned that some years later he was interviewed about the incident by a senior fire brigade officer. He does not know who the officer was or how he came to know of the case. That such belated interest should be shown in the case by a senior fire officer is strange when one considers that the fire brigade were not called to the scene at the time.

Don Carroll does not recall any medical expert giving evidence at the inquest. In all probability such evidence was submitted in writing.

If the police were sure that Jeannie was not a victim of SHC then why did they not mount a murder inquiry into Jeannie's death? The police, having been requested by the coroner to investigate the case, would have had to consider three possibilities: accidental death; suicide; or murder. The results of PC Leigh Marsden's investigations by implication ruled out both accidental death and suicide. If the authorities truly believed that SHC is merely a figment of overheated imaginations then the only possible cause of death remaining to be considered is murder. Jeannie's own sister, Kathleen Carroll said to me, 'There was no forensic investigation. No one came near. We could have done her in ourselves for all they knew.'

It is incumbent upon the police to investigate any suspicion of suicide or murder. Let us say, for the sake of argument, that Jeannie had been admitted to hospital with a large gash in her throat. Jack Saffin and Don Carroll reported that while Jeannie was seated in her chair, a large gash suddenly and without visible cause appeared in her throat. Four days later she dies in hospital of her injuries having said nothing. No suitable weapon could be found. In trying to help Jeannie both men became soaked in her blood. Would the actions of the police be the same in this case if Don Carroll and Jack Saffin had claimed that the wound had appeared in Jeannie's throat spontaneously? I think not. So! Why should the police treat the death of Jeannie Saffin from 'unknown causes' any differently? It seems obvious that their story was accepted by the authorities and so no further inquiries were made. In the cases of Henry Thomas and Annie Webb there were at least 'viable sources of ignition' present in the rooms on which to lay the blame – even though there was no proof that they were in fact the cause. It was enough that they were present. No such source could be blamed in Jeannie's case.

On the night of the 'Schofield's Quest' TV broadcast, dealing with SHC, a retired university lecturer phoned in to give the lie to the oft-recurring suggestion that SHC results from methane gas in the stomach. Philip Schofield read out his message to the effect that there is only a tiny amount of gas in the stomach and certainly not enough to sustain flames for more than a second or so. He also said there was far more gas in the stomachs of cows, so, if methane were the cause then we would see exploding cows all over the place. Don Carroll was watching that show and took umbrage over the fact that the subject was being treated with apparent levity, i.e. 'exploding cows'. That prompted him to contact the show. He hoped to tell his story and possibly give people some pause for thought. Both Don Carroll and his wife are determined to get recognition of the fact that Jeannie was killed by SHC. The establishment seem to be more concerned not to frighten the public rather than to find the true answer. Do not scare the public. I think 'the public' are made of sterner stuff. I could not imagine people running into the streets in panic at the prospect of suddenly igniting.

Though I am convinced the phenomenon occurs many times per year just in the United Kingdom, it is still no cause for general panic. There are many worse ways to die with all the pollution-induced cancers presently killing off thousands per month often in an extremely painful manner. All the evidence points to the victims being in a trance when the incineration takes place. Such a death would certainly seem to be both quick and painless, especially if the process were not interrupted.

To go back to Don Carroll's statement in the last chapter, there was also the matter of the smell. He said, 'The smell from the burning was absolutely horrible. I have never been able to get that smell out of my mind. It was like gases mixed.' Likewise in her statement about the incineration of Wilf Gowthorpe's hand, Sandra Stubbins said, 'The smell was terrible. I have never smelled anything like it. It was foul. It did not smell anything like a piece of meat burning, it was really horrible.'

The similarity of the two quotes is notable. Neither person has any knowledge of the other and they are describing incidents separated in time by nine years. I have already described the smell of a burning human body. It is similar to roasting pork and could not, by any stretch of the imagination be said to be foul or awful. Whatever Sandra Stubbins and Don Carroll smelled it made such an impression on both of them that they will never forget it – a smell that neither of them could properly describe having never experienced it before.

Don Carroll and his father-in-law Jack Saffin also both remarked on the roaring noise made by the flames that came from Jeannie's body. Kathleen Carroll told me how her father said on more than one occasion after the tragedy, 'You know Kath, I was in the First World War and I saw some flames but I never heard flames make that noise.' I was convinced that the flames had burst through Jeannie's abdomen and were coming out of her mouth as Don Carroll described them. However, the pathologist's report rules out such behaviour of the flames. I am not prepared to even suggest that the report was not true to fact. I had reasoned that the excessive burns to her hands resulted from her habit of always sitting with her hands in her lap. If the flames did burst through her abdomen then it is reasonable that her hands would have sustained considerable damage as they lay in the path of the flames. You will recall that I made reference to the fact that the right hand of the tramp, Bailey, seems to be missing in the fire brigade photographs. Having received Don Carroll's report of the death of Jeannie, wherein he states that the flames were apparently coming from her abdomen, coupled with the fact that her hands were terribly burned in less than a minute, I thought that the abdominal flames could have destroyed Bailey's hand. That could still be the case as the evidence shows that blue flames were issuing at force from Bailey's abdomen for at least seven minutes. The circumstances of Jeannie's burning cannot be quoted as reinforcing my theory as to the manner of the destruction of Bailey's hand, as her hands were obviously burning of their own accord.

My theory of the atomic flames outlined in the previous

chapter can still account for the burning of Jeannie. She was
sitting beside her father who was completely unaware of anything untoward until he suddenly saw a flash of flame out of
the corner of his eye and turned to see Jeannie on fire. The
burns surgeon noted that she must have been in contact with
an open flame for 'some little time' because the burns were so
deep.

As I have taken pains to explain in some detail previously,
when faced with something that is beyond our experience or
knowledge we tend to interpret what we see in the light of
what we already know. If we are to accept the pathologist's
report as accurate then Don Carroll could not have seen what
he thought he saw. I fully believe that Don Carroll is being
totally honest in his description of Jeannie's burning. He has
described what he saw bearing in mind that 'seeing' embraces
understanding. One of the indisputable facts is that Jeannie's
face was burnt down to the underlying fat. The burning could
not have been external. There was no fuel source to sustain
flames of sufficient temperature for a sufficient length of time
to cause such deep burns from the outside in. Suppose there
had been such a normal fuel source. What could possibly cause
Jeannie to quietly sit and sustain such terrible burns without
crying out? She was mentally retarded and had a mental age of
five or six years, and surely she would behave like a little child
if burned normally. She would be bound to scream out in
agony and thrash about. She would not sit still and quietly
burn from the outside in.

A full-depth burn resulting from burning inside to outside
with the total destruction of the skin would not appear to be
any different to full-depth burns inflicted in the normal manner, i.e. by the external application of fierce flames for some
time. In both cases the end result would be the skin burned off
exposing the underlying fat. There would be nothing to show
that the burning started below the skin rather than finishing
below the skin. The only clue to the fire commencing below

the skin is to be found in the fact that there was no external source of flames.

How could her father, sitting practically beside her, not notice these necessarily prolonged flames from an unknown mysterious source? The facts point to her being entranced like Jack Angel and Wilf Gowthorpe. For the most part she burned in several different places below the surface as did Jack Angel. He too had burns on various parts of his body apart from the major burns to his hand and arm. Unlike Angel and Gowthorpe, Jeannie's burning suddenly burst into flames having consumed the various layers of her skin. She had been sitting beside and behind her father, probably in a trance, while the burning was confined beneath her skin. Once the flames erupted her father was immediately aware of them both by sight and by sound. Both he and Don Carroll extinguished the flames with water after he dragged Jeannie out of her chair to the sink, burning his hands in the process.

Human fat is laden with water. The atomic flame process would produce great heat such that the water in the fat would be instantly converted into steam. Such a process would, in all probability, make quite a hissing or roaring noise such as that made by the water from wet chips falling into overheated cooking oil where it immediately explodes noisily into steam. When Don saw Jeannie breathing out flames like a dragon this could be accounted for by her breathing the flames in and out from her face. She might have been hyperventilating and exacerbating the effect somewhat like a circus fire eater.

The flames which appeared to be coming from her abdomen were more than likely coming from her hands which were also badly burned, possibly more so than her face. As she always sat with her hands in her lap it is quite possible that her hands were still in that position when her father pulled her out of the chair. Flames could not have been coming from Jeannie's abdomen because she only suffered 'superficial patches on abdomen'. The slight burns to her

abdomen could have resulted from the close proximity of her
two burning hands.

No matter how vehemently sceptics insist that SHC cannot
and therefore does not exist there is no way that Jeannie's
sparse clothing (even if ignited by any scientifically acceptable
means) could burn with such a roaring sound. What is there in
a cotton wrap-round apron and a nylon cardigan that could
support such roaring flames if they had burned? The evidence
of Don Carroll and the ambulancemen, who drenched
Jeannie's clothes with a liquid to prevent them sticking to her
body and transported her to hospital, is that, with the exception of her melted cardigan, her clothes did not burn to any
noticeable extent.

No evidence was called as to the extent of the burning of
her clothing at the inquest. The evidence of Don Carroll and
Police Constable Marsden made it quite clear Jeannie's burns
did not result from the flames of burning furniture or any
other materials in the kitchen. If SHC is not thought to be the
cause then the only possible source of the fire that caused such
horrific burns must have been her burning clothing, regardless
of the fact that there is no evidence to show that her clothing
did catch fire. Production of the clothes and the testimony of
the ambulancemen would have opened some extremely pertinent questions, questions which could only have been
answered by considering the SHC hypothesis.

I asked the police and the coroner to explain their opinions
on Jeannie Saffin's case. The coroner, Dr J.D.K. Burton
returned a verdict of death by misadventure. The legal definition of misadventure as defined in *Jowitt's Dictionary of English
Law*, 1977, is 'Excusable homicide, accidental killing resulting
from a lawful act. Examples: 1. a person is chopping wood
with an axe when the head flies off and strikes another person
causing their death. 2. a person is shooting a rifle at a mark and
undesignedly kills a bystander.' *The Oxford English Dictionary*
(second edition, vol. IX) defines misadventure thus: 'Homicide

committed accidentally by a person in doing a lawful act, without any intention of hurt.' Who is this person who was carrying out a lawful act and accidentally killed Jeannie Saffin?

When Dr Burton sent me copies of the inquest papers he also wrote a letter in which he informed me that 'human combustion' (*not* spontaneous human combustion) is common. He then gave a short explanation of the 'wick effect' wherein the clothes act as a wick. This explanation was rather pointless as the evidence showed that her clothes were hardly burned at all. He also mentioned that Eskimos use seal blubber (which is virtually water-free, unlike human fat) and wicks as lamps and also that he did not know what ignites marsh gas in the will o' the wisp. He further stated that though human flatus can be ignited he had never heard of it happening spontaneously. He concluded his letter stating that there was no suggestion of foul play, and he never comments upon the supernatural. I would have thought that the absence of any proof that Jeannie's death was accidental would of itself be *prima facie* proof that foul play was involved. It had to be one or the other. I wrote again to Dr Burton for clarification on the verdict of misadventure. The letter is reproduced in its entirety as follows:

Dear Dr Burton
Thank you for sending me the file on the death of Jean Saffin. Her family are still adamant that she was the victim of spontaneous human combustion. I have read and reread the inquest papers and all that I read supports the fact that Miss Saffin did not die as a result of her clothing catching fire by whatever means. In fact the evidence shows that her clothes sustained only minimal fire damage (statements by ambulancemen to hospital staff). The worst fire injuries were to her face and hands which were not clothed. It seems likely that Don Carroll is mistaken in his belief that flames were issuing from the

mouth and abdomen of the deceased. In all probability the flames were coming from her face and hands (which she normally held clasped in her lap) thus giving him an erroneous impression.

I have spoken to Police Constable Leigh Marsden who made the inquiries into the cause of her combustion. As he said in his statement he could find no possible source of ignition. He also said to me that he reported back to the CID that, in his opinion, the cause was indeed spontaneous human combustion.

Your verdict of misadventure implied an accident with some degree of negligence yet there is nothing in the inquest papers relating to an accident nor to any person having been careless in causing such accident. What sort of accident can cause a person to sit quietly, within a few feet of another person, while their hands and face burn down to the subcutaneous fat? That she was conscious is evidenced by the fact that when her father pulled her out of the chair and over to the sink, in order to douse the flames, she remained standing. Though her mental age was that of a five year old, she was capable of lucid speech and she certainly felt pain and would react to such pain as any five-year-old child. In view of the concluding paragraph of your letter I repeat that I do not subscribe to any belief in the supernatural. I am certain that SHC is a natural phenomenon requiring serious investigation.

The family of Jeannie Saffin are still unaware of the means by which she burned. If SHC is to be ruled out, would you kindly let me know on what evidence the verdict of misadventure was based?

I have also written to the Metropolitan Police to ascertain why no further inquiries were made when the source of ignition could not be found.

Yours faithfully, etc.

Dr Burton replied to the effect that the misadventure verdict means that death is not due to homicide. He said that such a verdict would be used were a person struck by lightning. He also said he had no intention of corresponding with me any further.

It seems that we are not going to be pen-pals after all. I also wrote to Commander David Kendrick, in charge of 3 Area, Metropolitan Police. I will not reproduce the whole letter as it mostly consists of the facts of Jeannie Saffin's incineration and subsequent death with which I have already dealt in detail. I stated that no source of ignition was found and so the prime cause of death had not been ascertained. I pointed out that the coroner had himself written in his inquest report that Jeannie's clothes had suddenly caught fire in some unknown fashion, and that further inquiries had not revealed a possible source of ignition. I concluded my rather long letter with the following three paragraphs:

> *I have this day written to Dr Burton inquiring as to what evidence he based his verdict of misadventure on. An open verdict seems more in keeping with the evidence or lack of it.*
>
> *I am curious as to why more diligent police inquiries were not made when no source of ignition could be found by the investigating officer. Either the lady was a victim of SHC or there is a more sinister explanation – she certainly did not set herself alight by any normal means. Her own sister (Kathleen Carroll) told me that there was no forensic examination made of the scene. She said that no one came to investigate apart from PC Marsden. She actually said to me, 'For all they know we could have done her in ourselves.'*
>
> *I wonder whether, at this late stage, any light can be thrown on the reason for the lack of any determined investigation into the primary cause of the death of Jean Lucille Saffin. I enclose a document, signed by Kathleen Carroll, authorising me to make inquiries on her behalf into the cause of the death of her sister.*

My letter was passed on to G.F. Searle, Divisional Commander, Edmonton Division, who replied to the effect that the facts were properly presented to Dr Burton over twelve years ago and that the facts and expert opinions given at the inquest were included in the inquest papers, of which I have a copy. So, there is no more to know. Without being able to ascertain the manner in which Jeannie was set on fire the police and coroner are certain that homicide was not involved.

The reader will recall that no experts ever visited the premises to investigate the cause of Jeannie's incineration. Police Constable Marsden, though hardly qualifying as an expert, carried out a thorough investigation of the premises. He concluded that there was no way that Jeannie Saffin could have caught fire in any mundane manner. I have no argument with his findings. The only expert opinions given to the coroner were those of the surgeon and pathologist at the hospital in which Jeannie died. Those opinions related purely and simply to the manner of her death as an aftermath of her horrendous burns and were submitted to the coroner in writing. Not one 'expert' was able to explain how she came by the burns in the first place. How she died, as the result of burns, was never in question. What was and still is in question is how she came to sustain those terrible burns without crying out and why she felt no pain?

I have attempted to get an admission to the possible existence of SHC by both the coroner and the police in the case of Jeannie Saffin. My attempt was in vain. The coroner accepted that she burned in the manner of the 'wick effect', though the evidence shows that her clothes did not burn anywhere near enough to initiate this. He also accepted that she burned in such a fashion when no possible source of ignition could be found, even though he adjourned the inquest so that a search could be made for the source of ignition.

The police state that 'the facts were properly presented' to the coroner. Would the police or the coroner have accepted that nothing untoward had occurred in the death of Jeannie Saffin if she had died in just as mysterious circumstances from poisoning, gunshot, knifewound or fractured skull, etc?

CHAPTER TWENTY-ONE

Static Flash Fires

Statement of Debbie Clark

It was about nine years ago, in 1985. I had been working for my mother all day. She had her own catering company. I had been working from the morning through to late evening. I had been working in the kitchen and serving food and running a buffet. When it actually happened it was outside and it was dark. I went out to get my handbag from my father's car and as I walked back down the drive I saw a flash. I thought it was someone with a torch. It happened again so I went back up the drive to see where it was coming from. I saw a man taking a dog for a walk so I assumed it was him. My father came out to see what was taking me so long. I told him that I kept seeing these flashes and I thought it was the man down the road. He walked back down the drive with me and he said it was me that was actually lighting up. I was lighting up the driveway every couple of steps.

As we got into the garden I thought it was funny at that point. I was walking around in circles saying 'Look at this Mum, look!' She started screaming and my brother came to the door and started screaming and shouting 'Have you never heard of spontaneous combustion?' They dragged me indoors and Mum said, 'Strip off'. So I started stripping off in the living room. She screamed again, 'That 's a nylon carpet, you don't do it there.'

She made me stand in the bath and get undressed. It never happened since. It was just the one occurrence. I think it was summer but I don't think it was particularly hot. I would have remembered if it was. I was not wearing any nylon clothing. I used to suffer a lot with static electricity so I tended not to wear anything nylon. I used to crackle with static when taking off my clothes and if I touched any metal thing it used to hurt me. I used to have a lot of trouble with electrical things. They would break down or blow up.

Statement of Dianne Clark (Debbie's mother)

It must have been in September, because it was dark. The first I knew about it we'd just finished doing the catering do. She [Debbie] was just coming down the driveway just flashing. The whole driveway was actually lit up with blue flashes. It was just as if someone had switched on a blue light. The whole yard was literally lit up with it. It just flashed and then went off. And as she walked along it kept flashing. It literally frightened the life out of me . I didn't know what to do. She was wearing a poly-cotton waitresses outfit. I thought it's got to be static electric so I thought, you know, get her undressed. I screamed at her to get her shoes off and it still kept going so I hassled her through and got her into the bath. I thought that the bath is wired to earth. It was a blue light you know what they call electric blue. She thought it was fun, she was laughing.

Statement of Susan Motteshead

It was in 1980 or 1979 and it was in the winter. I was then living in Cheshire. I was in the kitchen and it was very warm,

*that is the house was warm. We have central heating. I was in
the dining area of the kitchen/diner and there were no naked
flames of any sort in the kitchen. I had just washed and dried
my hair. I used to have a lot of static electricity when I was
younger. I used to get shocks from touching fridges and things
like that. I had just lost five and a half stones and I had bought
these pyjamas — they were terry towelling. They were the flame
resistant ones. I was stood in the kitchen and my daughter just
screamed out that my back was on fire. As I looked down it just
sort of 'whooshed' all over me. It was like yellow and blue
flames all over me. I was not burned at all. Not even my hair
was burned. I took off my pyjamas and my husband phoned the
fire brigade. I had a house full in the end, police as well. The fire
investigator took my pyjamas outside and tried to light them
with his lighter. He tried all ways to get them alight and he
couldn't. You could see that they were singed from top to bottom
and you could actually smell that they had been on fire. So they
were absolutely flabbergasted with it all and asked if they could
take the pyjamas away for tests. The pyjamas were newish.
They had been washed several times. I never got my pyjamas
back nor did I hear the result of the tests.*

Statement of Joanne Motteshead (Susan's daughter)

*It was a morning on a weekend in 1980. I was ten at the time.
My mum was in the kitchen. I was sat on a chair at the dining
table. I could see her because it was open-plan. She was facing
away from me. I can't really remember what she was doing. I just
saw these blue and orange flames and it wasn't burning her, it
was travelling up from the outside. She had pyjamas on. It was
so quick. It was around the bottom of the legs and it just
'whooshed' up. It did not make a 'whooshing' sound. When I
say 'whooshed' it's just how I described it going up. I screamed,
'Mum! You're on fire!' I just saw those flames going up. It did
frighten me. It frightened me for a long time afterwards. Every*

time I went to bed I thought I was going to set myself on fire.
She whipped them [pyjamas] off quick and then shouted for my
dad. My dad came running downstairs and we stood crying I
think – I was anyway. The fire brigade came out and investi-
gated it. They tried to set the pyjamas on fire. They wouldn't
burn. They weren't actually burned but you could smell it.

After reading the preceding four statements it must be obvious to anyone that body static can build up to quite
dangerous levels. Both the women involved had been more
than a little troubled with static electricity in their youth. I
am convinced that both ladies owe their present well-being
to the fact that neither of them was wearing nylon or acrylic
clothing – especially underclothes. In Susan Motteshead's case
she was extremely lucky to have been wearing only fire-
retardant terry towelling pyjamas. If the investigating firemen
could not set light to the pyjamas, even though they were
singed all over, then I am certain that had they been made of
a flammable cotton or nylon material then Susan's experience
might well have been her last. Such, was possibly the fate of
seventeen-year-old Jacqueline Fitzsimon. This case was excel-
lently documented by Jenny Randles and Peter Hough in
their book *Death by Supernatural Causes?* Their account of the
inquest into the girl's death is particularly valid as they were
both in attendance throughout the inquest. *Their account is*
thus first-hand.

In the winter of 1985, in Widnes, Cheshire, Jacqueline
Fitzsimon was attending a Youth Training Scheme cookery
course at Halton College of Further Education. She was walking down some stairs, arm-in-arm with two friends, Wendy
Hughes and Paula McGeever, when her back was suddenly
engulfed in flames. Two men, Neil Foy and Neil Gargan, both
mature students, together with three members of staff, quickly
smothered the flames. Jacqueline only complained that she had
burned her finger while endeavouring to remove her flaming

catering jacket with one hand while trying to protect her lacquered hair from the flames with the other. She seemed totally unaware of the fact that her acrylic jumper beneath the catering jacket had melted onto her skin. She was found to have 13 per cent superficial burns to her back from the melted acrylic and was not considered to be very ill. She was quite cheerful when interviewed by police officers two days later. However, she died two weeks later of 'shock-lung' involving inflammation of the bronchial tubes and septicaemia.

Just before being engulfed in flames, Jacqueline and her friends were passed on the stairs by two other girls, Rachel Heckle and Karena Leazer. Karena saw a strange glowing light over Jacqueline's right shoulder. The light appeared in mid-air and then apparently fell down her back. The two male mature students heard Jacqueline cry out and turned around to see her engulfed in flames. This report is similar to the statement of Joanne Motteshead when she saw the same type of flames engulf her mother's pyjamas.

One of the two mature students, John Foy, aged thirty-four, said, 'She looked like a stuntman on TV'. Both men had passed Jacqueline on the stairs only a matter of seconds before yet neither had noticed any sign of smoke or flame. How could a catering jacket go from showing no sign of fire to being completely engulfed in flames in a matter of seconds? Evidence of tests carried out on the same type of catering jackets showed that they will not burst into flames from smouldering. Not one of the witnesses had seen any form of smouldering or burning of the catering jacket before it burst into flames.

Robert Carson, the cookery lecturer, swore that all the gas rings had been turned off an hour before the tragedy. He also told the coroner, 'In any case, in twenty years I have never seen a catering jacket on fire.' Further evidence was given by a Home Office chemist, Philip Jones, to the effect that though he could ignite a catering jacket with a naked flame and the jacket would burn away in twenty-five seconds, he had been unable to make a smouldering catering jacket burst into flames even though he had exposed it to a strong air current. The coroner, Gordon Glasgow, asked Philip Jones about the possibility of a lighted cigarette being the cause of the ignition (the carelessly dropped cigarette is forever being pressed into service to explain away mysterious fires). Jones stated that it was extremely difficult to start such a fire with a cigarette despite popular belief to the contrary. He stated that he had managed to start the jacket smouldering by holding it close to the gas ring on one of the cookers in the classroom. He had also managed to keep the smouldering going by increasing the flow of air. He assumed that there would have been an increased air flow in the updraught of the stairwell on which Jacqueline collapsed.

Jones was asked by one of the solicitors present how close he had to place the jacket to the flame before he was able to initiate the smouldering process. The answer was a few millimetres. He was further asked how many times did the jacket burst into flames during the tests. The answer was none. Obviously the catering jacket performed as catering jackets are supposed to perform. They are made to be worn in situations of fire hazard and as such are not highly flammable. Jones' smouldering hypothesis was shown to be totally untenable. In the first instance, anyone leaning against the stove with the burner alight would be at least eight inches from the flame. The jacket would only smoulder when held within a few millimetres of the flames. Secondly the lecturer, Robert Carson, stated in his evidence that the gas rings had been turned off an hour before the tragedy.

As I demonstrated earlier, it is extremely difficult to get a smouldering piece of cloth to burst into flame. I am not so dogmatic as to claim it is impossible to do so. I could not do it at all but I would not rule out the possibility altogether of a smouldering piece of cloth bursting into flames. However, it is perfectly plain that a smouldering cloth bursting into flame is an exception rather than the rule. The Shirley Institute in Manchester (a textile research organisation), at the request of the Cheshire Fire Brigade, studied the case and prepared a thirty-page report describing how impossible it was for Jacqueline's catering jacket to have smouldered for five minutes before bursting into flame. The fire experts who compiled the report were never called by the coroner to give oral evidence and he did not, at any stage of the inquest, *make reference to their report*. Peter Hough later ascertained that though the Cheshire Fire Brigade submitted the report to the coroner it was returned to them as the coroner decided not to make use of it. No reason was given. For some unspecified reason the coroner preferred the view of the Home Office forensic expert, Philip Jones, than the investigation and statement of facts of the Shirley Institute.

The coroner's officer PC Jenion, who had accompanied Philip Jones to the college when he made his tests, was called to give evidence. He stated that he found no evidence of Spontaneous Human Combustion. As Randles and Hough remarked, he did not explain 'what that evidence might be, or how he would go about finding it.'

The jury returned a verdict of misadventure after the coroner summed up in favour of the view of the Home Office expert, Philip Jones. They concluded that Jacqueline had caught her jacket on fire, in a smouldering fashion, after leaning over a burner. So, a jacket which could only be made to smoulder by the Home Office chemist when he held it within a few millimetres of a naked flame, had somehow started to smoulder when a minimum distance of eight inches from a gas ring that was *not* alight. This miraculously smouldering jacket continued to smoulder for about five minutes unnoticed by any number of witnesses and then burst into flames despite the inability of the Home Office chemist to get a number of similarly smouldering catering jackets to burst into flame.

In view of Robert Carson's insistence that the rings had been turned off for an hour before the incident it is difficult to see how the jury could arrive at such a conclusion. In effect their conclusions were based on the assumptions of the Home Office chemist whose own tests proved the falsity of his assumptions.

It was assumed that there was an increased air flow on the stairway. It was also assumed that this increased air flow had fanned the smouldering catering jacket into flame. These assumptions were made despite the statement of the Home Office chemist that he had not caused a smouldering jacket to burst into flame by increasing the air flow. All this adds up to a great deal of assumption and in fact all the actual evidence of witnesses militated against such assumptions.

I must point out that Jenny Randles and Peter Hough, though styled as 'investigators of the paranormal', did not at any time claim that the case of Jacqueline Fitzsimon was an example of SHC. Before the inquest the media in general had been hyping the case as SHC. After the verdict they were equally unanimous in declaring that the case had been proven not to be SHC. It seems that none of the press were aware of the unanswered questions arising from the verdict, in the light of the sworn testimony.

This case is quite possibly one of Spontaneous Human Combustion. Though the victim's body did not combust it is likely that extreme body static caused the spontaneous combustion of her clothing. I prefer to call such happenings static flash fires. Such a name is far more descriptive and differentiates between them and the even more bizarre cases of actual body combustion. Had Susan Motteshead been wearing flammable cotton pyjamas over nylon or acrylic undergarments she too could have suffered the same fate.

I would not expect any coroner or jury to bring in a verdict of, 'death due to Spontaneous Human Combustion'. That would be unacceptable in the light of the current scientific attitude. All I ask is that the verdict accords with the evidence. If SHC is to be rejected then, rather than accept proven impossible causes of ignition, why not declare an open verdict, thereby admitting that the cause is unknown? All the evidence given at the inquest proves that the cause of ignition is indeed unknown. Let common sense prevail. The coroner in the Soudaine case, Brian Smith, found no problem in arriving at an open verdict while admitting that there was still much to be explained. What is wrong in admitting on occasion that we do not know the answer?

CHAPTER TWENTY-TWO

Preternatural Combustion in Oregon, USA

'The only lesson history has taught us is that man has not yet learned anything from history.'

ANON.

'Once is happenstance, twice is circumstance, three times is enemy action.'

ANON.

On Saturday 3 December 1994, several weeks after the 'Schofield's Quest' appeal for information relating to SHC, I received by post a four-page fax sent to Philip Schofield by Dr Dougal D. Drysdale, Reader in Fire Safety Engineering at the Department of Civil Engineering and Building Sciences, Edinburgh University. The fax was forwarded to me by Heidi Hannell.

Dr Drysdale had declined Heidi's invitation to appear on the show with me to argue the case for the 'wick effect'. In his covering letter, Dr Drysdale expressed his hope that the De Haan article (which he enclosed) would lay the myth of Spontaneous Human Combustion for all time. He also said that John De Haan is one of the foremost fire investigators in the USA.

Dr Drysdale said he had heard that I was intending to write a book based on information obtained from viewers of

'Schofield's Quest'. He stated that such information is hearsay and would have no scientific credibility. He continued by explaining that the SHC myth had arisen because the term spontaneous was added solely '. . . because in many (if not most) cases the source of ignition has not been identified'. He then finished by saying that the De Haan case is contrary to one of the underlying tenets of the myth that SHC only occurs in poorly ventilated rooms and that he hoped the information would be passed to me and I would be encouraged to, '. . . consider fully the implications of this case'.

Though Dougal Drysdale states that one of the myths of SHC is that it only occurs in poorly ventilated rooms I have never come across any references to poorly ventilated rooms. I have, however, on numerous occasions drawn attention to the coincidental and undeniable fact that Thomas and Webb were incinerated in virtually hermetically sealed rooms, but I have never claimed that poor ventilation, hence a lack of oxygen, was a *necessary requirement* in the process of SHC. I reiterate, yet again, the fact that because those two cases occurred in such poorly ventilated rooms the initially burning furniture ceased to burn due to the lack of oxygen. This allowed the process of SHC (which provides its own oxygen as well as hydrogen) to continue to completion unnoticed – i.e. torsos completely reduced to ashes. The process of SHC progresses quite happily in a well-ventilated room, the only problem then is that the furnishings continue to burn and the conflagration soon draws the attention of the fire brigade who promptly extinguish both the fire and the burning body before it can be reduced to ashes. Lack of oxygen is *not* an underlying tenet of SHC.

The last line of Drysdale's letter, asks Philip Schofield to encourage me to fully consider the implications of the DeHaan case. I must remain adamant that John DeHaan's article does nothing to explain SHC. It is in fact a classic example of 'preternatural combustion', as described by Professor Gee and Dr Gavin Thurston, and Dupuytren before them.

Early one morning in the month of February 1991, in the woods near Medford, Oregon, USA, two walkers came across the still burning body of a female adult face down in the fallen leaves of the woods. They raised the alarm and a local deputy sheriff was soon on the scene. The woman was obviously well beyond medical assistance so the deputy took various photographs of the burning body before extinguishing the flames. (Unfortunately the photographs are not available and were not included in the faxed copy.)

The victim had been stabbed several times in the upper regions of the chest and back. Both arms were away from the torso. Between mid-chest and the knees the body had been mostly destroyed. It seems that John DeHaan did not attend the scene himself as he refers to the crime scene personnel reporting that the bones of the pelvis and spine were not recoverable as they had been largely reduced to a grey powder. As I have stated elsewhere in this book, bones reduced to a grey powder indicate that the heat source was relatively low in temperature.

The victim was described as well-nourished – a common euphemism employed by pathologists for people who are considerably overweight. The victim's body thus had a high fat-to-muscle ratio which would make her a suitable candidate for preternatural combustion ('wick effect') providing the necessary criteria were present – they were, in abundance.

She was murdered, therefore she fulfilled the first requirement of being dead. The killer soaked her clothes and body with nearly a pint of barbecue starter fluid and set her on fire. And so the second requirement is fulfilled – that there is a source of ignition and a sustained burning at a suitably high temperature to render the water content out of sufficient fat so that the ash of the burned clothing is saturated with enough water-free fat to start the operation of the self-sustaining 'wick effect'.

The body was out in the open woods with an unrestricted

air supply. So the third condition is also filled in that there was an adequate supply of oxygen. I am certain that the surrounding trees prevented any forceful winds or even stiff breezes from extinguishing the observed low-level flames. I have a caravan which I keep on a site in the Forest of Dean. Often, when the wind is blowing strong on the open field site, my wife and I go for a walk in the forest. As soon as we enter the forest the wind magically drops away as though a door were suddenly closed. Though we can hear the wind in the treetops and see them swaying, at the floor of the forest hardly a breeze disturbs the leaves. A forest or wood wherein the trees are busily absorbing carbon dioxide and releasing oxygen, as a waste product, should provide ideal oxygenation for the support of the 'wick effect' unlike the oxygen-depleted sealed rooms of Thomas and Webb.

The victim's killer has been arrested, tried and sent to prison, having pleaded guilty. The lapsed time from when the killer admitted that he set the body on fire to the time it was extinguished covered a period of twelve to thirteen hours. DeHaan notes that there are many features of this case which can be found in 'so-called' cases of SHC. He is perfectly correct – there are many similarities. There are many similarities between a duck and a chicken. Such similarities do not mean that ducks must be chickens or vice versa. If the 'wick effect' is to encompass SHC then it must account for all the criteria of SHC – it does not.

As a scientist, DeHaan is aware of the dangers of similarity. For example, the active ingredient in a certain cough suppressant is dextromethorphan which is an analogue of codeine. It is harmless unless taken in massive doses. Levomethorphan is a narcotic five times stronger than morphine and deadly. They are similar, in fact they are so similar that the difference cannot be detected except by the use of a polarimeter. When tested in a polarimeter dextromethorphan bends light to the right and levomethorphan bends it to the left. Hence the prefixes of dextro- and levo-. D-sucrose is table sugar and of (dubious) nutritional benefit. L-sucrose though structurally the same has no nutritional benefit. Once again they bend light in different directions. Such can be the dangers in accepting similarities as evidence that things are the same. To be the same they must match in all respects even down to which way they bend light. Mistaking things that are superficially similar can lead to all kinds of catastrophe including death.

The account of the Oregon incineration details how the surfaces of the lower legs and the back of the neck showed signs of surface burning and scorching. These minor burns were thought to have occurred when the clothing on those parts of the body burned away. Such burns are *not* a feature of SHC. When, as in DeHaan's case, clothing burns away leaving minor burns that is indicative of the clothing burning independently of the body. In the cases of Thomas, Webb and Ashton, the bodies were reduced to ashes to a far greater degree yet none of the clothing on their unburned limbs was burned. Both the fire brigade officer, Roger Penney, and I remarked on how the trouser legs remaining on the unburned portions of the lower limbs of Ashton and Thomas were untouched, except for a thin burn line where the legs ceased to burn.

Why should the clothing of Thomas, Webb and Ashton only burn when in contact with the flames which consumed their bodies? Why did the burning of the clothes not proceed beyond the burned areas of the bodies? Such would be the normal mode of burning clothing, as clearly demonstrated in the Oregon case. Whenever a person's clothes catch fire they flare up extremely quickly. That is how people suffer such horrific burns when their clothes do catch fire. If clothing always burned at a slow rate then seldom would anyone die from burns resulting from the burning of their clothes. They would have plenty of time to remove their clothes before receiving fatal burns.

I cannot answer for the case of Ashton as I do not know how well the room was ventilated in which he was inciner-ated. However, I do know that Thomas and Webb burned to ashes in rooms which were starved of oxygen. Furnishings which had started to burn in those rooms ceased to burn once the oxygen level dropped too low. Such conditions of insufficient oxygen would explain why the victim's clothes only burned when in contact with the burning portions of the bodies.

In a 'normal' incineration of a corpse the clothes burn in the normal fashion i.e. a great deal faster than the water-laden corpse. If the corpse contains sufficient fat and the initial burning is prolonged by some artificial means, such as the application of a quantity of barbecue fluid, then the excessive water content of human fat is driven off and the clarified fat is then wicked up into the now charred remains of the vic-tim's clothing. Under these conditions, in the presence of adequate oxygen, the 'wick effect' takes over, the fat burns which continues the incineration far beyond the extent to which a body could normally be burned by the incineration of the clothes alone.

There is another possible, and perhaps more probable, rea-son for the trousers of Thomas and Ashton and the stockings of Annie Webb *not* burning. The trousers of Thomas were woven of a terylene mixture as far as I recall. I do not know what material Ashton's trousers were made of or Annie Webb's stockings. It is quite possible that they were made from man-made fibres. My own modest experiments demon-strated that man-made fibres do not readily burn unaided in the manner of cotton. Such clothing would burn as the flames of the burning body advanced and would cease to burn once the body stopped burning. Such a burning pattern rules out the 'wick effect' wherein the clothes must burn unaided with sufficient heat to clarify the fat. The resultant charred material must be suitably porous to act as a wick.

Man-made material melts into a solid plastic char entirely unsuitable for wicking up liquid fat by the capillary process. It is no doubt more than a coincidence that whenever the 'wick effect' is demonstrated the material used to wrap the fat is always cotton which just happens to make the best wick.

DeHaan states that the soft tissues of the right arm, torso and upper legs were 'consumed' along with the bones. I do not know what he means by 'consumed'. I would have thought it to have meant destroyed, reduced to powder. If this is the case then why did he specifically state that the bones of the pelvis and spine were largely reduced to a grey powder and could not be recovered? I suspect that the bones of the right arm and upper legs still maintained their integrity despite being severely burned. But the article is not more explicit.

DeHaan also states that the victim's burning clothing had melted sufficient body fat so that the clarified fat was able to burn when absorbed by the clothing thus simulating the burning of a candle. He does not give proper weight to the fact that nearly a pint of barbecue fuel was poured onto the clothing of the victim. It was the barbecue starter fluid that provided and sustained the initial intense heat required to render down the fat. DeHaan acknowledges in his article that human fat has a high water content. A human body would need to be clothed in a great deal of highly flammable clothing to sustain the necessary heat output for long enough to drive off the water content and render the fat both wickable and flammable.

DeHaan then uses some mathematical computations called the Heskestad relationship to calculate the heat output from the burning corpse. The calculations involve the height of the flames (as ascertained from the photographs taken by the deputy sheriff) and the diameter of the area of fire. He calculated a heat output of 25 to 30kW. He considers this to be a low heat output and if it occurred in a closed room would not generate enough radiant heat to ignite nearby combustible articles. Neither would such a low heat output produce a hot gas layer of any significance.

You will remember in Chapter 17 how Stan Ames demonstrated the manner in which the plastic TV set in Ashton's room could have been melted out of shape by the super-hot gases that rise to the ceiling and then descend. I commented on the fact that such a maelstrom of super-hot gases would have totally destroyed the room and the TV in a few seconds whereas nothing else in the room was touched by fire. DeHaan's comments prove that Ames' theory is totally out of order. He states that the heat output from a burning corpse is insufficient to produce the hot gases or the radiant heat necessary to melt plastic cabinets or TV control knobs several yards away. I have no cause to doubt DeHaan's calculations. In fact I readily concede that he is correct in his conclusions as to the heat output of a burning corpse. I also concede that bones can be reduced to ash at that low heat even though, for some unknown reason, they cannot be so reduced in laboratory tests. DeHaan admits that laboratory tests over prolonged periods at temperatures of 500°C have only succeeded in bringing about a partial conversion of bones to powdery calcium oxide. Some factor seems to have been missing from the laboratory tests.

Strangely enough, DeHaan insists that this ('wick effect') burning process is capable of reducing bodies to ashes in poorly ventilated rooms. He implies, however, that when the ventilation is reduced the heat output is also reduced. I have no argument with this, it is totally in accord with both common sense and the normal physics of combustion. I feel that DeHaan has cornered himself. He claims that the burning of a body by the 'wick effect' with adequate ventilation (he describes the open-air as unlimited ventilation) does not produce the necessary heat to melt distant plastic objects. He further implies that such occurrences in poorly ventilated rooms produce even less heat. It is a consistent factor in cases of SHC that the heat output is terrific and melts plastic objects at considerable distances from the burning body. DeHaan has ruled out the possibility of such occurrences. Am I to believe that I have not seen the molten control knobs on the TV set in Thomas's room or that the TV set in Ashton's room did not melt out of shape? DeHaan tells us that there is no such phenomenon as SHC and that the 'wick effect' explains all. Yet the 'wick effect' cannot account for the extreme amount of heat released in the circumstances which I and others perversely insist is SHC. He cannot have it both ways – either the 'wick effect' can generate the terrific amount of heat to melt distant plastic objects and convert bones to white, not grey, calcined ash or it is not the 'wick effect' that is melting those plastic objects and calcining those bones but some other phenomenon, i.e. SHC.

It is exceedingly easy to demonstrate the terrific amount of radiant heat that is required to melt plastic objects such as TVs and telephones several yards from the heat source. When next in the presence of a coal or gas fire just hold the palms of your hands out to the flames. You will feel the radiant heat. You will no doubt be able to hold your hands within twelve inches of the flames for quite a while before the heat becomes uncomfortable. Move your hands back to two feet distant and you will most likely be able to keep your hands at that distance without suffering any discomfort. Radiant heat obeys the same laws as other radiant energy such as light. It is subject to the law of the inverse square. If you double the distance from the heat source then the radiated heat at that distance is reduced to a quarter, if trebled then it drops to one ninth and if quadrupled it drops to one sixteenth. If Henry Thomas's incineration had resulted from the 'wick effect', the radiant heat output would have been somewhat lower than that from a coal or gas fire. The TV set was ten feet distant from the burning corpse which means that the radiant heat would be reduced to one hundredth. I have experimented with my own living-room open coal fire. It burns extremely well as it is supplied by underfloor draught, controlled by a butterfly valve. With the fire drawing well, and glowing, I have held my hands out at two feet distant without too much discomfort. Sitting eight feet from the fire I can hold my hands facing the fire without being able to discern any change in the temperature of my palms. A TV set would suffer no damage when situated ten feet from a corpse burning in the normal manner.

I have taken Dr Drysdale's recommendation on board and have considered the facts of this case most fully. The facts of the matter are that the Oregon case, which is entitled 'A Case of Not-So-Spontaneous Human Combustion', is precisely that. The 'wick effect' and SHC are two entirely different phenomena which share certain similarities. The argument has raged for many years, indeed centuries, over whether the phenomenon is SHC or the 'wick effect'. Dr Drysdale has, on this occasion, presented me with a classic example of the 'wick effect'.

I telephoned Dr Drysdale to thank him for providing me with the DeHaan article (and another chapter to my book). He told me that DeHaan is expanding the article and has now reduced the time factor to something under ten hours. The crime was committed in February 1991 and DeHaan dated his article 26 November 1994. The times of the murder and the discovery of the still-burning body are facts which should not be variable. When a murder is committed it is an event in space and time. Both those facts are absolutely basic and are among the first to be ascertained by the investigating officers. If the time of twelve to thirteen hours had held for nearly four years I find it strange that it should be amended at this late date. If such basic facts have since proved wrong then how much reliance can be placed on the other facts of the case?

The most relevant factor of SHC, the one that the sceptics just cannot accept the possibility of, is the spontaneous element of Spontaneous Human Combustion. They have no problem with the human combustion part. That is covered quite adequately by the 'wick effect' process. Though it is often difficult, even impossible, to pinpoint an external source of ignition in cases of SHC there is great reluctance to accept that there is no external source of ignition to find. An American general once said something to this effect: 'Once is happenstance, twice is circumstance, three times is enemy action.' He was quite right not to allow too many apparently coincidental mishaps to be written off as mere coincidence. When an apparent coincidence occurs time after time after time one should forget coincidence and start looking hard for the cause.

Dr Drysdale states in his letter that the word 'spontaneous' is often used because in most of the cases the source of ignition could not be found. It is not the case that occurrences of the 'wick effect' are being wrongly claimed as instances of SHC just because there is no immediately obvious source of ignition. Instances of SHC are so identified because the pattern of burning is totally different to normal burning, including the 'wick effect'. For instance, in SHC the clothes are burned by the burning body and do not burn beyond the burned parts of the body. In normal burning if the clothes catch fire they quickly burn away before the corpse starts to burn properly. SHC burnings always commence while the victim is alive as opposed to 'wick effect' burnings of already dead corpses. SHC burnings are at much higher temperatures than normal burnings and more significantly SHC can reduce a victim to ash when the ambient oxygen level is too low to support the burning of an ordinary candle or any other flammable material.

When cases of SHC are discovered it must be more than mere coincidence that in all such cases there is never any proven external source of ignition. In the instances of the 'wick effect', with which I am familiar, there has never been any doubt as to the cause of ignition. In each case the source was immediately obvious.

CHAPTER TWENTY-THREE

Cigarettes Can Kill?

When the sceptics or the authorities (usually one and the same) are explaining away awkward instances of SHC the ubiquitous carelessly dropped cigarette is mostly pressed into service as the trigger for the whole process of the 'wick effect'. I recently heard a discussion on BBC Radio Four in which the deleterious effects of smoking were under discussion. The usual cigarette manufacturers' medically qualified mouthpiece was stating that there is absolutely no scientific evidence that cigarettes even cause bronchitis let alone numerous types of cancer and many other diseases. Someone quoted 'government figures' showing that 200 people burn to death each year as the direct result of the carelessly dropped cigarette. He was more or less inviting the tame medical man to deny that the tobacco moguls were not responsible for those deaths.

I immediately homed in on the 200 deaths per year. Having never ever personally seen any cigarette burn result in more than a singed hole in clothing, furnishings or bedding I decided to carry out some experiments of my own. I was also extremely dubious of the ability of the type of electric fire which was supposed to have incinerated Ashton to set anything on fire. Ashton's fire was an antique. By the greatest coincidence (or synchronicity) my next-door neighbour, Stanley Hancock, possesses an immaculate antique fire with the exact same ceramic block supporting the same spiral electric element. Stanley kindly loaned the fire to me for my experiments.

First I made a cardboard support to fit on top of the fire. I then suspended a double-thickness paper tissue in front of the element which was already at full heat. Due to the backward leaning angle of the fire, the distance from the tissue to the heated element varied from one and a half inches at the bottom to two inches at the top. After fifteen minutes the tissue was burned black where closest to the element but would not catch fire. I then hung a piece of black cotton T-shirt material in the same position again for fifteen minutes and succeeded in scorching it. My experiment showed beyond any doubt that a radiant electric fire, the same as Ashton's, was incapable of setting any of his clothing on fire at the distance it was situated from his body.

Now for the much maligned cigarette – the avowed cause of so many individuals' fiery demise. For the first time in fifteen years I bought a packet of cigarettes. Though I did not inhale, by the end of my experimental session I was feeling decidedly sick. (I too have suffered in the interests of science.) I placed lighted cigarettes on four different types of material and failed totally to get any one of them to ignite into flame. The first was fluffy viscose material which smouldered away. When blown upon the glow brightened and smouldered faster though it would not burst into flame. It did leave a char which appeared suitable for wicking though I did not test its suitability. Acrylic tended to melt rather than glow and did not provide a suitable char for wicking. Nylon melted without any trace of glowing and once again was no good for wicking. Wool glowed and left char suitable for wicking. Cotton glowed best and most brightly when blown upon but still would not ignite.

Viscose burned fiercely when set alight with a match flame, so did acrylic. Cotton and wool also burned when set alight by a match flame. Nylon burned only as long as a naked flame remained in contact with the material. To set clothes, bed-clothes or furnishings alight with a lighted cigarette is apparently exceedingly difficult. I did not manage to set any of the materials alight using a lighted cigarette. I am not going to claim, purely on the basis of my own simple experiments with cigarettes and materials, that it is impossible for cigarettes to set such materials on fire. I will say, however, that it is exceedingly unlikely that such large numbers of people die the way they are alleged to. When a definite cause of ignition cannot be found the cigarette is always a convenient scapegoat. Are these people who supposedly burn away at the touch of a cigarette ever seen so to do? Of course not. Are any traces of a cigarette among the ashes ever found to give credence to the claim? Again of course not. It is all assumption. To paraphrase Dougal Drysdale, You cannot say that these people died through the agency of a carelessly dropped cigarette. No one has ever seen such an instance right from ignition, through to death and the final reduction to ashes.

Senior Divisional Officer David Leitch of Strathclyde fire brigade, claimed in his article, 'Logical Explanations Appear to Rule Out Possibility of SHC', (*Fire*, August 1986) that tramps wear multiple layers of clothes in cold weather which become impregnated with fat from greasy pies and chips and also meths and other spirits and so become far more easy to ignite. He wrote, 'In the event that a spark or cigarette became lodged in their clothing it would burn quite freely, possibly with a bluish flame due to the alcohol.' If they were to burn with a 'blue flame due to the alcohol', then they would need to have their clothes saturated with alcohol. This would require the tramp to be extremely careless and wasteful of his precious liquor. It would also require him to ignite very soon after such a massive spillage before the spirit could evaporate.

Any material soaked in alcohol and burning with a blue flame is not of itself burning. Only the alcohol is burning. Take the simple spirit lamp provided with most children's chemistry sets. The lamp consists of a cotton wick suspended in methylated spirits. When a flame is applied to the wick the alcohol in the wick burns brightly without consuming the wick itself. The wick only starts to burn when the spirit runs out. Too many sceptics rely on myths of common knowledge which prove to be totally wrong time after time. They should take note of the clangers that Aristotle dropped due to relying on his common sense rather than the evidence of his eyes. P.C. Jenion, the coroner's officer in the Jacqueline Fitzsimon case, having agreed that he had never seen a smouldering piece of cloth burst into flame insisted, 'But it's common knowledge, isn't it?'

It is not true that people such as I are continually propagating the 'myth' of SHC. In fact, the myths all go the other way. It is a myth that a person can catch alight from a cigarette coming in contact with their clothing. It is a myth that a cigarette can cause grease-soaked clothes to catch fire. It is also a myth that a cigarette can ignite clothing soaked in brandy or methylated spirits. If the clothes are saturated in the spirits the cigarette is extinguished. The same thing happens when a lighted cigarette is dropped into neat brandy or meths. The red heat of a glowing cigarette is at too low a temperature (approximately 550°C) to ignite the spirits.

At the same time as I carried out the experiments with the electric fire and cigarettes I also did some tests into the flammability of brandy and methylated spirits. Earlier in the book I stated that it was common knowledge that anyone soaked in methylated spirits or brandy having a lighted cigarette thrown at them would erupt into flame. Though it is common knowledge it is entirely untrue. Even senior fire officers make the mistake of subscribing to these unfounded yet commonly known 'facts'. As related above, David Leitch is quite sure that the meths- and grease-soaked clothes of tramps constitute ambulatory firebombs awaiting the merest spark or dropped cigarette to cause instant and fatal ignition.

Using some 70° proof brandy left over from the anointing of the Christmas cake I soaked a piece of cotton T-shirt. Having puffed a cigarette into a fierce state of glowing I gingerly placed the cigarette onto the brandy saturated cloth. The brandy was drawn up the glowing end of the cigarette by capillary action and the cigarette was promptly doused. I tried the same test several times each time with the same result. The brandy behaved just the same as the molten paraffin wax of a candle when the flame is snuffed. It is drawn up the wick by capillary action and extinguishes the glowing wick.

I repeated the tests using cotton and paper tissues with the same result. Both brandy and methylated spirit require a flame to heat the liquids sufficiently to convert them into gases which will combine with oxygen and burn. I also dropped lighted cigarettes into liquid brandy and methylated spirit with the same results – the extinction of the cigarette.

As it is obviously not quite so easy to ignite a person with a cigarette as is commonly assumed, what is the real cause of ignition of these 200 or so people per year? I had already deduced that the total number of cases of SHC in the UK yearly might possibly be in the region of 200. My deductions were based on the fact that the Home Office Pathologist, Dr G.S. Andrews, normally dealt with approximately six cases a year in his area in which the abdominal area was totally destroyed. These cases were, for the most part, blamed on the ubiquitous cigarette.

I assumed that the ignition point of brandy and methylated spirits must be higher than 550°C as a cigarette cannot ignite these spirits. I determined to find out the ignition temperatures. I failed to find the information at my local libraries so I asked Peter Sadler if he could help.

Peter soon informed me that meths ignites at around

450°C. This information really gave me pause for thought. It seems perfectly logical to assume that a cigarette, burning at 550°C, must ignite a spirit with an ignition temperature 100 degrees lower. I passed the paradox on to Peter Sadler. He carried out some experiments which showed that the answer lay in the amount of heat in, as well as the temperature of, the igniting medium. His full solution of the paradox is contained in Appendix B.

CHAPTER TWENTY-FOUR

The Burning Question

In June 1994, I went to London and filmed an interview for the Yorkshire Television production of 'Arthur C. Clarke's Mysterious Universe' programme, specifically the episode entitled, 'The Burning Question' which was later transmitted by Discovery Satellite Channel in the USA and then in Europe commencing in April 1995.

While the programme was well balanced and fair it did seem a little bland. I understand that this was because the programme was made primarily for American TV audiences. It seems that the sponsors of American TV shows carry a lot of clout and they do not like anything to be too controversial. Consequently the photographs of Bailey and Annie Webb were omitted although they dealt with both cases and I provided the photographs which the programme makers filmed. Yet again I was edited out when stating that the victims were alive at the start of their incineration. This was no doubt considered too strong for the stomachs of American TV viewers.

Professor Gee was briefly shown describing his experiment but it was left to a Dr Siva Loganathan to replicate the experiment with some pork from the local butchers. The doctor cut a piece of pork and fat about the size and thickness of a small bacon rasher. This he rolled up in a piece of cloth about the size of a tea towel so the cloth outweighed the meat and fat. A steel kebab skewer was then inserted into the meat and then clamped to a stand. The multi-layered roll of cloth was then set alight with a match and allowed to burn for some time. The cloth did not flare-up and burn away quickly because it was so tightly rolled.

When the end that was first set alight was burned out it was found that the meat was reduced to a blackened char, which is to be expected. Professor Gee had had to apply a Bunsen burner for about a minute to get his sample of human fat, covered with only a couple of layers of cloth to catch fire. In Dr Siva's demonstration he used so much cloth that a person being similarly clothed would be totally weighed down with the sheer mass of clothing. If this ratio of cloth to flesh were maintained for a victim of the 'wick effect' then a person weighing 140lb would be encased in over 200lb of clothes. This was yet again a demonstration that demonstrated nothing beyond the well-known fact that a small piece of meat can be burnt to a char if it is contained within sufficient burning fuel. Such a demonstration cannot possibly be extrapolated to show how a human can be reduced to ash, including the bones.

I hate to be picky but did the butchers not have any pork bones to use for a stiffener? After all, flesh is supported by bones, not kebab skewers or glass test tubes. It is notable that in all the demonstrations of the way in which bodies, including bones, can be reduced to ash by the 'wick effect', none of the demonstrators used bones to support the flesh and fat. Dr Alan Beard of Edinburgh University wrote in criticism of the 'QED' programme that they had tried burning an animal bone, wrapped in fat and covered with cloth, but had only succeeded in blackening the bone.

It may well be purely coincidental that a steel skewer was used. The normal reason for using steel skewers on meat and baked potatoes is to conduct the heat to the centre of the meat or potato and thus hasten the cooking. It is no doubt more than coincidence that the material used in all the demonstrations of fat-burning is cotton – the material that happens to burn and wick most readily. It is worth noting that after thirty years of scientific endeavour to prove that the instances of SHC are in fact occurrences of the 'wick effect', the experimenters have not advanced beyond burning a small amount of bloodless and boneless fat and meat in an excessive amount of cotton material to supposedly demonstrate the ease with which flesh and bone burn.

I have just checked some burning patterns using sheets of A4 copying paper. I set light to the first sheet held in a vertical position. The flames quickly consumed the sheet, taking just eighteen seconds. The second sheet I set fire to while holding it in a horizontal position. This time it took one whole minute to completely consume the sheet. The third sheet I rolled up into a tube much like Dr Loganathan's fat roll without the fat. I clamped the tube in a horizontal position and made several attempts to set fire to the one end. Each time the flame quickly died out once the lighted match was withdrawn. However, the paper continued to smoulder. After ten minutes only two and a half inches of a sheet measuring eleven and three quarter inches had burned away. At that rate it would take the complete roll forty-seven minutes to burn away. The same sized pieces of paper can take between eighteen seconds and forty-seven minutes to burn away and the only difference is whether the sheets are loose and vertical or rolled up and horizontal. The longest burning time is 156 times longer than the shortest. People do not normally wear their clothing around their limbs and torso, wrapped in a minimum of six tight layers.

The 'Mysterious Universe' programme also dealt briefly with the most famous American case of SHC – that of Mary Reeser, the 'Florida Cinderwoman'. Her son, Dr Richard Reeser, was interviewed and he could only express amazement at the incineration of his mother for which he has never been able to find any rational cause.

Mrs Reeser was sixty-seven years of age and weighed 170lb at a height of five feet seven inches, so she was somewhat overweight. She lived in an apartment in St Petersburg, Florida. At 8a.m. on Monday 2 July 1951, Mrs Reeser was found so completely incinerated in her wooden apartment that only one foot and shoe were found among her ashes which were mingled with the ashes and springs of the easy chair in which she had been sitting. There was evidence of some smoke and heat damage yet nothing else in the room had burned.

The local fireman, Nelson Aters, who attended the scene stated that the incident was totally inexplicable at the time and still is now. At the time all manner of experts examined the scene yet no cause could be found. The experts, such as fireman Aters, remained baffled.

Forty-three years later, Joe Nickell, of CSICOP, at the Fortean Unconvention 94 in London could state with absolute certainty that Mary Reeser had set fire to her nightdress having fallen asleep while smoking a cigarette. No one saw her smoking in her chair and no one saw her drop a lighted cigarette onto her nightdress. There would certainly not have been any evidence of such a happening among the sparse ashes. My own experiments have shown the improbability of clothing catching fire from a dropped cigarette. Had her clothing caught fire there was no way that a burning nightdress could generate sufficient heat to initiate the 'wick effect'. At most she would have been superficially burned and blistered.

The 'Mysterious Universe' programme ended with a visit to Ticonderoga, New York State, USA. In 1986, in a log cabin situated in the woods of Ticonderoga, a retired part-time fireman, George Mott was completely reduced to ashes. George Mott's son, Kendall Mott, had gone to his father's cabin in the woods one morning when his father failed to answer the telephone. He found the usual scene common to instances of SHC. The wooden cabin was undamaged by the fire that had reduced George Mott's body to ash. There was the usual smoke blackening to windows and walls. The bed on which the victim burned was partially burnt as was the wooden floor underneath, through which the ashes of George Mott had fallen. A somewhat heavily built man is reduced to ashes on a wooden bed and consequently burns through a wooden floor of a completely wooden cabin which yet fails to burn up. Is that normal?

Neither Kendall Mott nor the state trooper, Dick La Vallee, who attended the scene were in any doubt as to the cause of the incineration – it was SHC as far as they were concerned. There was no viable source of ignition to be blamed in this case and George Mott, having only one lung for some years, was a dedicated non-smoker. He had 'no smoking' signs exhibited in his cabin and he would not allow others to smoke in his home.

And so the programme ended, the latest in the present series of TV programmes resulting from a sudden, inexplicable upsurge of interest in the phenomenon of SHC. Though the producers of 'The Burning Question' omitted some disturbing yet highly relevant facts, such as the victims being alive when incinerating, they at least did not display any bias. Maybe one day a TV company will go so far as to commission a scientist to properly examine all the evidence that does not accord with the 'wick effect' hypothesis.

CHAPTER TWENTY-FIVE

A Paranormal Event?

I have insisted throughout this book that I do not subscribe to belief in the supernatural. I am convinced that whatever happens in the universe must be happening in accordance with the 'laws' of the universe and is therefore natural.

I will finish this book with an account of a happening that is even more of a mystery than SHC. I have spoken to the participants in this event, Bob and Beryl Smith of Burnley, Lancashire, and I am convinced that what they told me is the truth as they saw and experienced the event. Both Bob and Beryl are in their late sixties and are not the sort to indulge in pranks. They have no wish to hide their identities.

This incident was reported to me as a result of the 'Schofield's Quest' programme in 1994. Bob Smith was lying in bed around midnight about three years ago on a Sunday while Beryl was preparing a pot of tea. They insist that they have never smoked cigarettes in their bedroom in the thirty odd years that they have lived in their home, neither have they ever kept matches or lighters in the room. They are determined to keep the bedroom free from the smell of tobacco smoke.

Bob was reading a Sunday newspaper. He thinks it was the

News of The World. He was holding the paper up in front of himself as he lay in bed and was reading an article about the Manson 'family'. For those too young to remember, the Manson family was a group of degenerate hippies led by an evil common criminal named Charles Manson. They all lived together on a beat-up ranch in California or thereabouts. They used to go out on thieving forays at Manson's behest. Most of his followers were young women and they were all heavily into the drugs scene and revered Manson as some sort of Christ figure. They finally finished up breaking into the home of Roman Polanski, the film director and husband of the actress Sharon Tate. Polanski was away at the time when the Manson family dropped in and slaughtered Sharon Tate, her unborn child and several friends.

Bob was reading this report of the Manson family's depredations when he came to a reference to a gravestone in the backyard of the Manson ranch. The reporter had actually visited the ranch and found the gravestone. It seemed a strange situation for a gravestone so he read the inscription which was something like:

Here lies the body of [Bob cannot remember the name]
We burnt her bones
To rid the world of
Her evil flesh

Bob was holding the newspaper wide open, having just finished reading the inscription, when thick grey smoke started rising up from between the pages of the paper. He said,

At first I could not believe it. It just seemed that the paper was going to burst into flames at any moment. I shouted out to my wife at the top of my voice. She came dashing into the room just as I was flinging the paper down by the side of the bed. She could not believe what she was seeing when she saw the bedroom

*was full of smoke. It was certainly not imaginary smoke. It was
dense grey smoke with a horrible smell. She wanted to know
what the hell I had been doing. It sounded too ridiculous for
words as I explained to her what the cause of it was. I could
hardly believe it myself. The room was full of this foul smoke and
we had to open wide both the windows. I thought to myself,
'The first thing I must do is get rid of this newspaper.' Not just
out of the room, but out of the house completely. So I took it out
of the house and put it into the dustbin with the lid on and
moved the bin down to the bottom of the garden. We could not
give over thinking about it and it was a long time before we
could get off to sleep.*

*I have only told about two people about it and even they lis-
tened to me with a rather sceptical smile. If my wife had not seen
and smelled the smoke she would not believe me, but it's true.
I'm glad my wife came in and saw it. If she had not seen it and
I had told her what had happened she would have had me
locked up. The paper did not burn, in fact it did not even show
any sign of scorching. The dense smoke, which smelled indescribably foul, with something of a sulphurous quality to it, just
poured out from between the pages as long as I held it and filled
the bedroom. I cannot really describe the smell, it certainly did
not smell like a burning newspaper. I had been lying in bed
reading the newspaper for about an hour before the smoke
poured out of it. As I carried the paper to the dustbin it stopped
smoking.*

Beryl Smith verified what her husband had told me. She said,

*Well, Bob was in bed reading a newspaper story about a witch
I think it was. It was about Manson. I heard him shout out,
'Oh my God! Beryl!' I dashed into the bedroom, which was full
of smoke, and I saw this newspaper apparently smouldering.
There was smoke coming from it. There was no fire, just smoke.
The smoke smelled horrible. We never smoked in the bedroom,*

it was sacrilege to do so. It was very uncanny really. We had to open all the windows. We have not had the News of The World *since.*

The fact that the paper spontaneously exuded smoke is of itself remarkable but that Bob Smith had just finished reading the inscription from the grave of a murdered person, whose bones were seemingly burned, is stretching coincidence somewhat. I did not intend to include this incident as it does not seem to have any relationship with SHC. Then I realised that once again we have an instance where an indescribably foul smell was created which under normal circumstances should produce a totally different and far from unpleasant smell.

Conclusion

If by now you are not convinced of the existence of SHC then you should at least have strong doubts that the 'wick effect' can account for all the various criteria involved in the alleged cases of SHC. Throughout the course of my research into instances both of the 'wick effect' and SHC proper, I have only come across three proven cases of the 'wick effect'. The first was the case of the Countess Gorlitz, murdered by her servant Stauf and then partially burned by him in a near successful attempt to cover his crime. The second case was examined in detail by Professor Gee in 1965 which involved the eighty-five-year-old lady who had a stroke or heart attack and fell into an open coal fire and was substantially incinerated. Third and last is the well-documented case in the woods of Oregon, USA, in 1991, where a murder victim's body and clothes were saturated in barbecue starter fluid and set on fire destroying a large part of the torso over a twelve to thirteen hour period.

These three cases are proven examples of the 'wick effect' inasmuch as in each case the source of ignition is known, the victims were dead at the start of their incineration and their incinerations were all assisted by substantial external sources of fuel. These cases all conform to the criteria specified for the 'wick effect' by Dupuytren, Dr Gavin Thurston and Professor Gee.

All the cases of SHC considered in this book have failed to meet any of the necessary three criteria specified for the 'wick effect'. All the pathological evidence points to the victims being alive at the start of their incineration. No external source of fuel is present and there is no substantiated source of ignition. In the cases of Bailey and Jeannie Saffin careful examination by police and fire officers failed to find any possible cause of ignition. In all the other cases so-called viable sources of ignition were either not viable (such as the electric fire even if it had been switched on) or there was either no evidence to show that they had been involved or there was direct evidence to the effect that they had not been involved (i.e. Nigel Cruttenden's evidence that the gas stove showed no evidence of Soudaine having been in contact with it). In other cases it was shown to be a physical impossibility for the 'viable source' to have been involved (i.e. the unlit gas-ring and the catering jacket of Jacqueline Fitzsimon).

Following the broadcast of the 'QED' programme a letter was published in the *Radio Times*, dated 20–26 May 1989, under the heading 'Marred'. I quote a couple of extracts from that letter:

> It [the 'QED' programme] was, however, marred by the conclusions drawn, which were not justified by the content of the programme. That is: it cannot be said at the present time, that 'science' has explained beyond reasonable doubt what is happening in these unusual cases.

Also:

> In each of two exploratory tests carried out by Edinburgh University, in which an animal bone was packed around with fat

*and covered with cloth before burning, the result was to sub-
stantially carbonise the bone, but not to produce much, if any,
evident mineralisation.*

What is most interesting about this letter (one of four, all of
which criticised the programme) is that the writer was (Dr)
Alan Beard, Unit of Fire Safety Engineering, University of
Edinburgh. Though the name may not be familiar to the
reader the address should ring the odd bell or two. Drs Beard
and Drysdale were colleagues in the same department. They
were both involved in the initial 'QED' 'experiments' or
'demonstrations' testing the 'wick effect'. It is now clear why
no bones are used to provide rigidity in demonstrations of the
'wick effect'. 'Weigh not so much what men assert as what
they can prove.'

   One final thought on the reasons for the unrelenting opposition of the scientific Establishment to SHC. As I have earlier
stated the scientific method has been highly successful to date
in gathering knowledge relative to our world and even the
universe in general. The method has been so successful that
anything which cannot be readily investigated by the scientific
method is rejected as spurious. There are an ever-growing
number of books being written by academics and experimental psychologists and all manner of scientists that are
critical of the strict adherence to the scientific method. More
and more people are coming to realise that not everything is
amenable to examination by the scientific method. The quantum physicists started the ball rolling.

   The sceptics' attachment to the 'wick effect' hypothesis is
strengthened by the fact that it is amenable to examination by
the scientific method. (Even though, on their own admission
(and in TV demonstrations) scientists have not yet been able to
demonstrate in the laboratory how low-temperature slow-
burning can reduce bones to ash.) On the other hand, SHC is
totally unsuited to the scientific method of examination.

Maybe in a few more decades, when the scientific fraternity in general has finally awoken to the fact that there are other more suitable methods for the investigation of certain phenomena, we may finally solve the mystery of SHC and a lot more besides.

I have, within the last few days, been reading *In the Minds of Men* by Ian T. Taylor. Taylor gives an insight into the reason why the establishment scientists are so welded to the 'wick effect' hypothesis. Briefly he states that in any hierarchical organisation the ideas of the top élite are automatically propagated down through successive strata right to the bottom. In any government research laboratory or university, successful job applicants have first to show that they embrace the prevailing philosophy of the hierarchy. Once they become part of the hierarchy they have to maintain conformity in order to progress in both remuneration and promotion. Peer pressure guarantees conformity just as relentlessly as ever it did in the school playground.

If the reader still considers SHC to be impossible, for whatever reason, then take time to review the bare, undisputed facts of the plight of Jeannie Saffin. No possible cause of her ignition could be found or even suggested, yet her face and hands burned down to the subcutaneous fat. Her clothes did not burn to any extent nor did her hair burn. She did not cry out nor did she make any attempt to move though she was conscious and able to stand unaided when pulled out of the chair. There was no sign of the expected fire or smoke damage to be found in the room. Her father, seated a couple of feet away noticed nothing until he suddenly saw and heard the flames 'roaring' from both her hands and face. Contemplation of those facts alone should give any person pause for thought before dismissing SHC as an impossibility.

I have tried to find out what happened to the right hand of the tramp, Bailey. I wrote to the present coroner, Dr Sir M.B. Levine requesting information relative to the death of Bailey.

I received no reply. I have tried on numerous occasions, without success, to contact the fireman in the case, Jack Stacey.

I have asked H.M. Coroner for Kent, Brian N.D. Smith, whether or not coroners use the verdict of misadventure in a way other than defined in *The Oxford English Dictionary* and various legal dictionaries. He told me that about four years ago the family of some deceased person, whose death was ruled by a coroner as misadventure, appealed against the verdict. The judgement was that with regard to coroner's inquests misadventure was the same as accidental death. I do not know the details, though I must confess to being rather curious as to why it was considered necessary to confuse two entirely separate verdicts.

Before this strange ruling, if a person walking along a railway platform tripped and fell in front of a train, the resulting death would be accidental. If a person walking along the platform tripped and knocked another person into the path of the train the verdict would have been misadventure. Now, even though the two circumstances are entirely different, the two verdicts are to be considered synonymous and interchangeable. I would like to look into the case that resulted in such a strange ruling and see what anomalies were smoothed over as a result.

I shall research the case responsible for this ruling. Though we now have to accept that misadventure is synonymous with accidental death this still does not explain the verdict of misadventure in the case of Jeannie Saffin. How can a death be judged to be accidental when the cause of the flames that killed her is unknown? Though judges now see fit not to differentiate between accident and misadventure they can surely see that one has to know the cause before one can judge an incident as accidental. When the actual cause of the circumstances leading to death is unknown then the only proper verdict is an open verdict.

The sceptics are quite at home with the concept of human

combustion. They now have to take the final step and accept that, on occasion, the combustion is spontaneous. When no possible source of ignition is to be found, despite exhaustive searches, then it is only reasonable to accept the possibility of Spontaneous Human Combustion.

As I mentioned in the preface to this book I wish to collect as much evidence relative to SHC as possible. I would like to hear from any reader who has knowledge of a possible occurrence of SHC such as the cases featured in this book particularly where individuals are deemed to have died from excessive burns to the abdominal area because of a dropped cigarette or spark. I would also like to hear of any seemingly paranormal occurrences such as Bob Smith's smoking newspaper. Any accounts, short or long, together with your address and telephone number can be mailed to me, c/o Little, Brown. I guarantee complete confidentiality. Actual names will only be used with the express written consent of the people involved. All the named contributors to this book volunteered to be identified.

Appendix A

A typical mammalian cell is an enormously complex structure containing a mixture of small and large specialised proteins and organelles, constantly involved in complex creative processes as long as the cell is alive. It consists of 70 per cent water, 20 per cent protein plus its basic supporting structure. Such a cell produces at least a billion different proteins which is only a fraction of the almost infinite variety of its possible range of products. Because much organisation of its functioning is destroyed when attempts are made to study it, the details of its workings are poorly understood.

Each cell is a complete and complicated factory, manufacturing all the chemicals and creating the energy that keep the body alive and functioning. Mitochondria, which are free ranging in the fluid of the cell, take up 22 per cent of the volume in numbers, varying from 1,000 to 2,000 in almost every body cell.

The total power required for sustaining and energising all the living activities of human beings are generated by the mitochondria from the conversion of broken down food particles into energy. The true difference between living and dead flesh is the absence or cessation of mitochondrion activities. A body could be considered to be truly dead when every mito-chondrion has stopped its activities. (I wonder if the total energy active in mitochondria, in the form of electronic energy, is a possible measurable quantity that appears and dis-appears between the two states of an organism being dead or alive.)

In an attempt to simplify the description of the bewildering nature of the constituents and processes taking place at the microscopic level of SHC, it is presented in the form of the blown-up version. That, at least for me, makes it appear less difficult to visualise my basic theory of SHC and also helps to clarify the mechanisms suggested that may initiate the burn-ing processes when SHC occurs.

This is similar to the modern ploy of medical surgery, where the teaching hospitals have adopted the advanced tech-niques of virtual reality. Budding surgeons are now able, by means of VR, to stand alongside, say, a virtual image of a human heart the size of a small room. They are also able to enter inside it and take it apart bit by bit, examine it for any damaged parts as if they are carrying out surgery on a real heart in the theatre, but with this extra advantage of manipu-lating larger replicas of its parts and structures. The diameter of a human body cell is very small, its diameter is a fraction of a millimetre and large ones are just visible as the tiniest speck on a white background as seen by human eyes with 20/20 vision. The diameter of a mitochondrion is 50 times or so smaller than that of a normal human cell in which 1–2,000 of them exist at a time, each for only a short time. They are as uncon-scious of our existence as we are of theirs. They blindly carry out their purpose of converting energy from protein into a form that living things can absorb and sustain life with.

To enable the reader to visualise more realistically and relate more easily to the basic scenario of SHC, I have blown up the physical dimensions of the cell to that of the normal level of clarity, by magnifying the proportions by a factor of one thousand. The size of a human body cell now becomes the size of a golf ball, i.e. 40mm in diameter. The mitochondria now have a diameter of approximately 1mm.

The diameter of the average normal human torso at the level of the navel is about 30cm or 12in. The distance from the centre of the torso to the outside surface would average 15cm. The number of cells extending radially from the centre to the outer surface of the abdomen in a single line would number about 3,750. The area of the navel section of the torso is now equivalent to $70,686m^2$, equal to 10 standard football pitches. 40 million golf balls would be required to cover the area one ball deep, this equals the number of cells in a single layer of the average human torso at the navel. There are many millions of such layers in the total mass of the torso. The total number of cells in a torso is astronomical and each cell contains 1–2,000 mitochondria. The total is beyond comprehension. The average body contains 100 quadrillion (100,000,000,000,000,000) bacterial cells and another 10 quadrillion body cells, all containing their quota of mitochondria which power all higher forms of life with energy.

Each cell deep in the mass of cells is generally in physical contact touching five or six adjacent cells. If a cell deep in a mass of cells, for whatever reason, suddenly burned its hydrogen content, no oxygen or hydrogen would escape, even if its outer membrane was ruptured, because the gases would have combined before the heat was released to rupture the membrane. Heat energy would be conveyed to the adjacent cells. If the heat was sufficient to trigger some adjacent cells to burn in the same way then a chain reaction of burning cells could spread throughout the masses of adjacent cells with an exponential rise of temperature.

Because of the heat insulating properties of the mass of surrounding cells, the lack of oxygen and the fast accelerating numbers of cells heating up internally, no flaming would take place and the internal temperatures could rise to such a level to calcine bones before it reaches the surface of the body and runs out of cells to burn.

The above theory, describing the circumstances of how a continuous relatively small amount of heat energy accumulating in sufficient time can reach temperatures even comparable with those at the centre of the sun, is simply a question of heat insulation. One of the present difficulties of achieving nuclear energy by fusion is not the problem of supplying enough heat energy to get the appropriate atoms to high enough temperatures so that they react like those in the sun, but how to create the means to prevent the heat energy put into the atoms from leaking away.

Theoretically, if we had a perfect heat-insulating material encasing a heating element made of a material whose melting point is higher than the temperature of the sun, even with only a two kilowatt continuous supply of electrical energy, the temperature of the element would progressively rise until it disintegrated given sufficient time.

In the SHC process the supply of energy for its creation is self-contained and internally generated, somewhat like chemical energy, but quite unlike electrical heating which depends on a supply of energy from a separate external source. In the normal world, the bar element of an electric fire rises to a particular maximum temperature when the amount of heat energy being radiated away equals the amount of electrical energy being supplied to it.

My suggested theory of the SHC process is based on the same basic laws that control the function of heating devices. What triggers SHC in the first place and sustains the process is the mystery we are attempting to solve. One possibility stems from the everpresent saturation of the universe with high energy cosmic particles. The whole earth and its inhabitants, including humans, every second of every day constantly throughout their lives are being showered by various types of different masses of high energy particles that pass right through our bodies and down through the earth with energies as high as 10^{20} (1,000,000,000,000,000,000,000) electron volts. The simplest of the instruments used to detect these high energy particles are called Geiger Counters.

If a cosmic particle passes between two parallel electrically charged plates in a vacuum, it triggers an electrical discharge across the plates that can be measured and recorded. In the light of this well-known process I suggest that by probability the energy existing in a particular mitochondrion in a human cell may, at a particular instant, be at a high point of its electrical potential when it is struck by a high energy cosmic particle. This could result in a rise of temperature from the sudden discharge of the stored energy inside the mitochondrion igniting the oxygen and hydrogen gasses into flameless heat energy, which by a continuing chain reaction, triggers discharges in the other 1,000 or more mitochondria in the cell, thereby heating the first cell to a destructively high temperature. This could result in a knock-on effect on the adjacent cells which would carry on travelling towards the outer limits of the body. The probability of such an occurrence is not high but during a life span of 70 years it could happen, as it seems to, in a few of the six billion humans presently alive. From this postulation, SHC should also occur in animals, but information of this is apparently not available or known.

During the destruction of the first cell most of the mitochondria would be destroyed inside the cell just before it ruptured, affecting only the surrounding cells with its glowing carbon residues of the heat energy without flaming, but becoming hot enough to trigger the energy of the cells in contact with it. The accumulating chain reaction from cell to cell, in ever increasing numbers of burning cells, would soon encompass the whole mass of the body in a relatively short time.

As all the mixtures of oxygen and hydrogen are used up from burning inside each cell's outer membranes reducing them to carbon, none of the gasses are expelled outside the cells and leave only the greasy carbon ash from the unique type of intense smouldering that has taken place inside the cells without an external supply of oxygen. It is only when the burning gets closer to the surface of the body to make contact with atmospheric oxygen that the characteristic blue flames of SHC would appear.

The intense temperature developed may be due to the speed of the ever-increasing rate of the energy generated inside the cells as the heat develops exponentially. It may also be due to the high efficiency of the heat insulating properties of the unburned masses of the myriad cells contained in the torso between the burning cells and the surface of the body.

In the case of SHC, although the same basic laws of thermodynamics apply, it is the peculiar nature of the source of its energy; the (at present) unaccountable means that initiates its occurrence; and our lack of knowledge of what living matter really is, that makes SHC appear as the ultimate horror and drives normally rational people to deny its existence. However, we do know that SHC happens. It is a fact of life (or rather death) in the physical world.

Appendix B

The purpose of this appendix is an attempt to explain why a lighted cigarette at, presumably, a temperature in the region of 550° C (the temperature of red heat) fails to ignite materials soaked in methylated spirits with an ignition temperature of around 450° C. I was intrigued by the fact that I could not ignite meths or brandy with a lighted cigarette. I was told by Peter Sadler that the ignition temperature of meths was in the region of 450° C and I already knew from earlier experiments in tempering hand forged steel that the temperature of red heat was around 550°C. I told Peter of the seeming paradox and he kindly set to and solved the paradox.

The terms 'Temperature' and 'Heat' are by no means identical, and for clarity, particularly in relation to the ignition of inflammable liquids, these terms must not be assumed to mean the same thing. It is all too easy to assume if one sample of water has a higher temperature than another that as it is hotter, it must therefore contain more energy, this is not necessarily true. A tumbler of water at 80°C is very much hotter than a bath of water at 40°C, but there is very much more heat energy contained in the bath than the tumbler. The terms 'hot' and 'cold' are subjective and are due to feeling sensations when humans make physical contact with things that are at higher or lower temperatures than the human body.

Temperature is no more than the measure of the average amount of mechanical energy contained in the movements of the individual atoms that make up the material world in all its three states of solids, liquids and gases. Temperature is an equivalence measure of the average mechanical energy of the individual atoms. The heat energy content of a gas, liquid or solid is the total internal energy of all the individual atoms that make up the total system. Put simply, heat represents the total quantity of energy we call heat, while temperature indicates the average energy in the motions of the individual atom. This is more apparent if we imagine heating a small piece of wire say one millimetre in diameter and ten millimetres long to red heat, say 550°C and plunging it into a litre of normal cold tap water. The increase in the temperature of the water could barely be detected. But, if we heat a round bar of the same metal, say 60 millimetres in diameter and 120 millimetres long, to the same temperature and plunged it into a similar litre of cold water, the water would explode into steam instantaneously.

I believe that this indicates the same mechanism of a glowing cigarette being doused in an inflammable liquid. It is the limiting amount of heat content available in the glowing cigarette, and the short length of time it stays at 550°C when it makes contact with the liquid. I feel fairly sure that, if the total heat energy contained in the glowing cigarette was up to the necessary critical amount required, any inflammable liquid would have exploded. Ignition seems to depend not only on the temperature applied, but also on the amount of heat energy available when attempting to raise the temperature of an inflammable liquid to its ignition point.

I did, in fact, carry out a simple experiment to check that methylated spirits would ignite at 550°C provided there was sufficient heat energy contained in the ignition source. I heated a small steel washer to red heat and dropped it into a small amount of meths and the meths ignited. I repeated the test with a minimal amount of meths and found that the same washer, heated to the same degree, caused the meths to burst into a large clear flame. I also found that by converting the meths into a mist of fine droplets it ignited much more explosively. This was a logical progression from the previous test.

Index

acausal connections, 7, 40
alcohol, 42, 45, 76, 225
Ames, Stan, 138–46, 154, 218
Andrews, Dr G. S., 25–6, 102–4, 227
Angel, Jack, 163–8, 177, 187, 195
Arnold, Larry E., 163, 167, 176
Arthur C. Clarke's Mysterious Universe, 9, 84, 229
Ashton, Alfred, 82, 106, 137, 138, 139, 152–5, 216, 217, 219, 223, 224

Bailey, tramp, 40, 42, 75–81, 88, 104, 129, 132, 136, 137, 145, 177, 199, 229, 239, 241
ball lightning, 7, 86–7, 90–91, 99, 133
BBC Breakfast Television, 126–7
BCS (battered child syndrome), 85–6, 91
Beard, Alan, 108–9, 229, 240
Bentley, Dr J. Irving, 22, 115–17
Bentley, Ron, 123
Bleak House, 4, 16, 113, 133
Brothwell, Don, 52–3
Burton, Dr John, 185–6, 196–201

candle effect, *see* wick effect

carbon monoxide, 26, 36
Carlson, Shawn, 71
causes (possible cause of SHC), 42–3, 104–5, 169–74, 175, 176,
      177, 188, 191
Chamberlain, Clive, 103–4, 144
cigarette (as cause of death), 26, 61, 89, 109, 207, 223–8, 232,
      251–3
Clark, Debbie, 202–3
cremation process, 117, 135–6, 143, 144
Cruttenden, Nigel William, 148–50, 239
CSICOP, 109–10, 115, 123, 162, 165, 232

DeHaan, John, 53, 211–20
Di Bandi, Countess, 123–5
Dickens, Charles, 4, 16, 113
draught, 18–20, 34, 39
Drysdale, Dougal, 108–9, 127–8, 133–46, 212–13, 220–21, 225,
      240
Dupuytren, 42, 44, 45, 112, 213, 239
Durham, Inspector Colin, 37–8

fire (as cause of death), 23, 35–6, 151–2, 154, 223 *see also* cigarette
Firth, Dr, 95
Fitzsimon, Jacqueline, 205–9, 226, 239
Fortean Unconvention, 6, 115, 123, 162, 232

Gee, Professor, 9, 41, 91, 95–103, 108, 134, 144, 212, 229–30,
      238–9
Gowthorpe, Wilfred, 157–64, 166, 167–8, 177, 187, 192, 195

Halliday, David X., 10, 43–4, 136–8, 142
house fires, 121–3
Hunt, Theresa, 131–46, 155

Jones, Bill Treharne, 37–9, 99
Jung, Carl, 7, 40

Krogman, Dr Wilton M., 119–21

Krook, 4, 16, 113
Kurtz, Paul, 109

Lavoisier, Antoine, 55, 63, 90
Lavoisier Syndrome, 22, 54–63, 90
Leadbetter, Stephen, 42, 44, 45
Leitch, David, 7, 225, 226
Lewes, George Henry, 113–4

Marsden, Constable Leigh, 185, 189, 190–91, 196, 198, 200
meteorites, 7, 55–6, 62, 63, 90
Mott, George, 232–3
Motteshead, Susan, 203–5, 206, 209

New Scientist, 6, 42–3, 52, 54, 104
Newsnight, 9, 37, 40–2, 76, 81, 84, 131
Nickel, Joe, 115–7, 123, 162, 163, 232

Ogston, Alexander, 44–6

Paxman, Jeremy, 126–7
Penney, Roger, 152, 154, 215
preternatural combustion, *see* wick effect
prolonged human combustion, *see* wick effect
psychic trigger, 176, 188

QED, 9, 10, 44, 84, 126, 131–46, 149–50, 152, 154, 155, 230, 239, 240

Reeser, Mary, 119–21, 231–2

Sadler, Peter, 169, 170, 227–8, 251–3
Saffin, Jeannie, 88, 168, 177, 179–88, 189, 190, 193–201, 239, 241, 242
Schofield, Philip, 156, 211–12
Schofield's Quest, 156, 169, 181, 191, 211–12, 234
Shirley Institute, 116, 208
smell (following SHC), 21, 31, 148, 158, 167–8, 182, 192–3, 236–7

Smith, Beryl, 234
Smith, Bob, 234, 243
Soudaine, Barry, 82, 106, 137, 138, 147–52, 210, 239
Stacey, Jack, 40, 42, 75–81, 129, 177, 242 *see also* Bailey, tramp
static electric flash, *see* static flash fires
static flash fires, 13, 176, 202–10

Thomas, Henry, 3, 14–30, 32, 34, 36, 37–8, 39, 40, 42, 43–4, 51,
    52, 54, 83, 84, 97, 98, 102, 103, 104, 106, 119, 125, 132, 134,
    136, 137, 139, 153, 156, 166, 168, 191, 212, 214, 215, 216,
    219
Thomsen, Dr Mogens, 111, 113
Thurston, Dr Gavin, 76, 91, 95, 97, 213, 239
Tomorrow's World, 105
trance, 79, 158–9, 166–7, 187, 192, 195

verdict
    — accidental death, 26
    — asphyxia, 78
    — misadventure, 181, 196–7, 208
    — open, 152, 210
victims (of SHC), 176 *see also* Angel, Jack; Ashton, Alfred; Bailey,
    tramp; Clark, Debbie; Di Bandi, Countess; Fitzsimon,
    Jacqueline; Gowthorpe, Wilfred; Krook; Mott, George;
    Motteshead, Susan; Reeser, Mary; Saffin, Jeannie; Soudaine,
    Barry; Thomas, Henry; Webb, Annie Gertrude

Webb, Annie Gertrude, 31–6, 37–8, 39, 83, 97, 102, 103, 104, 124,
    125, 132, 136, 137, 168, 191, 212, 214, 215, 216, 229
Westrum, Dr Ron, 6, 63, 84–6, 90, 92, 111, 120–21, 132
wick effect, 5, 8, 9, 12, 23, 29, 39, 41, 45, 46, 53, 62, 81, 83–4, 88,
    91, 93–106, 107, 108, 112, 117, 120, 130, 132, 133–46, 150,
    152, 162, 174, 197, 200, 211–222, 223, 230, 231, 232, 233,
    238, 239, 240–1